POLITICAL ORDER AND POWER TRANSITION IN HONG KONG

Political Order and Power Transition in Hong Kong

Edited by
Li Pang-kwong

The Chinese University Press

ISBN 962–201–783–5

THE CHINESE UNIVERSITY PRESS
The Chinese University of Hong Kong
Sha Tin, N.T., Hong Kong
Fax: +852 2603 6692
+852 2603 7355
E-mail: cup@cuhk.edu.hk
Web-site: http://www.cuhk.edu.hk/cupress/w1.htm

Printed in Hong Kong

To those who devote their time and efforts
to work on an overlooked, undervalued
but socially important field of research —
Hong Kong studies.

Contents

Preface

The smooth transfer of sovereignty and the efficient governance of Hong Kong both before and after 1997 have been the paramount concerns of all walks of life in the territory. So too for the academics. These concerns have driven me to think of holding a conference to take stock of our current research efforts and to solicit ideas on the governing of the post-1997 Hong Kong.

An International Conference on Political Order and Power Transition in Hong Kong, jointly organized by the Centre for Public Policy Studies and the Centre for Asian Pacific Studies, Lingnan College, was therefore held on 18–19 September 1996. This book is the logical outcome of the said conference. After review by peers in Hong Kong or abroad, nine conference papers were revised and included in this book. In this connection, I am most appreciative the efforts of eleven anonymous reviewers who critically commented on at least one chapter each of this book.

My appreciation is also extended to The Chinese University Press, for their kind assistance in publishing, editing and proofreading the manuscripts; to my Lingnan colleagues, Phoebe Cheng, David Ji, Dorothy Kok, May Leung and Raymond Ng, for preparing the said conference; and to Brian Bridges and Virginia Man, for proofreading the manuscripts.

Li Pang-kwong
September 1997

Contributors

CHEUNG Bing-leung, Anthony is the Head and Associate Professor in the Department of Public and Social Administration, City University of Hong Kong. His main research interests are: civil service studies; para-governmental organizations; privatization and administrative reforms. His recent publications on Hong Kong public sector reforms appeared in the *International Review of Administrative Sciences, International Journal of Public Sector Management,* and *International Journal of Public Administration.* Dr. Cheung is active in public service, being presently member of the Hong Kong Housing Authority, the Consultative Committee on the New Airport and Related Projects, and the Standing Committee on Disciplined Services Salaries and Conditions of Service. He was elected to the Legislative Council in 1995.

Brian HOOK is a senior member of the academic staff of the University of Leeds where he teaches in the Department of East Asian Studies. He was a founder member of the original Department of Chinese Studies of which he was head between 1979 and 1982, and from 1985 to 1988. Between 1958 and 1963 he was a member of Her Majesty's Overseas Civil Service in the Government of Hong Kong, serving as Assistant Secretary in the Secretariat for Chinese Affairs, and subsequently in the Colonial Secretariat. From 1980 to 1991, he was Editor of *The China Quarterly.* He has edited both editions of *The Cambridge Encyclopedia of China.* In 1995 he was University Fellow and Visiting Professor at the David C. Lam Institute for East-West Studies. His chief interest is the history of the People's Republic of China, and his recent publications examine the arrangements for the retrocession of Hong Kong, on which he plans a full-length study.

IP Po-keung is Professor and Dean of the School of Arts and Social Sciences, The Open University of Hong Kong. After graduating from The Chinese University of Hong Kong, where he studied philosophy and sociology, he studied history and philosophy of science at the University of Western Ontario, Canada and got his doctoral degree there. His major publications include: *Foundations of Democracy — A Dialogue* (with S. W. Man); *Ecological Crisis and Environmental Conversation Strategies* (with W. T. Hung); *Human Rights — Theory and Practice*; *Logic and Methodology*; *Thinking and Rational Thinking* (with K. P. Yu), *Beyond Money: Perspectives on Business Ethics*. His current research interests are: ethical and social implications of technology, applied ethics, and the development of civil society in China and Hong Kong.

LAI Wai-chung, Lawrence, is Associate Professor in the Department of Real Estate and Construction (Surveying), the University of Hong Kong. He is member of: Royal Australian Planning Institute; Hong Kong Institute of Planners; Chartered Institute of Transport; Registered Professional Planner. His major research interests are: property rights and other economic aspects of planning; economics of sustainable development; office decentralization. His publications included: *Zoning and Property Rights*; *Hong Kong in China: Real Estate and the Economy* (with Professor Walker and Dr. K. W. Chau); *Town Planning in Hong Kong: A Critical Review* (forthcoming); and his journal articles appeared in *Progress in Planning*, *Town Planning Review*, *Third World Planning Review*, *Land Use Policy*, *Asian Economic Journal*, etc.

K. K. LEUNG is Associate Professor in the Department of Applied Social Studies, City University of Hong Kong; a Guest Associate Professor in Peking University; the President of the Foundation of China Studies and the Director of the Centre of China Studies. His research interest is political sociology in mainland China, Taiwan and Hong Kong.

LI Pang-kwong is University Lecturer in the Department of Politics and Sociology and Director of the Research and Survey Programme, Lingnan College. He has published articles on the electoral politics of Hong Kong in edited volumes and journal, such as *Hong Kong Tried Democracy*, *The Other Hong Kong Report*, *The 1995 Legislative Council Elections in Hong Kong* and *Asian Perspective*. Currently, he is working on a book on electoral dynamics and institutional changes of Hong Kong.

LO Shiu-hing teaches Hong Kong politics in the Department of Politics and Public Administration, the University of Hong Kong. His research interests focus on the politics of Hong Kong and Macau. His major publications include: *The Politics of Democratization in Hong Kong* and *Political Development in Macau*.

TANG Shu-hung studied at The Chinese University of Hong Kong, B.Soc.Sc. (Economics), University of Toronto, M.A. (Economics), and McMaster University, Ph.D. (Economics). He is Professor and Head of Economics Department, Hong Kong Baptist University. He is also the author of *The Hong Kong Finances in the Transitional Period*.

Steve TSANG is Louis Cha Fellow and Dean at St. Anthony College, Oxford University. He is also Director of the College's Asian Studies Centre. His most recent books on Hong Kong are: *Hong Kong: Appointment with China* and *A Documentary History of Hong Kong: Government and Politics*.

Introduction

Political order has been one of the paramount goals pursued by people regardless of their political inclination. In the context of Hong Kong, the importance of political order has been gaining even more emphasis in the bumpy process of the sovereignty transfer from the United Kingdom to the People's Republic of China (P.R.C.). The contrasts between order and change have painted a mixed picture of stability and uncertainty in the extended 13-year period of the power transition, starting from the conclusion of the Sino-British Joint Declaration in late 1984 to the formation of the Hong Kong Special Administrative Region (HKSAR) of the P.R.C. on 1 July 1997.

As a non-sovereign political entity, Hong Kong's political destiny has been shaped mostly by exogenous, rather than endogenous, political forces. The contributors in this volume have, in one way or the other, taken this special status into consideration by incorporating China's and Britain's considerations and calculations towards Hong Kong into their studies. By doing so, the readers should be better able to comprehend the complex process of power transition.

The first two chapters discuss the broad context of the complex Britain–China–Hong Kong interrelationships. Taking into consideration British internal political dynamics, Brian Hook examines the peculiar situation faced by the British Government when formulating its policy towards Hong Kong in the postwar period. Hook argues that the presence of China and its attitude towards Hong Kong have, in one way or the other, set the parameters of any possible political reforms initiated by the British and Hong Kong Governments. After surveying the major political reforms attempted since 1945, Hook advances his view on the Sino-British controversy over the 1994–1995 electoral arrangements, the last attempt at reform during the British rule over Hong Kong.

Steve Tsang analyses the politics of democratization in transitional Hong Kong. In evaluating the role of the major players in the transitional political game, Steve Tsang regards Britain as the declining force, China as the rising force, and the people of Hong Kong as the ineffective force in framing the post-1997 Hong Kong political order. The withdrawal of the British administration, which has acted as a buffer between the Hong Kong people and the Chinese Government, he argues, may require the people of Hong Kong to stand up for what they want within the "rigid framework" set by the Chinese Government.

The next five chapters examine the dynamics within and between the key elements of Hong Kong's political system and society. Accompanying the transition of Hong Kong from a British colony to a Chinese HKSAR is the need to design a new framework for the post-1997 governance. Li Pang-kwong evaluates the institutional design of the HKSAR political system with an emphasis on the executive-legislature relationships. Li analyses the constitution-making process of the Basic Law with a view to reveal the calculations of the competing political forces in the process. From his point of view, the "executive-dominated" system with a segmented legislature would not serve to ease the conflicts, which have emerged in both the electoral market and the legislature of Hong Kong. He advances several ways to strengthen the linkages among the voters, the legislature and the executive so as to encapsulate the said conflicts.

Cheung Bing-leung, Anthony, discusses at length the role of the senior civil service in the governance of Hong Kong and the reasons why the administrative elite could enjoy such a privileged position before the 1980s. Although challenged by the aborted British attempts at introducing representative government in the 1980s and 1990s, the bureaucratic authority would continue to play a significant role in the HKSAR governance, Cheung argues, because of the Chinese preference "for an executive-led system with the civil service in charge."

Although the British Hong Kong Government encouraged the development of representative government, the corresponding input mechanisms have yet to mature. Given the current state of development, K. K. Leung argues that the label "political party" does not fit well in the unique political situation of Hong Kong where free elections would coexist with a "no-majority-party" system both "before and after 1997." Instead, he suggests employing the concept of "political fraction." By employing Douglas Rae's fractionalization index to comprehend the voting patterns of various "political fractions" in the Legislative Council's sessions of 1991–1995, he predicts that a more fragmented legislature, with multipolar fraction competition, would emerge.

Whether adopting the label "political party" or "political fraction," the emergence of the political "opposition" forces since the 1980s seemed inevitable. Lo Shiu-hing discusses the evolution of political opposition forces in Hong Kong. Using the concepts and typology of political opposition developed by Guillermo O'Donnell and Philippe Schmitter, Lo tries to analyse the dynamic relations both among factions of political opposition as well as between the political opposition and the P.R.C. in the democratization process in Hong Kong. He concludes that regardless of the co-optation efforts made by the P.R.C., factions of political opposition would press ahead their demands with different strategies.

Relating to the development of political opposition forces is the issue of whether a civil society has emerged in Hong Kong since the 1970s. After discussing the different mode of state-society relationships, Ip Po-keung advances his "state-driven" thesis in accounting for the development of civil society in Hong Kong. Focusing on the institutional aspect, Ip assesses the state of civil society in Hong Kong through the examination of autonomy and legal entitlements of its citizens. He then argues that as "public space becomes more entrenched and pronounced," the civil society of Hong Kong will only "be tamed, but not be crushed."

The final two chapters examine specific aspects of public policy in the transitional period. Tang Shu-hung reviews the fiscal policy of Hong Kong before 1997 and the possible impact of sovereignty transfer on it. Arguing that the British Hong Kong Government had adopted a conservative fiscal policy, as reflected in generating huge fiscal reserves and in controlling the size of the public sector, he further envisions that the HKSAR Government is highly likely to adopt an even more conservative budgetary planning and management. It is because the Chinese officials have regarded the rising welfare expenditure in the last years of colonial rule as violating the principle of "living within our means" of Article 107 of the Basic Law.

Lai Wai-chung, Lawrence, discusses in his chapter the land use policy in Hong Kong. From the viewpoint of contractual right, Lai first surveys the practice of contractual planning and the plan hierarchy in Hong Kong. He then presents the possible conflicts between contractual rights and administrative zoning. Supporting the low income tax regime and the government welfare spending, the land revenue is so vital that the government has to maintain the contractual foundation of the land market. In this connection, he argues, there would be a role for the leasehold land system to play in the government planning mechanism.

In sum, the above contributors have touched on some of the major topics that deserve the attention of our society. If these chapters have contributed anything at all to the readers of this book or have caused any debate on certain issues afterward, the purpose of this book would be achieved.

From Repossession to Retrocession: British Policy towards Hong Kong 1945–1997

Brian Hook

In 1945, following the end of the Second World War, Hong Kong started along the final stretch of road in its history as a British Crown Colony. At that time, nobody could predict with any degree of certainty the way ahead, the distance to be covered and the time it would take to reach the ultimate destination, namely the retrocession to and the reunification with China. Nor could anyone predict with any level of confidence the future conditions: how rough, how tortuous they might become. It was clear however, from discussions among the principal allies fighting the war against Japanese imperialism in the Pacific theatre, the United States, China and Britain that sooner or later, and quite possibly sooner rather than later, China would regain sovereignty over Hong Kong.

That writing was, as the saying goes, on the wall. From 1943 until his death in April 1945 shortly before the war ended, President Roosevelt and his sinophilic administration had been receptive to and to some extent persuaded by the arguments deployed by Generalissimo Chiang Kai-shek and his skilful advisers, among them the Chinese foreign minister T. V. Soong and the renowned ambassador to Britain Wellington Koo, of the case for Britain's voluntary relinquishing its rights in China.[1] China was

---

[1] Chan Lau Kit-ching, *China, Britain and Hong Kong 1895–1945* (Hong Kong: The Chinese University Press, 1990), pp. 293–323; Kevin P. Lane, *Sovereignty and the Status Quo* (Boulder: Westview Press, 1990), pp. 41–60.

an ally. The U.S. was, by conviction, anti-imperialist and anti-colonialist. Britain's morally indefensible imperial position in China, reflected in China's need to seek the retrocession of mainland foreign concessions, the reversion of foreign settlements, the extinguishing of extraterritorial rights, the termination of the lease on the New Territories and the resumption of the exercise of sovereignty over the colony of Hong Kong, seemed, in the circumstances in the wartime alliance, wholly inappropriate.

From 1941–1945 Britain under pressure from the U.S. to revert international settlements, renounce extra-territoriality and retrocede concessions fought a tenacious rearguard action to preserve its position, particularly that in Hong Kong and the New Territories. The final round of pressure exerted by the determined leaders of the Nationalist government on Britain came as it became clear the Japanese forces were facing defeat. Chiang Kai-shek advocated that it would be entirely appropriate if the surrender of the Hong Kong garrison was to be received by his military representatives and not by those of the erstwhile colonial power. In the event, Roosevelt's successor, President Truman, responding to British, notably Churchillian-inspired opposition to the plan, viewed in London as a clever manoeuvre designed either to deny or curtail full formal repossession of the colony, demurred. Britain sent a fleet under Admiral Harcourt to receive the surrender of the garrison after the Japanese conceded defeat on 14 August 1945.

After sixteen days sailing the fleet reached Hong Kong harbour and, on 16 September having accepted the surrender of the Japanese commander on behalf of Great Britain and Chiang Kai-shek as supreme commander of China's war theatre, Harcourt formally regained possession of Hong Kong for Britain. A symbolic repossession by China, whatever, in the circumstances of the late 1940s it might have led to in practice, did not for the time being occur. Nevertheless, the markers that had been put down by the Kuomintang (KMT) during the war were there for all to see. It was evident, therefore, from the time of the British repossession in 1945 that Hong Kong had set off along what may be referred to as the final stretch of the relatively short road of its colonial history.

The final length of road to the ultimate destination of reunification with China was, as we now know, to stretch from 1945 to 1997. For Hong Kong to have endured for another fifty or so years as a British possession on the south-eastern tip of the Chinese land mass, increasing the length of its colonial history by half as much again when viewed from the precarious vantage point of 1945, is nothing short of astonishing. Indeed it would have been seen as rash to lay odds on the survival of Hong Kong in its present form beyond say two years.

Not only did it survive but it flourished. History will record by the eve of the retrocession in 1997 in the approach to the final milestone along the road to reunification it had become a prosperous and stable community living under the rule of law. It had a uniquely evolved colonial political system delivering in substantial measure the freedoms associated with democracy but not, as yet in the full sense of the concept, the normally accepted relevant democratic institutions. Education, health and welfare systems were generally as good as those in many developed democracies and a good deal better than some. The material standard of living reflecting physical conditions in the territory was generally good: accommodation, because of the shortage of space and the density of population, was conventionally in small high-rise apartments; public transport was well organized, well-run and inexpensive; the private ownership of cars though popular was unnecessary; the levels of growth and employment the record would confirm were, when compared to other areas, enviable.

The remarkable socio-economic success of Hong Kong, the measure of which can be illustrated by reference to published indicators, can only be fully and properly understood when considered in the light of the policies adopted by Britain and China over the stretch of history from the repossession by Britain in 1945 to the retrocession by Britain to China in 1997. The main indicators of socio-economic success are:

- average annual real GDP growth of 8.5% from 1974 to 1984, and 6.0% from 1984 to 1994,
- per capita GDP of some US$22,000 in 1995 exceeding that of Britain and Australia and second only to Japan in East Asia,
- the world's eighth largest trading economy,
- the largest container port in terms of container throughput, and
- ranking among the leading financial centres in the world, in terms of external banking transactions and stock market capitalization.[2]

The degree of contemporary socio-economic success implies that British policies for Hong Kong, including those decided in London and those generated and implemented in Hong Kong by the colonial administration,

---

[2] *Background Facts* (London: Hong Kong Government Office, August 1995).

over the final stretch of its colonial history were, on balance, at the very least, not significantly incorrect or inappropriate. Some policies it will be shown could have been better formulated; some could have been better implemented; some could have come earlier or gone further; some, it may be argued, could have been improved by the conscious development of a more democratically representative system of government pitched at a level acceptable to China.

The gradual introduction of a democratically representative system of government did not start until the early 1980s. By that time not only had Hong Kong passed the milestones along the road to 1997 marking prosperity and stability, but China had also signalled the limits beyond which it would not tolerate progress towards democratization. British policy, for that reason, from then on until the divisive controversies of 1992–1994, in that context, was formulated with the expressed views of the leadership of the People's Republic of China (P.R.C.) in mind. This, in practice, was no different to the situation that had obtained, albeit accompanied by a lesser threat from a lesser power in circumstances that were more favourable to Britain, from 1945 onwards. It was, indeed, progressively so in what was to become the long stretch of road from 1949 onwards.

The aim of this chapter is, therefore, to identify and discuss what, in fact, constitute for want of a better term, the milestones of British policy for Hong Kong along the road from repossession to retrocession. The theme of the chapter is that while it is relatively easy, superficially and in an uninformed fashion to pick holes in the fabric of the history of British policy towards Hong Kong for the half century or more after 1945, thereby exposing certain weaknesses, and leading to the adoption of an overly judgmental approach to the record, the serious historian must adopt a more balanced approach. It is therefore important when evaluating British policy in this period clinically and unemotionally to examine the relevant issues and to give due weight to the social, political and economic realities of Hong Kong, and to the constantly changing international balance of power before attempting to make any judgement as to its merits and demerits.

1945–1952

The background factors to the formulation of British policy towards Hong Kong in the immediate postwar period were determined by a range of important considerations. Britain itself, although with its allies victorious in the war, was on its knees economically. The war had seriously eroded the belief in and functioning of the empire. Moreover the growth of nationalistic and patriotic forces in many parts of the imperial system indicated that it could not be sustained in its then existing form.

At home, the demand for social reform had been reflected in the surprising electoral defeat of Churchill in 1945. He had been the wartime leader without whose vision, patriotic leadership, stirring oratory and pugnacious political characteristics, the war might have gone the other way. He was summarily rejected by the people in 1945; they chose, instead, to elect a Labour government under Attlee. The domestic agenda was to create a democratic socialist system incorporating the nationalization of the commanding heights of the economy and the installation of a government-funded social welfare and health system with corresponding shifts in the ownership of the means of production, supply, distribution and in the levels of taxation.

These background factors are seldom well understood outside Britain. The reality was that the rather grand outward manifestation of empire had actually concealed the acuteness of an ongoing class struggle. In the postwar circumstances this was consistent with widespread social deprivation, an inordinately unequal distribution of wealth and the deficient structure of the education, health and welfare systems. For many, the war, though a gruesome experience, had also been an educative one. Hence the popular rejection of Churchill and the support for the Labour Party's social and political agenda. Abroad, this agenda was reflected in measures to meet demands for change to and reform within the empire.

For Hong Kong, this agenda was reflected in attempts to make its governance more representative of the wishes of the people. Under instructions, the Governor, Sir Mark Young, promoted the idea of organizing a powerful semi-autonomous Municipal Council that would go some way towards meeting the aims. He did not succeed for several reasons. Firstly, while it was supported by some expatriate business people who saw it as a replication of the advantageous (i.e. non-bureaucratic) aspects of governance in the British concession in Shanghai, the colonial administrators viewed it as a potential infringement of their role. The view was that it could reduce the scope for the existing colonial administration. Secondly, there was the fear that the Municipal Council would initially contend with and, by virtue of the electoral mandate, eventually dominate the Legislative Council (Legco). Thirdly, there was the fear that the KMT, at the time the dominant political force in China, would succeed, by hook or by crook, in getting their supporters elected to the Municipal Council, raising the spectre that had been exorcized by Churchill in the run-up to the Japanese capitulation, namely a *de facto* assumption of sovereignty.[3]

At about the same time, the response from Singapore to the instructions to consider reforming the system of governance was to recommend changes to the legislature. Since Hong Kong and Singapore shared some characteristics (but not others), this served to sow seeds of doubt in London as to the appropriateness of the idea of a Municipal Council.[4]

In the light of all these considerations it is not surprising Young failed in his efforts. His successor, Sir Alexander Grantham took up the baton, possibly with less enthusiasm than his predecessor, in 1947. By this time, the political scene in China was beginning to change. It no longer appeared self-evident that the Civil War which had broken out would result in a victory for Chiang Kai-shek. Elements within the British Labour Party viewed the Chinese Communist Party (CCP) as mainly "agrarian reformers," and therefore the possibility of a victory by the People's Liberation Army (PLA) did not necessarily evoke the same degree of alarm and despondency as it did in the U.S. The latter, as has been noted, had developed a special affiliation with the KMT.[5] The socialist view was however, not shared by the British compatriots of the China coast community and the dominant British expatriate presence in Hong Kong.

As the course of the Civil War unfolded and it became obvious that the tide had turned against the KMT, the question was posed as to whether the PLA would liberate Hong Kong too. In the event, that was not the case. Inexplicably, it seemed, the PLA halted its advance at the northern frontier of Hong Kong on 17 October 1949 by which time the founding of the P.R.C. had already been proclaimed by Mao Zedong and the Republic of China (R.O.C.), under his adversary Chiang Kai-shek, had retreated to Taiwan. It is not surprising the view was emerging in London that the time was less than opportune to pursue constitutional reform in Hong Kong. In

---

[3] N. J. Miners, "Plans for Constitutional Reform in Hong Kong, 1946–52," *The China Quarterly*, Vol. 107 (September 1986), pp. 463–82; Chan Lau Kit-ching, *China, Britain and Hong Kong*; Kevin P. Lane, *Sovereignty and the Status Quo*, Note 1; Steve Tsang, *Democracy Shelved: Great Britain, China, and Attempts at Constitutional Reform in Hong Kong, 1945–1952*, (Hong Kong: Oxford University Press, 1988).

[4] N. J. Miners, *ibid.*; Steve Tsang, *ibid.*

[5] Chan Lau Kit-ching, *ibid.*; Kevin P. Lane, *ibid.*

fact, at the time, the Hong Kong garrison had been heavily reinforced, suggesting that Britain intended to resist any invasion. In the circumstances, while the outcome of any PLA invasion *per se* would not have been in doubt, an invasion would have been deemed an act of international belligerency and not sanctioned by the commander of the local theatre of war and could have provided a pretext for the U.S. to escalate the war, an eventuality the nascent P.R.C. would in any event wish to avoid.

Although there remained in Hong Kong and in London some support for reform, the issue had already become very complicated.

The complexity is evident from the shift away from the concept of a powerful semi-autonomous Municipal Council as envisaged in the Young plan in the summer of 1949. Instead, unofficials on Legco, fearing a clash between their nominated body and a subordinate but elected body, advocated abandoning the plan for the latter and the introduction of a number of elected members to a reformed Legco in which there would be an unofficial majority. This raised many questions including:

- the franchise for Legco elections,
- the risk of voter manipulation and the use of the forum as a platform for anti-British or anti-government rhetoric,
- the formation of communal electorates,
- calculations of voting behaviour on Legco,
- the implications for governance of an unofficial majority which could defeat the administration on local policy issues,
- inter-ethnic block-voting power,
- the issue of the development of ministerial-type responsibilities (initially raised in 1947 by Secretary of State Creech-Jones in a series of recommendations for constitutional reform in Hong Kong) and, in due course,
- the appointment to Executive Council (Exco) of elected members of Legco whose loyalty might be in doubt.

The full implications of these questions duly emerged and resulted, in 1950, in yet another revised scheme. Grantham thus proposed the unofficial majority sought by Legco in 1949 should be achieved by what was perceived as the safer course of nominated unofficials and unofficials indirectly elected by various corporate bodies (i.e. functional constituencies) rather than by nominated and directly elected unofficials. Under the scheme the administration could no longer avoid defeat in Legco on local issues but it could continue to prevail on international political issues involving

British interests in Hong Kong. As the scheme was the least liberalizing so far, it had to be carefully packaged to secure acceptance.

Having agreed on this, British policy was again deflected by events outside Hong Kong. The entry of Chinese forces into the Korean War in November 1950 coincided with the adoption of the scheme. The Foreign Office being consulted, advised against unnecessarily provoking renewed P.R.C. denunciation of the British position in Hong Kong and no progress was made until the end of 1951. By then Britain had a Conservative government, and there was renewed agitation for constitutional reform in Hong Kong as the situation had eased in Korea. On balance, it appeared to the Governor that to postpone further the promise of reform made in 1946 would be more damaging than to provoke another barrage of communist propaganda. This view was summed up by the Colonial Office in a letter to the Foreign Office, as, in all the circumstances, "the balance of dis-advantage now lay on the side of continued inaction."[6] This was convincing and the proposals were approved by the British Cabinet in May 1952.

That was, however, not to be the end of the matter. In a matter of weeks the unofficial members of Exco and Legco urged the Governor to induce the British government to drop the scheme, which it did. The reasons for abandoning, for the third time since 1945, a scheme for democratic reform (each less liberal than the other, and none so radical as to embody the recommendations made by the Secretary of State Creech-Jones in 1947) are obscure. Ostensibly, on the third occasion the unofficials feared the onset of greater political activity as the nature of the regime in the P.R.C. became clear. Moreover, to have introduced constitutional change in such circumstances could have been seen locally as a signal that Britain was preparing to exit. Equally, externally, the P.R.C. may have signalled, through interlocutors, that Hong Kong was secure for the time being provided there was no constitutional reform. While such speculation does not explain the first two local initiatives that induced modifications or abandonment of the proposals, it could explain the sudden and unexpected *volte-face* by the councillors in 1952.

Although Britain chose to present the abandoning of the scheme as a postponement of constitutional reform, announcing as a consolation that

---

[6] N. J. Miners, "Plans for Constitutional Reform in Hong Kong"; Steve Tsang, *Democracy Shelved*.

the number of elected seats on the Urban Council would increase from 2 to 4, in effect the issue was not revisited until the 1980s. In practice, the preoccupation with the need to avoid unnecessarily provoking China remained as a major criterion in the formation of policy for Hong Kong in London and in policy formation and implementation by the administration in Hong Kong. Moreover, when the question of constitutional reform was eventually revisited, it is significant that many of the issues that surfaced between 1945 and 1952, to which reference is made above, resurfaced with similar delaying effect.

The difference between the "post-repossession stage" of contemplated constitutional reform and the "pre-retrocession stage" is, of course, that the future of constitutional reform in Hong Kong from 1984 onwards was a matter that had to take into consideration not only British and Hong Kong interests but the interests of the future sovereign and British obligations under the 1984 Sino-British Agreement.[7]

Nevertheless it is worth noting, before considering the interim period of three decades, that a number of the issues militating against constitutional reform between 1946–1952 remained as impediments affecting the substance, pace and reach of constitutional reform from 1984 to 1992.

1952–1982

For the next thirty years British policy towards Hong Kong was dedicated to the management of the inherited situation. Nobody knew the length of the tenure. Few in Britain and Hong Kong would have bet on the survival of Hong Kong for more than a year or two for the first two decades of the following three decades. In 1972 however, when the P.R.C. resumed the China seat in the United Nations, and requested the exclusion of Hong Kong from the list of territories awaiting self-determination, there was an indication that the expiry of the lease on the New Territories was to be the date by which the future would have been settled.

In the first decade, British policy was to support the Hong Kong administration in dealing with the heavy burden of a refugee influx from

---

[7] *A Draft Agreement between the Government of the United Kingdom of Great Britain and Northern Ireland and the Government of the People's Republic of China on the Future of Hong Kong.* White Paper by HMG London 26 September 1984, reproduced by The Government Printer, Hong Kong, 1984.

China that swelled the territory's population from something over 600,000 in 1945 to 2.5 millions in 1958. There was, as Sir Jack Cater confirms,[8] very little funding available from dedicated budgetary provision in Britain for financing projects in the colonies and what was made available was on terms for repayment. In Britain itself, although the rationing of essential foodstuffs such as meat, fats, sugar, eggs, cheese, and clothing had ended in 1954, having been in force for fourteen years, the postwar economy was in a parlous state.

When the British economic recovery began, it was on terms agreeable to the strong Trades Union movement within a semi-socialist system that took full employment as a precondition. Consequently, Britain entered the 1960s as a declining imperial power with the dismal prospect of an increasingly uncompetitive, labour-intensive industrial base, plagued by inter-union job demarcation disputes, exposed to the increasingly capital-intensive, restructured, highly competitive industries of Western Germany and Japan on the one hand and to the labour-intensive, low-cost, non-unionized exploitative industries in the nascent manufacturing economies on the other.

Hong Kong fell into the latter category. Its role as an entrepôt in the imperial system, the farthest reach east of the fleet, had ceased with the trade embargo on the P.R.C. imposed at the time of the Korean War. It had plentiful cheap labour however, arising from its being a sanctuary for refugees from China. Among them were diverse talents and experienced industrialists from Shanghai who were to promote the development of the manufacturing base.[9] British policy in Hong Kong was to meet the challenge of the refugee influx, graphically illustrated by the tens of thousands of squatter huts in dreadful conditions in the foothills of Hong Kong, Kowloon and the New Territories (NT). The solving of the problem of people as it was called[10] was of the utmost urgency. Its imperfect but admirable solution, made imperative by the disastrous Shek Kip Mei fire in 1953, was in the construction of resettlement and low-cost housing estates with planned provision for manufacturing units and the beginnings of the manufacturing base.

---

[8] Private correspondence with Sir Jack Cater.

[9] Wong Siu-lun, *Emigrant Entrepreneurs: Shanghai Industrialists in Hong Kong* (Hong Kong: Oxford University Press, 1988).

[10] *A Problem of People* (Hong Kong: The Government Press, 1960).

An important aspect of British policy in Hong Kong was the interventionist approach which the administration had to take to deal with social issues, and the generally non-interventionist approach adopted for the economy, save for the economic infrastructure. This was started by Sir John Cowperthwaite during his period as Financial Secretary but came to be epitomized in the policies of his successor Sir Philip Haddon-Cave. One area of the economy in which the administration had to intervene was however, in ensuring a supply of land for the development.

The best example of the latter aspect of British policy is to be found in the development of the industrial and manufacturing base in Tsuen Wan. At the time, the capacity for the rapid production of land through reclamation was not as great as it was to become in the 1990s in the Port and Airport Development Strategy (PADS). It was necessary to make land available from existing sites. Land was relatively plentiful in the NT but the traditional owners were conservative farmers or lineage clans unwilling to part with land. The government could, of course, legally resume land but to do so on the scale required would have been to invite social unrest with unpredictable consequences.

To satisfy the demand for land for manufacturing and social use in Tsuen Wan and subsequently elsewhere in the NT, the administration devised an ingenious voucher system that became known as Letters B. The system originated with the District Officers of the time, Denis Bray, Hal Miller (now Sir Hal Miller), and David Akers-Jones (now Sir David Akers-Jones). Briefly, by surrendering an agricultural site for developmental purposes the NT owner was guaranteed a developmental site at a time of the former owner's choosing, the area being determined by a ratio of 5 to 2.

This entitlement was expressed in the form of the so-called Letters B. Thus the owners, with the prospect of sharing in the appreciation of land values as development increased, were less reluctant to sell land. Moreover, there developed a market in Letters B which was a further incentive since, besides being exchanged for development land which involved paying a premium for the difference in land values, they could also be sold for cash to developers. This appealed to a gambling or investment instinct. It is arguable that without this ingenious device, and the confidence of the owners in the integrity of the British administration, the development of the NT and of the manufacturing base in Hong Kong would have been a very tortuous process.

In the event, it was not. While Britain could take some pleasure in the territory's economic recovery, as manufacturing replaced the stagnating entrepôt economy, inexpensive Hong Kong imports brought protests from its own ailing textile industry. The exploitation of Hong Kong workers was a focus for the protests. This charge was not without substance though it seemed locally to be a price worth paying and there was little to be done about it if Hong Kong was to survive. The friction between Hong Kong and Britain on this account continued as the British textile industry was inevitably down-sized and quota restrictions were put in place in the general context of Multi-Fibre Agreements (MFA) under the General Agreement on Tariffs and Trade (GATT).

In retrospect, British policy towards Hong Kong from 1952 to the early 1960s, spanning the remaining six years in the office of Sir Alexander Grantham and the whole of the period of Sir Robert Black (1958–1964) was reasonably successful. It eschewed politics. Constitutional reform had been abandoned and the administration, reflecting the British government's policy, settled for the development of the system that became best known for the description applied by Professor Ambrose King: the administrative absorption of politics.[11] The soundness of that approach, undemocratic as it was, is clear from the success achieved in avoiding the overt transfer of the rivalry between the CCP and the KMT to the streets of Hong Kong. The two occasions when such rivalry showed the dangers that existed from any relaxing of the policy were the downing of the airliner the Kashmir Princess[12] in 1955 and the riots in 1956.[13]

On this basis, and with large foreign exchange gains from the fore-runner to the modern tourist industry, the rest and recreation furloughs of the U.S. forces deployed to implement John Foster Dulles' containment policy in East Asia, together with overseas Chinese investments, Hong Kong passed the early milestones along the road to a high degree of autonomy and prosperity. Within these parameters, apart from the extension of British legislation chiefly to enable Hong Kong to function in the international arena, British policy towards Hong Kong was in fact the

---

[11] Ambrose King, "Administrative Absorption of Politics in Hong Kong: Emphasis on the Grass Roots Level," *Asian Survey*, Vol. 15, No. 5 (May 1975), pp. 422–39.

[12] Gary Catron, "Hong Kong and Chinese Foreign Policy 1955–60," *The China Quarterly*, Vol. 51 (July–September 1972), pp. 405–24.

[13] Gary Catron, *ibid.*; Steve Tsang, "Target Zhou Enlai: The Kashmir Princess Incident of 1955," *The China Quarterly*, Vol. 139 (September 1994), pp. 766–82.

policy of the local administration, what is today often referred to as the British Hong Kong Government, acting to all intents and purposes autonomously.

The successor to Sir Alexander Grantham was Sir Robert Black who governed from 1958 to 1964. In turn, he was succeeded by Sir David Trench (1964–1971). Both were Colonial Service governors. They were career officers in the former Colonial Service and had served elsewhere in the empire, the former as Colonial (Chief) Secretary in Singapore, where he had been incarcerated by the Japanese imperialists during the Pacific War, and the latter was Governor in the Western Pacific. They were to be the penultimate and ultimate Colonial Service governors of Hong Kong. Indeed, reflecting the "wind of change" as Prime Minister Macmillan had described the urgent decolonization process in his famous speech,[14] the Colonial Administrative Service had already been subsumed into Her Majesty's Overseas Civil Service (HMOCS). The great office of empire, the Colonial Office, had been subsumed into, or swallowed by its occasional rival in the history of Hong Kong,[15] the Foreign Office, now renamed Foreign and Commonwealth Office (FCO), in the onward transition from empire to commonwealth.

All the succeeding governors of Hong Kong, Sir Murray MacLehose, Sir Edward Youde, Sir David Wilson, until the appointment of the politician, the Rt. Hon. Christopher Patten, were FCO appointees. None of them had any prior experience of territorial administration. All of them, with the exception of Mr. Patten, had experience of Sino-British diplomacy. Mr. Patten's rich and varied experience was gained in a party political role and in high ministerial office. There was, it should be noted, the interregnum of the very experienced colonial administrator Sir David Akers-Jones in late 1986 to early 1987 whom many thought would have made an excellent governor. No other candidate had a similar grasp of Hong Kong affairs. This occurred after the untimely death in office of Sir Edward Youde. Then, the British Government of the day, led by Mrs. Thatcher, and guided by her influential foreign policy advisor Sir Percy Cradock, ultimately reaffirmed the view, implicit in the Trench appointment being

---

[14] Macmillan was British Prime Minister 1957–1963. One of the aims of his government was independence for colonies, expressed in his "wind of change" speech in Capetown, 3 February 1960.

[15] Chan Lau Kit-ching, *China, Britain and Hong Kong*.

the last "Colonial Service" governor of Hong Kong, that the making of British policy towards Hong Kong would, until the final stretch of the approach to retrocession, increasingly become a matter of foreign policy.

By the time Trench succeeded Black the policies of the 1950s had enabled the rich talents involuntarily assembled in Hong Kong to promote the transition from stagnant entrepôt to the beginnings of a dynamic manufacturing economy. The authoritarian aspects of unrepresentative government adopted in the past had, to the extent they were mitigated by the development of Kaifong associations representing the views of neighbourhood and other social groupings, served the place reasonably well. Yet, the gap between government and the governed remained to be adequately and convincingly bridged. The inadequacies were exposed in the 1966 riots which, although triggered by increased ferry fares, were symptomatic of the administration's failure politically to bridge what may be deemed a credibility gap.[16] Indeed, there was a popular view, never successfully dispelled in Hong Kong, that the task of the administration was, by one means or another, blatantly or conspiratorially, to make a profit for Britain.

The existence of the credibility gap had been spotted by the administration but the danger had not been removed. It was, of course, inherent in an unrepresentative system. Among those to comment on it were recent senior administrative transferees from former colonies that had gained independence, particularly from Africa. Known as "African retreads," their enthusiasm for progress towards greater democracy did not gain great support within the administration. The prevailing view was that Confucianist and Legalist aspects of Chinese culture rendered the problems of Hong Kong *sui generis* and therefore, it was inappropriate indiscriminately to apply that which would be culturally alien.

This view was a general basis for the rejection of the Dickinson Report in 1966. As it happened, reflecting the administration's wish to bridge the gap, a working party had been established in April 1966 to look into the question of practicable alternatives for the development of a system of local administration, in view of the existing urban areas and the plans for new towns in the NT. It was under the chairmanship of W. V. Dickinson who was a very able transferee from the Gold Coast (Ghana) at the time of its

---

[16] *Kowloon Disturbances 1966, Report of Commission of Inquiry* (Hong Kong: Government Printer, 1967).

independence. The report of the working group, composed of the chairman, five members and a secretary, went into details to outline ways in which local government might be organized.[17] It was, in practice, an acknowledgement of the increasing complexity of governing the disparate areas of Hong Kong, and another look at ways to create a framework for a more progressive, democratic form of administration which would nurture the concept of responsible citizenship. Three decades on, the exercise would be regarded as being aimed at promoting the development of civil society.

The need for progress had been highlighted by the riots before the report was delivered. In the event, the findings in the report were unconvincing owing to the expressed ambivalence of members of the group. These included those of Mr. John Walden, subsequently a champion of progressive administration, and the then leading local administrator, Mr. Paul K. C. Tsui, later Secretary for Chinese Affairs (then ranking third in the administrative hierarchy). Four members attached reservations. The report deserves more attention in the postwar history of Hong Kong than it has received. Although it was effectively marginalized, shelved and overtaken by the scheme for district administration, it represented another example of the dilemma faced in the five decades of the British administration of Hong Kong from repossession to retrocession: to reform or to change within tradition. As the following sections show, there was no escape from the dilemma. When the attempt was finally made it was too late and it led to confrontation with the P.R.C.

The administration chose the latter course but not before the reality of Hong Kong being a borrowed place in borrowed time had been demonstrated by more disturbances. The 1967 riots were much more serious than those in 1966. They were a local reaction to the Cultural Revolution in China, caused by ultraleftist anticolonialist agitators. Britain having been one of the first nations to recognize the P.R.C. had relatively recently raised its representation to the level of ambassador.[18] Nevertheless, it was a major target for the destructive actions of ultraleftist and mob violence in Peking (Beijing).[19] Apart from demonstrating the vulnerability of British Hong Kong to the effects of political developments in China,

---

[17] *Report of the Working Party on Local Administration* (Hong Kong: Government Printer, 1967).

[18] Percy Cradock, *Experiences of China* (London: John Murray, 1994).

[19] *Ibid.*

latent xenophobia and social unrest arising from poor living and working conditions, all negative factors combining to challenge the British administration in 1967, the quelling of the rioting revealed solid support from broad sections of the population including the police force which remained loyal throughout the crisis.

The experience was responsible for the government's reaction. When the dust settled, Hong Kong was steered down the road of change within tradition. The dangers from propelling the territory into reforms, *terra incognita*, such as those referred to in the Dickinson Report, that could also provoke the P.R.C., appeared as self-evident as did the need for better channels of communication between the citizens and their government. Britain had, by the skin of its teeth, retained the administration of Hong Kong while the Portuguese administration of Macau had caved in under the combined pressure of local anticolonial forces and others taking advantage of the power struggle at the centre.

The official reaction was to bridge the gap by extending the practice of appointing District Officers, the eyes and ears of central government in the rural areas, to the urban areas.[20] Throughout the disturbances, it had been evident that apart from cross-border incursions from China, the rural NT had remained relatively stable. The key to this was seen to be the effectiveness of the District Officer (DO) system. At the time the NT was divided for this purpose into a number of districts under a District Commissioner and treated separately from the established urban areas. These districts were Tsuen Wan, Tuen Mun, Yuen Long, Tai Po, Sai Kung and Islands. At the base of this system were some 500 villages which elected, under a male franchise, some 900 representatives to form 27 Rural Committees whose chairmen and vice-chairmen, in turn, formed a major part of the Heung Yee Kuk (Xiangyi Ju), a powerful consultative body influential in the formation of government policy in the NT.

Clearly it was not possible precisely to replicate the NT structure in the urban areas, but from the 1970s there was increasing functional symmetry and managerial similarity between the rural and urban areas of Hong Kong. In this process, the new towns in the NT had a catalytic effect. There, the DOs had gained rich experience in the coordinating and consultative

---

[20] *The City District Officer Scheme, Report by the Secretary for Chinese Affairs* (Hong Kong: Government Printer, 1969).

process involved in creating new towns. There followed throughout the 1970s, under a new governor, Sir Murray MacLehose, the introduction of a greatly expanded system of consultation and local administration leading ultimately in 1981, with the rationalization of district administration, to the creation of District Boards. These became the lowest level of the three tiers of representative government in the pre-1997 system.[21]

These policies and many others that greatly benefited Hong Kong were pursued under Sir Murray MacLehose. As already noted, he was the first of three governors appointed from the diplomatic service. As such, he had a greater familiarity than his predecessors did with the thinking on Hong Kong in the FCO. For one without experience of territorial administration his achievements were formidable. For example, he set about indirectly to distribute the increasing wealth of Hong Kong in a more equitable way: housing, social services, education, recreation and anti-corruption policies made Hong Kong a better place to live in for the majority of its population.

The success and prosperity of Hong Kong was in fact in sharp contrast to the decline in Britain and China. It also enabled Hong Kong to enjoy a high degree of autonomy. There were, however, always limits to the scope of the autonomy enjoyed by the local administration. Britain did not, for example, give Hong Kong control over its immigration policies. Here, there were three main areas of contention: the rights of Hong Kong citizens, as British subjects to enter Britain; the policy towards illegal immigrants from the P.R.C.; and the policy towards illegal immigrants from Vietnam.

Britain had, as already noted, pursued labour-intensive economic policies after the war, availing itself, while it still enjoyed captive colonial markets, of workers from what euphemistically became known as the New Commonwealth.[22] Once the number entering under the 1948 Immigration Act, which itself had sought to restrict the availability of full British nationality, conferring the rights to go to and to live in Britain (entry and

---

[21] *Green Paper: A Pattern of District Administration in Hong Kong* (Hong Kong: Government Printer, June 1980); *White Paper: District Administration in Hong Kong* (Hong Kong: Government Printer, January 1981).

[22] Until 1948 British nationality was a status enjoyed by people born in countries under the British sovereignty; they could go to and live in Britain. After 1948, Nationality Acts restricted full British nationality. The trend reflected the status of newly independent Commonwealth nations and the wish to restrict the immigration of "new" Commonwealth citizens to Britain.

abode) became unsupportable, because of the drain on the revenues levied under a semi-socialist high tax, increasingly uncompetitive economy, the immigration law was changed. Although the immigration from Hong Kong had never been a problem, the rights enjoyed by Hong Kong citizens who, incidentally, by virtue of British control had no right to retaliate through reciprocal amendments to their domestic legislation, were adversely affected by British National Acts of 1963, 1981 and changes to the latter in 1986.

In effect, in the context of rights accruing from nationality, British policy for Hong Kong discriminated against Hong Kong citizens. The fear was that an insupportable number might, unless the immigration status was eroded, under certain circumstances, move to Britain. Successive legislation, withdrawing British Dependent Territories Citizens' (BDTC) right of abode in 1963, replacing this category in 1985 by the transitional category of British National (Overseas) (BN(O)) showed the trend of the policy. It was the British reneging on what he saw as moral obligations with respect to nationality that led to Mr. Lo Tak-shing dramatically to resign from Legco and Exco in 1985.

Britain's policy towards Hong Kong was also reflected in measures taken on illegal immigration from China and Vietnam. While measures to deal with the former were agreed with the local administration, those measures to deal with the latter were determined by Britain having regard to its perceived international interests, particularly the Anglo-American links, rather than the interests of the local administration. In 1980, the Reached or Touch Base Policy[23] for Chinese illegal immigrants was abandoned, yet the Port of First Asylum policy[24] for Vietnamese illegal immigrants was retained. This led to growing public resentment against a British policy that was an imposition on the Hong Kong taxpayers, a source of social disruption and an affront to local people whose relatives seeking

---

[23] The policy on illegal immigrants between 1974 and 1980: if they reached the ceded territory of Hong Kong or Kowloon they could stay. From 1976 to 1980 over 500,000 arrived.

[24] The British government policy requiring Hong Kong to offer shelter to Vietnamese refugees for whom Hong Kong was the first landing place. Between 1975–1981 Hong Kong provided temporary asylum for 105,000 refugees. In 1982 Hong Kong adopted a closed camp policy to deter immigration and in 1988 a screening policy to exclude economic migrants.

entry to Hong Kong would be summarily deported while people from Vietnam with no ties at all to the territory were admitted. To add salt to the wound, Britain escalated the Hong Kong taxpayers' contribution to the cost of maintaining the British garrison, one of whose main responsibilities was to control illegal immigration. Between the early 1970s and 1978 as a result of pressure from the Select Committee on Expenditure of the British Parliament, the contribution rose from 29% to 75% of actual costs (i.e. including those of dependents and support services).

These negative aspects of British policy were however, more than counterbalanced by the positive aspects in the 1970s. In 1979, the Governor, whose reputation had been greatly enhanced by the evident success of his policies, went to Peking to discuss the future of Hong Kong. From the British point of view the future of Hong Kong beyond 1997 should be settled sooner rather than later. There was, moreover, no possibility of maintaining the ceded territory if the leased territory was to revert. It was seen as an opportune time for Britain but in the event it was not so for the P.R.C. The latter was still hoping, first and foremost, to promote reunification with Taiwan in the circumstances surrounding the U.S. derecognition of the R.O.C. and the formal recognition of the P.R.C. P.R.C. policy was reflected in Ye Jianying's proposals and in the development of the concept of "one country, two systems." In this context, although the message from Deng Xiaoping to Hong Kong was encouraging, it was necessary to wait until 1982, by which time U.S. politics had ruled out any progress regarding China's reuniting Taiwan, before Britain was able formally to raise the question of the future of Hong Kong.

1982–1996

The history of the subsequent negotiations leading to the signing of the Sino-British Agreement is well known. Suffice to say that the P.R.C. ruled out, from the start, any renewal of the lease or any question of Britain's exchanging sovereignty for the right of continued administration. In those circumstances, the policy of the British negotiators was to achieve as detailed an agreement as humanly possible in the belief that the outcome would be binding and confidence in the future of Hong Kong would be maintained up to and beyond 1997. As events unfolded the period to 1997 was to cover the terms of office of three governors, Sir Edward Youde, Sir David Wilson and the Rt. Hon. Christopher Patten.

In the context of Britain's Hong Kong policy, the main question that has arisen concerns the issue of continuity. Throughout the period from the repossession of Hong Kong to the signing of the Joint Declaration (JD) in 1984, the aim of the policy had been to manage the inherited situation in what was perceived to be the best interests of business and residents. The grounds for this were that such interests were linked, that profit for the former would promote growth from which the latter, with sound administration, would benefit too. Did the British at any of the several milestones along the final stretch of the road from repossession to retrocession deliberately, and, as the phrase goes, with malice aforethought, change aim? If so at which stage and with what new target in sight?

The charge that they were preparing to do so was made as early as 1985 by Xu Jiatun, then head of the Xinhua News Agency (XHNA), the vehicle of the Hong Kong and Macau Work Committee of the CCP. He identified the ongoing development of representative government as a departure, by the British, from what had been envisaged in the negotiations leading to the agreement.[25] To those committed to such a development this seemed an unacceptable interference as the agreement specified that the legislature of Hong Kong Special Administrative Region would be constituted by elections. Indeed, many had chosen to be convinced by this provision that the agreement was a good one. Their confidence had been boosted by the promise implied in that single statement and by the linked assertion that the executive would be accountable to the legislature.

It is now clear from the reaction of the Chinese side and recent observations by the chief British negotiator, the very able and experienced former ambassador to the P.R.C., Privy Councillor and advisor to Prime Minister Thatcher (1984–1991) and, (until 1992) Prime Minister John Major, Sir Percy Cradock, that the statement was meant in very general terms and had been included "at a very late stage in the negotiations." It had been agreed following a plea made in a letter from the then British Foreign Secretary Sir Geoffrey Howe to his Chinese counterpart, Foreign Minister Wu Xueqian. That it was framed in very general terms, without any attempt clearly to define how such a system would be generated, reflected the position of the Chinese side. Indeed, according to Sir Percy when, at an earlier stage in the negotiations, the British negotiators had

---

[25] Statement by Xu Jiatun at a press conference called by him shortly before the second meeting of the Joint Liaison Group, reported in *Xinwan Bao* (Hong Kong), 22 November 1985.

mooted the idea of democracy for Hong Kong, the immediate response of the chief negotiator Ji Pengfei had been to say emphatically "bu xing" (meaning no).[26] While the circumstances of the inclusion of the statement had been made clear to Exco in Hong Kong, which, at the time was more concerned with the issue of nationality, over which, as noted, Mr. Lo Tak-shing was subsequently to resign, they were neither self-evident nor had they been made clear to those on the outside in Britain and Hong Kong. Their perception of the agreement was formed from the gloss put on it by the British politicians and the media. The conservative leadership was obviously keen to present it for what it was: a considerable feat of negotiation.

In retrospect, it is evident there was no need for, say, Sir Geoffrey Howe or any other British politician to have presented the terms of the agreement in greater detail. Sir Geoffrey did not perform a feat *of legerdemain* or Welsh wizardry in presenting it to Hong Kong, the British parliament and the world. Moreover, although there were ambiguities, they could be ascribed to the teams having gone as far as their instructions permitted in 1984. On balance, it did not appear likely that in the approach to 1997, under the continued leadership of Deng Xiaoping and Zhao Ziyang, such ambiguities would become the source of irreconcilable contradictions.

On the eve of retrocession, this view of British policy is acceptable neither to the P.R.C. nor to many of the politicians who, in the meantime, have emerged to lead Hong Kong. Taking the views of the latter first, it is clear that those who formed the United Democrats and the Democratic Party, such as Martin Lee Chu-ming and Szeto Wah and a number of independents including Emily Lau and Christine Loh, who represent the middle class and middle class values and aspirations in Hong Kong, interpreted the JD rather differently. They saw it as a guarantee of a high degree of autonomy of Hong Kong, to be achieved in the approach to 1997 through the realization of a democratic system of representative government. This was the view they, and their increasingly numerous supporters in the 20–50 age group, chose to take of the JD. They campaigned accordingly and with increasing effectiveness while the British government and the Hong Kong

---

[26] I am grateful to Sir Percy Cradock for this amplification of the circumstances surrounding the inclusion of these commitments in Annex 1 of the Agreement.

administration sought, through Green and White Papers issued during the periods in office of Sir Edward Youde and Sir David Wilson judiciously to manage the situation.[27]

The view of the P.R.C., or rather, Britain's perception of the view of the P.R.C., was of the risks inherent in rapid constitutional development in Hong Kong. The constitutional changes advocated by the reformists had not been sanctioned in the negotiations and had not been tried during the years of Britain's tenure in Hong Kong. Indeed, in various forms they had been proposed and rejected in the 1945–1952 period. Some of the reasons for rejecting them appeared as cogent in the 1980s as they had been earlier. These included notably the risk of the legislature being dominated by political forces opposed to the sovereign power and the administration being unable to get its policies approved by a hostile legislature. The reforms proposed appeared to presage the introduction of an untried system at a late stage in the history of British Hong Kong. The outcome, at the very best, would be disruptive and unpredictable; and at the very worst, it could be disruptive and damaging. If Britain permitted the development of the system along the lines advocated by reformists, the governance of Hong Kong and possibly its economic performance would be affected, as would the future relationship between the central government and the HKSAR.

By 1989, these views of the reformists and of China were already far apart. In between, the view from Britain was to attempt to bridge the gap through consultation and by reaching a compromise on the pace and reach of constitutional reform ultimately to be sanctioned by the Basic Law (BL). Unfortunately, the consequences of the crisis in China in 1989 made the gap virtually unbridgeable. The suppression of the democracy movement and the abrupt fall from grace of Zhao Ziyang traumatized the Hong Kong population and its nascent political leaders. People of all persuasions, to differing degrees, expressed shock, horror and condemnation of the killings in Tiananmen Square. Many of the leaders of the democratic movement in

---

[27] *Green Paper: The Further Development of Representative Government in Hong Kong* (Hong Kong: Government Printer, July 1984); *White Paper, The Further Development of Representative Government in Hong Kong* (Hong Kong: Government Printer, November 1984); *Green Paper, The 1987 Review of Developments in Representative Government* (Hong Kong: Government Printer, May 1987); *The Development of Representative Government: The Way Forward* (Hong Kong: Government Printer, February 1988).

Hong Kong were particularly outspoken in their support for the student movement in the P.R.C. and in their condemnation of the methods employed to suppress it.

With the benefit of hindsight, the response of the democrats in Hong Kong can be explained partly by the shock of the political and military reaction in the P.R.C. and partly by the unfulfilled expectation that communist systems throughout the world were collapsing. The judgement was proved to be correct for the U.S.S.R. and its satellite countries but seriously incorrect for the P.R.C. Consequently they incurred the unremitting wrath of the leadership under Deng Xiaoping and Li Peng, and Hong Kong was identified and condemned for its role as a base for subverting the political system of the P.R.C.[28] This verdict was reflected in the text of the final version of the Basic Law approved in 1990.

The crisis in China had a "significant impact on British policy" towards Hong Kong. Coincidentally, the Foreign Affairs Committee (FAC) of the British House of Commons was scrutinizing the conduct of British policy towards Hong Kong at the time of the crisis. It took evidence in Hong Kong and, before the breakup of the Deng-Zhao coalition, visited Peking. The 1989 FAC report was condemned for its pusillanimous attitude to the question of Hong Kong British Citizens' rights of abode in Britain but praised for its support of a faster pace of democratization, the planned repatriation of Vietnamese refugees, the provision of a Bill of Rights and for the renegotiating of the question of the presence of the PLA in the HKSAR.[29] The FAC is not part of the government but its views carry weight. On this occasion, the British government, under pressure from its own supporters, the opposition and increasingly, the media, had to act. In fact, it did so judiciously. It did not initiate unilateral steps to promote democratization beyond that agreed in ongoing consultation with the P.R.C. Faced by a serious loss of confidence in Hong Kong of which the brain drain was the most conspicuous indication, it did, however, unilaterally endorse the initiation of three measures: the Port and Airport Development

---

[28] Chen Xitong, *Renmin Ribao* (Beijing), 10 July 1989. The most conspicuous example of the impact of the crisis on the second draft of the BL (February 1989) is to be found in Article 23 where there was the addition of a clause requiring the HKSAR Government to pass a law banning subversion.

[29] House of Commons, *Foreign Affairs Committee Second Report: Hong Kong* (Session 1988–89) (London: HMSO, 1989).

Strategy (PADS), the British Nationality Selection Scheme (BNSS) and the Bill of Rights.[30]

Within a short space of time, these aspects of British policy, designed to bolster confidence in Hong Kong, were condemned by the P.R.C. The PADS was seen as a manoeuvre to siphon off reserves through contracts awarded to British companies and to saddle the P.R.C. with sovereign debt. The BNSS which gave 50,000 heads of household full British Citizenship, implying that up to 250,000 Hong Kong people could emigrate at the time of their choosing, was viewed as a stratagem for the creation of a "fifth column" of British "sleepers" in the HKSAR system. Their role would be to sustain British influence beyond 1997. The Bill of Rights was regarded as a calculated attempt to subordinate the BL to its provisions. There were grounds for that view since, although the BL confirmed the provisions of the International Covenant on Civil and Political Rights (ICCPR), the International Covenant on Economic, Social and Cultural Rights (ICESCR) and labour conventions as applied in Hong Kong would remain in force, in practice they had not been applied absolutely.

These were important milestones along the road from repossession to retrocession. The way ahead had become far more difficult than predicted. Those difficulties were reflected in the snail-like progress in the Joint Liaison Group (JLG). The BNSS was established amidst much opposition from the P.R.C. It was a precedent for provisions adopted by other countries such as Switzerland and France which feared the outflow of talent would damage the operation of their locally based interests. Together, the scheme and such provisions succeeded in stemming the loss of talent until the return of confidence after Deng Xiaoping's southern progress in 1992. The Bill of Rights was also a target of criticism. As enacted after the appearance of the BL, it dilutes some of the provisions of the ICCPR, and largely ignores the ICESCR. It is, however, through an amendment to Letters Patent, entrenched in Hong Kong law, meaning it could not easily be changed before 1997 and it is superior to existing Hong Kong law, meaning such law has to be interpreted in the light of the criteria established by the Bill.

---

[30] *Address by the Governor, Sir David Wilson, at the opening of the 1989–1990 session of the Legislative Council, 11 October 1989.* The British government ruled out the possibility of granting the right of abode to 3.25 millions entitled to BDTC and instead announced the BNSS in late 1989, after continuing pressure from Hong Kong.

The most protracted objections (1989–1995) were, however, reserved for PADS. Whether any or all of the criticisms for this aspect of British policy could have been avoided had there been, for example, prior consultation in the wake of Tiananmen incident is highly debatable. In the event, Sir Percy Cradock and Governor Sir David Wilson continued to negotiate on constitutional reform, in particular the number of directly elected seats to Legco, and on the PADS. Regarding the latter, Sir Percy succeeded in arranging for Prime Ministers Li Peng and John Major to sign a Memorandum of Understanding (MOU) in 1991. The MOU facilitated progress on the ten core projects of the PADS.

The implications of constitutional reform were evident in the results of the 1991 elections which gave the United Democrats and their supporters a major presence in the legislature. In the shadow of the suppression of the democracy movement in China, their success was not unexpected. Britain chose not to accede to the claims of the United Democrats that their leaders should be appointed to Exco. The reason given was that the requirement of oath of confidentiality remained an impediment. In fact, the P.R.C. was opposed to their inclusion. The two prominent leaders Martin Lee and Szeto Wah had been condemned in 1989 for supporting counter-revolutionary activities.

The 1991–1995 term of the Legco was significant not only because it involved, for the first time, directly elected members but also for the requirement to reach a decision on Britain's Hong Kong policy for the 1995 elections for the 1995–1999 Legco. The aspect of the policy that was to capture the headlines concerned the measures to implement the constitutional reform to enable the Hong Kong system directly to converge with the HKSAR system prescribed in the BL. The formulation and implementation of British policy became the main task of the last governor, the Rt. Hon. Christopher Patten who succeeded Sir David Wilson in 1992.

The announcement of the retirement of the governor was made at the end of 1991 and his successor was not named until after the British general election in April 1992. Although the appointment of a politician appeared to herald a change in policy, according to Sir Percy Cradock it was not so.[31] Based on experience gained from the appointment of Lord Soames in the case of Rhodesia-Zimbabwe, it was thought that such an appointment

---

[31] Private discussion with Sir Percy Cradock, August 1996.

would be appropriate for the final period. The new governor arrived in July 1992 and announced his constitutional package in October 1992. The salient points of the package concerned the manner in which a fully elected Legco and the accountability of the executive to the legislature would be achieved in accordance with the JD and the BL in 1995.

Among them were the separation of Exco and Legco, the creation of nine new functional constituencies (FC) on a broad franchise and the broadening of the franchise for existing FCs, lowering the voting age to 18, abolishing the appointed membership of Municipal Councils (MCs) and District Boards (DBs) and the formation of the 1995 election committee from elected DB members. The package was revealed by the British Foreign Secretary Douglas Hurd to his Chinese counterpart Qian Qichen, at one of the regular biannual meetings that had been a product of the MOU negotiations. Qian requested time for consultations before the governor made the proposals public. In a departure from established practice, this was refused. The package was announced at the opening session of the 1992–1993 Legco.[32]

The controversial history of this constitutional package is also well known. Consultations started in 1993, stimulated by the administration's initiating the legal process to ensure that all stages affecting the three tiers of representative government, the District Boards, Municipal Councils and the Legco, could be completed by the end of the 1993–1994 session. After seventeen rounds of Sino-British talks, no agreement was reached. The British side, by now faced with threats that the P.R.C. would set up a "second stove" or centre of power with a view to dismantling the three tiers of representative government at the point of retrocession, proceeded unilaterally to submit the draft legislation to Legco.

Among P.R.C. grounds for challenging British policy, at the time closely identified with the governor who was regarded as having a private agenda, were that the package was in breach of the JD, the BL and of a confidential agreement in 1990 on the formation of the Election Committee. The P.R.C. was not without support for its vigorous opposition. Britain had not reached agreement through consultations and had proceeded unilaterally; the franchise for the FCs was a significant departure from

---

[32] *Address by the Governor, the Rt. Hon. Christopher Patten at the Opening of the 1992–93 Session of the Legislative Council.*

existing practice. There was support from Sir Percy Cradock on those grounds and for the view that had there not been agreement between Britain and China covering all aspects of the 1997 constitutional arrangements in the BL, the final draft providing for twenty directly elected seats in the 1995 Legco elections would not have been approved.[33]

The question remains: did Britain significantly depart from its policy by presenting such a divisive package to Legco in the teeth of P.R.C. opposition? The dominant view, formed by the FAC in 1993[34] is that it did not. The British lawyers asserted there was no breach of the agreement, nor of the provisions of the BL. The report noted that after the crisis in 1989 circumstances had changed, that the new governor had a different style but that policy had remained consistent. Another way of answering the question is to consider the damage that had been suffered and ask: would Britain have risked national interests by a change of policy that survived intact by a single vote in the legislature, in the knowledge that the reforms would not survive beyond 1997?

Implicit in this response is that Britain could hardly afford lightly to have risked benefits that would accrue from a share of the China market. Nor would Britain lightly have squandered the benefits to Hong Kong of the concept of the "through train," on which all legislators would have ridden to complete their term in the post-1997 HKSAR legislature. Instead, it is implied, a significant change in policy actually occurred after the crisis in the P.R.C. in 1989 and in the corridors of power there rather than in those in Britain. Subsequently, and consequently, British policy, taking into account British, Hong Kong and international factors, was formed to restore confidence and maintain social, political and economic progress consistent with the needs of Hong Kong in the final approach to 1997.

Those needs included the adoption of proposals for representative government which were fair and open and in the judgement of the British government acceptable to the people of Hong Kong.[35]

---

[33] Private discussion with Sir Percy Cradock, August 1996.

[34] House of Commons, *Foreign Affairs Committee, First Report, Relations between the United Kingdom and China in the Period Up To and Beyond 1997*, session 1993–94, Vol. 1 (London: HMSO, 1994).

[35] Douglas Hurd, Secretary of State for Foreign Affairs and Commonwealth Affairs, *White Paper, Representative Government in Hong Kong* (Hong Kong: Government Printing Department, February 1994).

As Sir Robin McLaren, who led the British team for fifteen of the seventeen rounds of talks in 1993 put it:

> I find it very difficult to believe that any British government, whichever political party formed the government, and whoever was Prime Minister, Foreign Secretary or Governor, would have been willing to hold those elections (in 1994 and 1995) in a way which was not demonstrably fair and open, and acceptable in Hong Kong. There is room for argument about what is fair and open — they are not absolute terms — but in the end a judgement had to be made ... It was made not because Britain's policy towards China and Hong Kong had changed, as critics like to allege, but precisely because it had remained the same ... based on a sense of responsibility for and towards the people of Hong Kong, and a desire to secure the best possible future for them in Hong Kong.[36]

This argument is in part convincing; it does not, however, convincingly account for the departure from established policy in the significant extension of the franchise for FCs, nor for the conflict of views that has emerged on the British side. Among the dissenting views are those of the principal British negotiator of the JD and the MOU, Sir Percy Cradock, set out at length and eloquently before the FAC in 1993. His view is not only of a changed approach but also of a departure from the agreements. The changed approach he would argue has led to policies that are in effect worse, in the long run, for Hong Kong than the alternative based on P.R.C. preferences. This suggests the composition of the post-1997 reconstructed tiers of representative government and of the upper levels of the Civil Service for example, could be less suited to the needs of Hong Kong and the interests of Britain than the pre-reform alternatives would have been. Thus, the effect of the reform has been divisive, leaving those associated with it such as former Secretary for Constitutional Affairs Michael Sze, at a disadvantage. Worse still, the departure from the agreements could create a precedent which will be used to justify similar departures after 1997. If this were to be the case the value of the details in JD for which the negotiators strove in 1982–1984, would be significantly reduced. Such controversies over the final milestones of British policy from repossession to retrocession are unlikely to be settled in, or indeed soon after, 1997.

---

[36] Sir Robin McLaren, "Hong Kong and the Sino-British Relationship" (The Hong Kong Lecture delivered at the University of Hong Kong, 19 November 1994).

Moreover, although Britain departs then, there remain interests in, responsibilities and obligations to Hong Kong which will sustain a continuing British Hong Kong policy that, in turn, will influence Sino-British relations for many years to come.

2

Realignment of Power: The Politics of Transition and Reform in Hong Kong

Steve Tsang

The reaching of an agreement over the future of Hong Kong by Britain and the People's Republic of China (P.R.C.) in 1984 opened a new chapter in the political history of Hong Kong. This Agreement stipulates that the non-elective Crown Colony system of government in the territory would have to be reformed sufficiently to allow its "legislature ... [to] be constituted by elections" at the time of the Chinese take-over in 1997.[1] It also declares that from the day the Agreement comes into force, a "transitional period" will begin until the actual transfer of sovereignty. During this period "the United Kingdom will be responsible for the administration of Hong Kong with the object of maintaining and preserving its economic prosperity and social stability," to which "China will give its cooperation."[2] Although these two provisions do not appear to conflict with each other, in practice they require democratic Britain to be responsible to reform Hong Kong's legislature in a way which socialist China will support. In view of the opposing political persuasions of the two signatories, the Agreement in effect put them on a collision course but forbade them from crashing into each other. The situation was further complicated by the fact that introducing elections to the legislature would involve handing over certain political

---

[1] *A Draft Agreement between the Government of the United Kingdom of Great Britain and Northern Ireland and the Government of the People's Republic of China on the Future of Hong Kong* (Sino-British Agreement) (Hong Kong: Government Printer, 1984), p. 15.

[2] *Ibid.*, p. 13.

power to the local population. The politics of transition in Hong Kong was therefore conditioned by the realignment of power among Britain, China and, as a result of political reforms, the people of Hong Kong. There was, however, no agreement as to how this should be achieved.

From China's point of view, the transitional period serves the purposes of preparing Hong Kong to be retroceded to China and of enhancing the interests of China as defined by the leadership in Beijing. It has no other value. All the concessions made to Britain in the Agreement of 1984 were conceded in order to secure the return of this precious and somewhat vulnerable piece of valuable real estate without undue damage being done to it. Thus Beijing feels entirely justified to call the shots in the politics of transition in Hong Kong, but has decided to allow as large a degree of flexibility as possible in Hong Kong in order to further its own best interests. In other words, to Beijing, the British Government in Hong Kong should serve as its custodian in the transitional period and not attempt anything disapproved by itself.

Britain does see its role in the transitional period as that of a custodian, but that of its own and of Hong Kong's rather than Beijing's best interests. Britain recognizes the need to secure the blessings of China for its policies in Hong Kong during the transition but does not intend to be China's hatchet man. To Britain the rationale for the Agreement was to enable itself to withdraw from Hong Kong with honour. For this purpose it was necessary "to secure an agreement which meets the needs and wishes of the people" there and "would ensure lasting stability and prosperity for Hong Kong."[3] As sovereign power until 1997 Britain felt when it signed the 1984 Agreement that it had considerable latitude to run the territory as it saw fit through the Hong Kong Government. To the British the transition is to ensure that the pieces are in place for the Chinese take-over so that little need to be done apart from a formal hand-over of sovereignty in 1997. As the personal representative of the Crown the Governor of Hong Kong has not abdicated his position and authority, though he is in general terms prepared to be sensitive to the wishes and needs of China, the prospective new sovereign.

The people of Hong Kong are divided over the prospect of Chinese take-over in 1997. Some are pleased to see the end of British imperial rule

---

[3] *Sino-British Agreement*, p. 7.

and reunification with mother China, others are not. But even among former groups some are also unwilling to see Hong Kong being absorbed into the P.R.C. A wide spectrum of views exist. The emerging trend since 1984 is a rising desire among local residents to have a say over their own future, though they are divided as to the best way to achieve this goal. To some, democratization is the obvious answer. Others prefer to please the new prospective sovereign and to be co-opted into the power structure set up by the Chinese, just as the former elites of Hong Kong had managed to do through the good office of the British colonial establishment. Some of the "old guards" who were part of the establishment in 1984 also tried to fight a rearguard operation to protect their vested interests. In contrast to the previous decades when local politics could be seen as having been absorbed by administration, the picture began to change significantly in 1985 and a new brand of politics emerged in due course.[4]

As Hong Kong entered the period of transition, the need for political reform and the forces unleashed by the Sino-British Agreement caused the alignment of political power to be altered. This chapter examines this process by looking into the roles played by the three principal actors, Britain, the people of Hong Kong and the P.R.C. In the context of this inquiry the Hong Kong Government is considered to be part of the British establishment rather than the civil authority representing the people of Hong Kong. It is because the subject matter concerned involves relations with the P.R.C. for which Britain is responsible, and which requires the Hong Kong Government to work closely with Her Majesty's Government (HMG) in London. The close consultations between Government House and Whitehall in this matter does not imply the Hong Kong Government has become less autonomous in the management of its domestic affairs. This chapter ends with some reflections on the forces behind the process to realign political power in the transitional period.

The Declining Force: Britain

The ratification of the 1984 Agreement marked the beginning of the end of British pre-eminence in the politics of Hong Kong. Although its

---

[4] For the concept of administrative absorption of politics, see Ambrose King, "Administrative Absorption of Politics in Hong Kong: Emphasis on the Grass Roots Level," *Asian Survey*, Vol. 15, No. 5 (May 1975).

sovereign right to rule continues until 1997, the signing of the Agreement demonstrated clearly the British intention to pull out and hand over power to the new sovereign. Unlike the usual process of decolonization elsewhere in the British empire, the British withdrawal requires them to transfer power not to the local people but to a new metropolitan power, the P.R.C. By the Agreement, Britain would relinquish in 1997 sovereignty over Hong Kong to the P.R.C. which, in turn, would empower the people of Hong Kong through the Basic Law to form a Special Administrative Region (SAR). Whatever the public rhetoric, this had to be achieved regardless of the wishes of the local people.[5] Despite conducting an exercise ostensibly to assess public acceptability of the Agreement in 1984, the British had made it "clear beyond any possibility of misunderstanding" that there was "no possibility of an amended agreement" and that the only alternative was "to have no agreement" because the Chinese would not reopen negotiations.[6] The implication was that while Britain had tried and would continue to try to secure the best deal for itself and for the people of Hong Kong, it conceded that China had the advantage of being able to exercise a kind of pocket veto on this matter.

The political reality above notwithstanding, HMG, the British Parliament and the Hong Kong Government engaged in what appears in retrospect remarkable wishful thinking in 1984. In Hong Kong a major political reform package was being examined carefully during the last stage of the Sino-British negotiations. In July, two months before the Sino-British Agreement was initialled, a Green Paper was published in which the Hong Kong Government pointedly stated the main aim of this reform. It was "to develop progressively a system of government the authority for which is firmly rooted in Hong Kong, which is able to represent authoritatively the views of the people of Hong Kong, and which is more directly accountable to the people of Hong Kong."[7] The consultation exercise was followed by the publication of a reform package in a White Paper in

---

[5] Ian Scott, "Political Transformation in Hong Kong: From Colony to Colony," in *The Hong Kong–Guangdong Link: Partnership in Flux*, edited by R. Y. W. Kwok and A. Y. So (Hong Kong: Hong Kong University Press, 1995), pp. 193–94.

[6] *Sino-British Agreement*, p. 7.

[7] *Green Paper: The Further Development of Representative Government in Hong Kong* (Hong Kong: Government Printer, 1984), p. 4.

November, again a month prior to the formal signing of the Agreement. When Parliament debated the draft Agreement in December, one after another, most members who voiced support for the Agreement did so on the understanding that democratization would be introduced as part of the deal. It was not a partisan issue. In order to secure the support of Parliament, Minister of State Richard Luce told the House of Commons that Britain would "build up a firmly-based, democratic administration in Hong Kong in the years between now and 1997."[8] Luce's colleague, Baroness Young admitted in the House of Lords that Britain had decided to proceed slowly rather than quickly when the Green Paper was revised into the White Paper in the autumn that year. However, she assured the House that the "White Paper proposals are entirely consistent with the provisions in the draft agreement ... which specified that the Legislature of the Hong Kong SAR shall be constituted by elections."[9] In spite of Young's recognition of the need to dovetail with China's plans for Hong Kong as from 1997, the British establishment proceeded on the basis that Britain would have a free hand to reform the political system of Hong Kong within the framework defined by the Agreement. In other words, in 1984 the British establishment deluded itself by refusing to recognize that by signing the Agreement, the old alignment of power between Britain and China over Hong Kong had been changed significantly.

The British establishment's remarkable display of confidence in its ability to steer political developments in Hong Kong did not last, however. Within a year HMG and the Hong Kong Government had to admit in practice that China could exercise a *de facto* veto over any British plan for democratization in Hong Kong. In November 1985, shortly after the Hong Kong Government introduced the limited political reform outlined in the White Paper of 1984, China's representative in Hong Kong, Xu Jiatun, took the initiative to accuse the British of breaching the Agreement.[10] Xu stressed the need for political reforms in Hong Kong in the transitional period to converge with the Basic Law for the SAR, for which the drafting

---

[8] *Parliamentary Debates: House of Commons*, Vol. 69, No. 23, 6 December 1984 (London: Her Majesty's Stationary Office, 1984), p. 470.

[9] *Parliamentary Debates: House of Lords*, Vol. 458, No. 17, 10 December 1984 (London: Her Majesty's Stationary Office, 1984), p. 85.

[10] *Cheng Bao* (Hong Kong), 22 November 1985.

process had just begun.[11] However clumsy Xu was, his bold initiative was in fact of considerable significance. From a legalistic point of view, the proper basis for ensuring convergence between British and Chinese rule over Hong Kong must be the Agreement itself and not the Basic Law. The latter is a document to be promulgated, albeit by the Chinese National People's Congress on its own authority, as required by the Agreement for the purpose of implementing its terms.[12] By insisting that convergence be based on the Basic Law, an entirely Chinese concern, Xu in effect put aside the Sino-British Agreement and demanded the right for his government to exercise a veto. As Sir Percy Cradock, at the time an adviser to the British Prime Minister, admits in his memoirs this meant the Chinese "would decide what to put in the Basic Law and the British would converge with it."[13] The British rationale, explained by Cradock, was to ensure "major changes in government during the transitional period" would "remain in force beyond the hand-over."[14] Convergence has become a guiding principle of British policy over Hong Kong ever since.

The subsequent debates in Hong Kong over the pace and extent of democratization, particularly the controversies over the introduction of directly elected seats to the Legislative Council (1987–1988) should be seen in this context. The Hong Kong Government on its own had already abandoned its policy that "major reform was 'inopportune'," a policy which was in place between 1952 and 1981.[15] HMG, for its part, had gone further and, as illustrated above, had committed itself in Parliament to introduce democracy to Hong Kong. On their own, the two governments had no reason to reverse their policy of political reform. However, following Xu's forceful accusation, British Foreign Office Minister Timothy Renton also received confirmation of China's views about convergence when he visited Beijing in January 1986.[16] Consequently he tried to dampen public

---

[11] *Ibid.*; Xu Jiatun, *Xu Jiatun Xianggang Huiyilu*, Vol. 1 (Taiwan: United Daily News, 1993), pp. 172–74.

[12] *Sino-British Agreement*, p. 14.

[13] Percy Cradock, *Experiences of China* (London: John Murray, 1994), p. 218.

[14] *Ibid.*

[15] Steve Tsang, *Democracy Shelved: Great Britain, China, and Attempts at Constitutional Reform in Hong Kong, 1945–1952* (Hong Kong: Oxford University Press, 1988), p. 213.

[16] Mark Roberti, *The Fall of Hong Kong: Britain's Betrayal and China's Triumph* (New York: John Wiley & Sons, 1994), p. 162.

demands for further democratization in Hong Kong.[17] By then the British had in practice accepted the existence of a Chinese veto and started to back-pedal. Nevertheless, the British had committed themselves in the White Paper of November 1984 to review in 1987 the question of introducing direct elections to the Legislative Council in 1988.[18] A review had to be conducted. The British also adhered to the principle of convergence as they considered "co-operation over Hong Kong's future lies at the heart of the present close and cordial relations between the United Kingdom and China."[19] In light of the above, it is understandable that the Hong Kong Government "used discredited submissions and surveys to support its view that 'more were against than in favour of direct elections in 1988', a highly dubious conclusion."[20] It was not a coincidence that the number of directly elected members to the Legislative Council approved by the Hong Kong Government in 1988 "accord[ed] with the figure published in the first draft of the Basic Law" later that year.[21] However manipulative the British were on this occasion, they were not malicious. Their action was dictated by the tipping of the balance of power in favour of China, and also by Britain's assessment at the time that it was the lesser of the two evils — the other was to lose China's cooperation.

The Tiananmen incident of 1989 traumatized Hong Kong and almost subverted the British plan that by agreeing to converge on the Basic Law, Britain would have "a further opportunity of ... ensuring that evolution in the final years [of British rule] would survive the transition."[22] Following the military crackdown in Beijing, strong public opinion and the Foreign Affairs Committee of the House of Commons urged HMG to "seize the initiative so as to establish in Hong Kong in advance of 1997 the institutions and systems best designed to guarantee Hong Kong's future autonomy and

---

[17] *Hong Kong Standard* (Hong Kong), 22 January 1986.

[18] *White Paper: The Further Development of Representative Government in Hong Kong* (Hong Kong: Government Printer, 1984), p. 9.

[19] *White Paper on the Annual Report on Hong Kong 1987 to Parliament* (Hong Kong: Government Printer, 1988), p. 1.

[20] Ian Scott, *Political Change and the Crisis of Legitimacy in Hong Kong* (Hong Kong: Oxford University Press, 1989), pp. 296–97.

[21] Percy Cradock, *Experiences of China*, p. 227.

[22] *Ibid.*, p. 218.

stability."[23] Even Prime Minister Margaret Thatcher recognized that there were "strong moral arguments for doing so."[24] But she resisted the calls to push ahead with democratization regardless of Beijing's views. For his part Hong Kong Governor Sir David Wilson continued to take the view "that 'whatever is the percentage of direct elections laid down in the Basic Law [would be the percentage] [sic] in our final election under British administration'."[25] What the British did in the aftermath of the crackdown in Beijing was to suspend normal business with the Chinese authorities including ministerial exchanges. However, as Foreign Secretary Sir Geoffrey Howe explained, HMG remained convinced that the future of Hong Kong "must depend on a successful and secure partnership with the Government and people of China."[26] Convergence was suspended temporarily, not abandoned as a policy.

The Tiananmen incident also provoked "a confidence crisis" in Hong Kong.[27] In response, HMG and the Hong Kong Government "outlined a package of measures ... to restore confidence."[28] These included a bill of rights for Hong Kong, the granting of the right of abode to 50,000 Hong Kong families, the launching of the massive Port and Airport Development Strategy (PADS), and increasing the number of directly elected seats to the Legislative Council in 1991. As Governor Wilson told the people of Hong Kong, all of these were intended to "demonstrate your government's commitment to the future."[29] None was meant to antagonize Beijing. Indeed,

---

[23] House of Commons, *Foreign Affairs Committee Second Report: Hong Kong* (Session 1988–89) (London: Her Majesty's Stationary Office, 1989), p. xii.

[24] Margaret Thatcher, *The Downing Street Years* (London: Harper Collins, 1993), p. 495.

[25] *Foreign Affairs Committee Second Report* (1988–89), p. xii.

[26] Hong Kong Government Office (London), "Parliamentary Debate in the House of Commons on 6 June, 1989" *Parliamentary Information*, 511/12, No. 69, statement by Sir G. Howe.

[27] Joseph Cheng, "Prospects for Democracy in Hong Kong," in *The Broken Mirror: China After Tiananmen*, edited by George Hicks (Harlow: Longman, 1990), p. 278.

[28] Frank Ching, "Toward Colonial Sunset: The Wilson Regime, 1987–1992," in *Precarious Balance: Hong Kong between China and Britain, 1842–1992*, edited by M. K. Chan (Hong Kong: Hong Kong University Press, 1994), p. 180.

[29] *Hong Kong 1990* (Hong Kong: Government Printer, 1990), p. 22.

HMG was so keen to "pick up the threads of business with the Chinese leaders" and restore the policy of convergence that Cradock was secretly sent to Beijing as a personal representative of Prime Minister Thatcher in December 1989.[30] The Chinese leaders showed "a feeling of anger, and a complete failure of understanding, over the reactions of Hong Kong people to the student movement and its suppression."[31] They were suspicious that the British proposals were "in fact a sign of a conspiracy to exert pressure on China."[32] The less than positive Chinese reaction, and the strong public expectations in Hong Kong and in Britain of a strengthening of safeguards for the future of the people of Hong Kong, forced HMG and the Hong Kong Government to appear to take a stronger stand towards China than they actually did. For a short time after June 1989, the two governments appeared to have seized the initiative and to be conducting their policies towards Hong Kong without reference to Beijing's wishes.

As the dust of the Tiananmen incident and the collapse of communism in Eastern Europe and the Soviet Union settled and as the Chinese leadership recovered its confidence in its control over the country, China took a harder line towards the British over Hong Kong. There was little that Beijing could actually do immediately to derail the bill of rights and the right of abode package. However, the massive and long-term nature of financing required for PADS gave Beijing a useful lever to regain the upper hand *vis-à-vis* London. Unable to persuade Beijing of its good intentions over PADS, the British tried to break the deadlock by making a major concession. Prime Minister John Major ended the West's suspension of summit meetings with China imposed in response to the Tiananmen incident, and restored credibility to the Chinese Government by paying an official visit to Beijing in September 1991. Major secured a memorandum of understanding for the airport core project, and an agreement "to intensify consultation and co-operation over Hong Kong issues in the approach to 30 June 1997."[33] Nevertheless, Beijing did not allow the status quo anted in Sino-British relations to be restored and insisted publicly that any major

---

[30] Percy Cradock, *Experiences of China*, pp. 229 and 231.

[31] *Ibid.*, p. 230.

[32] *Ibid.*, p. 231.

[33] Foreign and Commonwealth Office, *Documents on the Prime Minister's Visit to Peking, 2–4 September 1991* (no publication details), "Memorandum of Understanding."

policy matter that would straddle 1997 would have to be approved by Beijing before implementation.

This Chinese demand to be given a public veto over development policies in Hong Kong despite Britain's major concession appeared to have angered or at least greatly disappointed the Prime Minister, who must have come to the conclusion that a policy adjustment was needed. This would explain his decision to remove the two leading advocates for the policy of accommodating China shortly afterwards. Wilson was removed from the governorship of Hong Kong and Cradock was retired as an adviser to the Prime Minister. Major must have decided to stiffen British's handling of its policy over Hong Kong. When Major appointed Christopher Patten, a former cabinet minister and close colleague, Governor of Hong Kong in mid-1992, the latter was undoubtedly sent with a mandate to review Britain's Hong Kong policy. At that time there were great expectations for a quicker pace of democratization in Hong Kong. As the House of Commons Foreign Affairs Committee recognized, "doing nothing about electoral arrangements was not an option."[34] The political reform proposals which Patten put forward in October 1992 bore the marks of a cleverly devised scheme. They were intended "to extend democracy while working within the Basic Law."[35] Patten in fact tried to push to the absolute limit of democratization not expressly prohibited in, which in the common law tradition means not violating, the Basic Law.[36] Not familiar with the Chinese, Patten probably did not realize that in Chinese legal tradition, what is not permitted is prohibited. In other words, his carefully devised scheme would in the Chinese view amount to breaching the Basic Law even though they could not cite chapters and verses to back up their views. Nor did Patten appear to believe the Chinese would actually put the well-being of Hong Kong (and therefore China's own interests) at risk and demolish in 1997 his proposed reforms because these had not received prior approval from Beijing. Judging on the basis of his proposals, Patten had not intended to reverse the policy of convergence or provoke Beijing. However, as a

---

[34] House of Commons, *Foreign Affairs Committee: First Report: Relations between the United Kingdom and China in the Period Up To and Beyond 1997*, session 1993–94, Vol. 1 (London: Her Majesty's Stationary Office, 1994), p. xlvi.

[35] Christopher Patten, *Our Next Five Years: The Agenda for Hong Kong* (Hong Kong: Government Printer, 1992), p. 41.

[36] *Foreign Affairs Committee: First Report*, pp. xxxix–xl.

political heavyweight in Britain he did change the emphasis, alter the way
with which Britain dealt with Beijing, and push further than British mandarins had attempted hitherto.[37]

Britain's policy towards Hong Kong was toughened after October 1992
primarily in response to the virulent attacks which the Chinese levelled at
Governor Patten. It was because London felt it was presented with the
choice between supporting the Governor or "surrender[ing] the argument
to China."[38] In spite of the steady decline of Britain's power over Hong
Kong *vis-à-vis* China, it felt that it had no option but rally behind its man
on the spot and make a stand. Britain has not in fact abandoned convergence
but, as will be explained later, the Chinese policy to ignore Governor Patten
had greatly reduced the value of the policy of convergence. China increasingly worked to marginalize Britain's influence over Hong Kong affairs
after negotiations over the Patten proposals were broken off in 1994. Nevertheless, as the metropolitan power Britain will continue to be responsible
for the administration of the territory through the Hong Kong Government.
Given China's desire and need for a smooth take-over which requires
British cooperation, it has accepted that Britain still has a significant though
declining role to play in Hong Kong politics in the run-up to the actual
transfer of power in mid-1997.

The Rising Force: China

The relative decline of Britain as a factor in Hong Kong politics was
matched to an extent by the rise of China. As the prospective new sovereign
which has the ultimate say in what will be permitted at the end of the
transitional period, its policy towards Hong Kong has become an increasingly dominant factor in the local political scene. However, this has not
been a simple linear development.

To begin with, since China's objective was to take over Hong Kong
and benefit from it economically, it had to work within the political environment which it found in Hong Kong in the earlier half of the 1980s.
As Joseph Cheng rightly observed at the time, the "vast majority of Hong
Kong's 5.5 million people hope to preserve their freedom, way of life and

---

[37] *Ibid.*, p. xlvi.
[38] *Ibid.*, p. xlix.

standard of living," and were worried that China would not "refrain from interfering in the territory's domestic activities."[39] A successful take-over by China would therefore largely depend on China's ability to persuade the local people that China would not interfere with their affairs. This provided an important counter-weight to Britain's conceding the advantage to China of prescribing the parameters for political reform inherent in its policy of convergence.

China's policy towards Hong Kong since the early 1980s has in fact been based on the principle of allowing "maximum flexibility within a rigid framework."[40] This policy was laid down at the beginning of the Sino-British negotiations by Deng Xiaoping who considered that the basis for a solution, the Chinese recovery of sovereignty, was "not a subject that could be discussed."[41] Within this rigid framework he was willing to negotiate with the British the other two crucial issues involved, namely: the way by which China would administer Hong Kong in order to maintain prosperity and stability after 1997 and arrangements to ensure a smooth transition.[42] This was the foundation of the policy known as "one country, two systems." In other words, China would permit Hong Kong to maintain the status quo for fifty years and enjoy "a high degree of autonomy," provided Hong Kong would continue to be deemed by the Chinese leadership as economically beneficial and not harmful to its claim of sovereignty. The implication of this policy is that China would for its own interests hold back from intervening in local politics during the transition. The existence of a brief honeymoon period in Anglo-Chinese cooperation in the first half of 1985 testifies that this policy was implemented seriously at first.

Since the British were then engaged in reforming the political system in Hong Kong the situation changed quickly, however. By late 1985 China had become highly suspicious of Britain's intentions behind its efforts to introduce political reforms in Hong Kong. As seen by China's representative

---

[39] Joseph Cheng (ed.), *Hong Kong: In Search of a Future* (Hong Kong: Oxford University Press, 1984), pp. 12–13.

[40] Steve Tsang, "Maximum Flexibility, Rigid Framework: China's Policy towards Hong Kong and Its Implications," *Journal of International Affairs*, Vol. 49, No. 2 (Winter 1996), p. 414.

[41] Deng Xiaoping, *Deng Xiaoping Wenxuan*, Vol. 3 (Beijing: Renmin Chubanshe, 1993), p. 12.

[42] *Ibid.*, pp. 12–13.

in Hong Kong at the time, Xu Jiatun, the reforms were deemed a British pre-emptive strike intended to achieve "major changes in the [coming] thirteen years and no changes in the [following] fifty years," and to present China with a *fait accompli* while it was only beginning to draft the Basic Law.[43] It was in this context that he publicly accused Britain of breaching the Agreement in November 1985. The initial reservation which Beijing had over Xu's initiative indicates it was a departure from the established policy. It was only after the British responded by conceding convergence would be based on the Basic Law that Beijing vindicated Xu.[44] The tipping of the balance of power to China's favour as a result was not foreseen but welcomed by the Chinese leaders including Deng Xiaoping himself.[45]

Once the Chinese realized that they had in effect acquired a pocket veto over political developments in Hong Kong, particularly through the drafting of the Basic Law, they used it to force the British to converge on their position, most noticeably over the 1987 review for reform examined earlier. Nevertheless, the Chinese could not ignore the rising public demand for democratic changes in Hong Kong. It had to win the hearts and minds of the local people in order to ensure a smooth transition. The drafting process of the Basic Law was thus used as the centre-piece for their united front efforts in the territory. Although at no point did China give up directing the drafting process, it did make considerable concessions to public opinion.[46] Even Hong Kong's leading critic of Beijing, Martin Lee, who took part in the drafting process until 1989 admitted relatively early in the process that he "felt both the mainland and Hong Kong members of the Drafting Committee cooperated happily together."[47] The final product undoubtedly represented what Beijing found acceptable, but the Basic Law would not have been the same without the extended consultations. As illustrated by the drafting process until 1989, China avoided letting its

---

[43] Xu Jiatun, *Xu Jiatun Xianggang Huiyilu*, Vol. 1, pp. 172–73.

[44] *Ibid.*, pp. 175–77.

[45] *Ibid.*

[46] Xianggang Wenhuipao (ed.), *Jibenfa de Dansheng* (Hong Kong: Wen Wei Publishing, 1990), pp. 54–55 (statement by T. K. Ann).

[47] Li Zhuming, *Li Zhuming Minzhu Yanlunji* (Hong Kong: Tianyuan Shudian, 1989), p. 163. This statement was made at the second full meeting of the Drafting Committee on 20 April 1986.

steadily rising influence dominate Hong Kong politics completely. This self-restraint allowed scope, however limited it was, for the residents of Hong Kong, particularly the political activists, to concurrently expand their roles in local politics. By and large Beijing played the political game in Hong Kong in accordance with the rules laid down by the British administration.

The Tiananmen incident of 1989 caused a major change to China's attitude. Until then Deng and his government had the confidence "that the Communist Party-dominated system of the P.R.C. was superior to Hong Kong's capitalist system."[48] This was necessary to allow an *imperium in imperio* to practise a system fundamentally hostile to its survival, which is inherent in the policy to permit capitalism to continue in Hong Kong as a part of socialist China.[49] The public challenge to Deng's authority in Tiananmen and the subsequent collapse of communism in Eastern Europe greatly weakened such confidence. After the military crackdown, Deng ordered the party-state to "uphold socialism staunchly and pre-empt peaceful evolution."[50] The support which the people of Hong Kong gave to the Tiananmen demonstrators was seen as subversion by Beijing.[51] Feeling insecure, China tightened its control over the drafting of the Basic Law and toughened its terms.[52] As explained in the earlier section, Beijing also took a harder line towards the British and used PADS to regain the upper hand over Hong Kong. Beijing wanted to make sure that Hong Kong would not be used as a base for what it saw as an international conspiracy called "peaceful evolution" to subvert Chinese socialism.[53] It is ironic that the

---

[48] Deng Xiaoping, *Deng Xiaoping Lun Xianggang Wenti* (Hong Kong: Joint Publishing, 1993), p. 6.

[49] Deng Xiaoping, *Deng Xiaoping Wenxuan*, p. 217.

[50] *Ibid.*, p. 344.

[51] *Baixing* (Pai Shing Semi-monthly), Vol. 195 (1 July 1989), p. 52; Percy Cradock, *Experiences of China*, pp. 229–30.

[52] Ming K. Chan and David Clark (eds.), *The Hong Kong Basic Law: Blueprint for "Stability and Prosperity" under Chinese Sovereignty* (Hong Kong: Hong Kong University Press, 1991), pp. 21–29.

[53] The Chinese believe John Foster Dulles first used the term "peaceful evolution" in the 1950s to describe a strategy to bring down Communism by peaceful means.

Chinese leadership became more aggressive over Hong Kong when its self-confidence reached a low point.

It was in this context that Governor Patten's reform proposals of October 1992 were received in Beijing. The Chinese misunderstood not only the real thrust of the proposals but also the British intention.[54] In the words of Lu Ping, Director of the Hong Kong and Macau Affairs Office, the proposals were deemed an attempt "to turn Hong Kong into a semi-independent entity with a vain hope that this will influence political developments in China."[55] This was elaborated on by Foreign Minister Qian Qichen, who linked the proposals to an alleged conspiracy to create "one China and one Taiwan" and to interfere with "the so-called human rights issues of Tibet" in order to "create disorder" for the P.R.C.[56] The basic policy line was stated by Premier Li Peng: "It was totally unacceptable [to China] to make any counter-proposals or reach any compromise on the basis of the Governor's political reform proposals."[57] Nevertheless, in view of the need to win over the support of the Hong Kong people, China entered into negotiations with Britain over the Patten proposals in April 1993 after a long delay. When the British finally broke off negotiations after seventeen rounds, Beijing responded by proceeding to, in Lu Ping's words, "build a new kitchen."[58] This meant China would set up the first SAR legislature regardless of the political reforms undertaken under Governor Patten. By then, in 1994, China had concluded that Britain had abandoned the policy of convergence and it must therefore work out its own arrangements for the take-over — with or without British cooperation.[59] The fact that Britain still, as explained earlier, adheres to convergence and tries to reach working compromises with China indicates that China has relatively greater say in dictating the political agenda in the final years of the transition, though Britain has not been reduced to an irrelevant

---

[54] For Beijing's failure to understand the scope of Patten's proposals, see Steve Tsang, "Maximum Flexibility, Rigid Framework," pp. 424–25.

[55] *Wen Wei Po* (Hong Kong), 28 January 1993.

[56] *Ta Kung Pao* (Hong Kong), 19 March 1993.

[57] *Wen Wei Po*, 24 November 1992.

[58] *Wen Wei Po*, 4 January 1993.

[59] British Broadcasting Corporations, *Survey of World Broadcast*, FE/1935 F/1, Xinhua News Agency Report of 1 March 1994.

factor either. The need for a successful take-over means that China still seeks British cooperation where it will serve Chinese interests.

The Ineffective Force: The People of Hong Kong

The Sino-British negotiations of 1982–1984 epitomized the political impotence of the people of Hong Kong. They did "not have a direct voice in the negotiations" over their future and were not allowed to vote on its outcome.[60] Even when their Governor (Sir Edward Youde) stated that he represented them, Beijing publicly and "very firmly slapped him down."[61] This political powerlessness during the negotiations "served as the catalyst to the political awakening of Hong Kong."[62] In the immediate post negotiations period, it was "the tiny but growing group of political activists" who saw and seized the 1985 reform "as their opportunity to obtain and wield political power."[63] In the second half of the 1980s, politicking by activists, heightened interest and coverage in the mass media, and emergence of a series of major debates on public issues ranging from the building of the Daya Bay Nuclear Power Plant to further electoral reforms steadily increased public interest in taking part in local political debates and activities. Although the local people were maturing fast politically, on balance they had an attitude of ambivalence towards democratization.[64] This permitted the British to accommodate the Chinese and put off, among others, introducing direct elections into the Legislative Council in 1988 without provoking a political crisis. The decisive shift of public opinion in favour of democratization occurred only in 1989 in response to the Tiananmen

---

[60] Robert Cottrell, *The End of Hong Kong: The Secret Diplomacy of Imperial Retreat* (London: John Murray, 1993), p. 108.

[61] *Ibid.*

[62] Steve Tsang (ed.), *A Documentary History of Hong Kong: Government and Politics* (Hong Kong: Hong Kong University Press, 1995), p. 227.

[63] Lau Siu-kai and Kuan Hsin-chi, "The 1985 District Board Election in Hong Kong and the Limits of Political Mobilization in a Dependent Polity," *The Journal of Commonwealth and Comparative Politics*, Vol. 25, No. 1 (March 1987), p. 83.

[64] Lau Siu-kai, "Institutions without Leaders: The Hong Kong Chinese View of Political Leadership," *Pacific Affairs*, Vol. 63, No. 2 (1990), p. 206.

incident, though many remained doubtful if it could be an effective bulwark against Chinese interference in local affairs after 1997.[65]

Throughout the 1980s the people of Hong Kong, their interest groups and activists merely played a peripheral role in the politics of Hong Kong and its future. This appears out of step with the fact that Britain was willing to open the local political arena to public participation, and "the colonial government had displayed tremendous capacity to adapt its methods of government to social changes."[66] The reality was that, as explained above, even after the reform of 1985 there was still public ambivalence to democratization. Furthermore, Hong Kong had failed to produce "a group of popular and organized *indigenous* [italics original] leaders as the guardians of its interests, as confidence-boosters and as guarantors of the success of the vaunted 'one country, two systems' approach to Hong Kong's political future."[67] It was not until April 1990 that the first political party, the United Democrats of Hong Kong, was founded "to take an active part in politics, to win the support of the people and to hold public office thereby putting into practice our beliefs and political platform."[68] But this happened only after "earlier doubts about the political readiness of the Hong Kong people for participatory politics dissipated" during the Tiananmen incident.[69] Even the pioneering United Democrats merely responded to a rising public demand. The lack of effective and far-sighted political leadership thus accounted to a considerable extent for the limited role which the local people played in the politics of the transition.

The "big change of opinions" towards democratization in Hong Kong in 1989 also prompted Britain to negotiate with China to increase the number of directly elected seats to the Legislative Council before 1997.[70] The increase of directly elected seats from 10 (as provided for in the White

---

[65] Lau Siu-kai, "Institutions without Leaders," p. 207.

[66] Lau Siu-kai, "Colonial Rule, Transfer of Sovereignty and the Problem of Political Leaders," *Journal of Commonwealth and Comparative Politics*, Vol. 30, No. 2 (July 1992), p. 225.

[67] Lau, Siu-kai, "Institutions without Leaders," p. 191.

[68] Steve Tsang (ed.), *A Documentary History of Hong Kong*, p. 228 (declaration on the founding of the United Democrats).

[69] *Ibid.*, p. 227.

[70] Percy Cradock, *Experiences of China*, p. 231.

Paper of 1988) to 18 in 1991 was the result. This suggests that a more assertive population, particularly if ably represented and organized by an adept political leadership, could have secured for themselves a greater say in local politics and perhaps even in the pace or extent of political reform.

The above notwithstanding, the hostility of the P.R.C. to Western democratic ideas imposes a limit to the scope, extent and pace of democratization in Hong Kong and thus restricts the role which the local population can play.[71] The limit is, however, not a rigid and unchangeable one. In fact, Beijing has continued to accommodate local opinions in its own way. It ought to be recognized that even after the overtly anti-Beijing elections to the Legislative Council resulted in a fiasco for pro-Beijing candidates in 1991, and the implementation of the Patten reforms against its wishes, Beijing continued to let its supporters take part in the 1995 elections, and accepted a second humiliating defeat.[72] This tolerance is based on the policy of exercising maximum flexibility within a rigid framework. One way by which the people of Hong Kong can persuade Beijing to allow them a larger scope of autonomous power, or a quicker pace of democratization, is to assure the latter that they will "restrict [their] politics to [their] own boundary and take no part in the wider Chinese politics."[73] As long as Beijing feels secure that its sovereignty over and its basic interests in Hong Kong are not at risk, it is willing to accommodate the wishes of the local people. The derailing of the "through train" in 1994 means Beijing no longer counted on British cooperation as it did in the past, though it would continue to secure it where possible. As a result, Beijing has become more dependent on the cooperation of the local people for a smooth transition than previously. However, no political party has emerged to provide the leadership to grasp this opportunity to enable the local people to play a more important role. Such a party would have to be

---

[71] Deng Xiaoping, *Deng Xiaoping Wenxuan*, p. 220.

[72] See Leung Sai-wing, "The 'China Factor' in the 1991 Legislative Council Election," in *Hong Kong Tried Democracy*, edited by Lau Siu-kai and Louie Kin-sheun (Hong Kong: Hong Kong Institute of Asia-Pacific Studies, 1993), pp. 187–224; and Steve Tsang, "A Famous Victory Leaves Hong Kong with a Hangover," *Parliamentary Brief*, Vol. 4, No. 1 (October 1995), pp. 77–78.

[73] Steve Tsang, "Political Problems Facing the Hong Kong Civil Service in Transition," *Hong Kong Public Administration*, Vol. 3, No. 1 (March 1994), p. 144.

able to persuade Beijing of the harmlessness of reforms to its interests on the one hand, and to obtain public confidence and trust in Hong Kong on the other hand. The Democratic Alliance for Betterment of Hong Kong can fulfil the first requirement but not the second while the Democratic Party can achieve the exact opposite. The people of Hong Kong have thus remained remarkably ineffective in the politics of transition and reform which affect themselves more than anybody else.

Conclusion

The increasing importance of the P.R.C. and the declining influence of Britain in Hong Kong politics are inherent in the logic of the transition. Once Britain conceded in 1984 that China would take over sovereignty in thirteen years' time, China was on a rising curve in its power relations with Britain over Hong Kong, but China's rise was not proportional to Britain's fall. Much as the Chinese rejected the idea that a "three-legged stool" existed, the people of Hong Kong could not be dismissed as a factor in the realignment of power.[74] A triangular power alignment existed in practice as the new framework for power politics in and over Hong Kong during the transitional period. It is not a static relationship and has been readjusted by the interplay among Britain, China and the politically active people of Hong Kong. According to the Sino-British Agreement which gave rise to the Joint Liaison Group, a body supposed to continue to monitor the implementation of the Agreement, this triangular relationship should continue in some form until the end of the century. However, despite the provisions in the Agreement, the actual role of the Joint Liaison Group after June 1997 remains unclear. While Britain will remain interested in Hong Kong, it is highly unlikely that China will let Britain have a major role to play after the transfer of sovereignty.

In the transition the main limit to the ascendancy of China's power is its need and desire for a successful take-over, which cannot be achieved without the cooperation of both Britain and the people of Hong Kong. This is very much reflected in the political situation since 1994, when the idea of convergence has lost much of its original meaning. As explained earlier, China no longer rested its policy on the foundation of convergence as it

---

[74] Xu Jiatun, *Xu Jiatun Xianggang Huiyilu*, Vol. 1, pp. 83–84.

mistakenly believed Britain had abandoned it. The new Chinese policy to create a provisional legislature appears to be intended to make a statement of principle rather than to serve China's, let alone Hong Kong's, best interests. From Beijing's point of view, this "new kitchen" has to be set up because Britain had "violated" the Agreement, the Basic Law and various memoranda exchanged in 1990.[75] In making this statement of principle Beijing has also in fact breached the principle laid down in its own Basic Law, in which a provisional legislature has no place.[76] This appears to have been an unintentional mistake, as China evidently intends to adhere to its original plan for the take-over as much as possible. Its basic policy remains that of exercising maximum flexibility within a rigid framework.

The limit to Britain's decline as a political force in Hong Kong rests on the fact that it is responsible for the administration of the territory until mid-1997 and is very good at it. While China has prepared itself to step in and take over from the British, the prospect remains extremely unappealing as a premature end of British rule will gravely damage Hong Kong's stability, order and prosperity. The conscientious way by which Britain runs Hong Kong has earned it grudging admiration from the local people, many of whom also resent Britain for many different reasons.[77] Some feel betrayed — either by the Agreement or by the many post-Agreement concessions Britain made to China. Others remember and object to the old days of colonial privileges which British expatriates used to enjoy. Although specific British policies have their own harsh critics in Hong Kong, the overall British record is generally accepted as a very positive one.[78] This partly explains why, despite the rise of a kind of Chinese nationalist feeling in the last decade, the Hong Kong Government "still commands a fairly high level of trust among the people" whereas "the

---

[75] BBC, *SWB*, FE1935 F/1, 2 March 1994 (Xinhua domestic report of 1 March 1994).

[76] The Basic Law leaves the forming of the first SAR legislature to the "Decision of the NPC on the Method for the Formation of the First Government and the First Legislative Council of the HKSAR," adopted on 4 April 1990. Neither document authorizes the forming of a Provisional Legislative Council in place of the First Legislative Council.

[77] Lau Siu-kai and Kuan Hsin-chi, *The Ethos of the Hong Kong Chinese* (Hong Kong: The Chinese University Press, 1988), pp. 82–85.

[78] Steve Tsang, *A Documentary History of Hong Kong*, pp. 4–9.

Chinese government is mistrusted by the Hong Kong Chinese."[79] Be that as it may, China's rigid view of sovereignty will not permit Britain to remain a major force in Hong Kong politics after the transfer of power.

There are two principal factors which prevented the people of Hong Kong from playing a more significant role in transitional politics. The basic limitation is China's reluctance to permit democratization and what it entails in Hong Kong. However, China has demonstrated a willingness to make some concessions if it would not feel threatened as a result. The absolute limit of China's tolerance was not tested because Hong Kong does not have an indigenous leadership which can represent the local people effectively and reassure Beijing at the same time. Britain has not been a major factor in denying political participation to the local people, even though it is formally responsible for the slow pace of democratization. Britain would have asked China for greater democracy for Hong Kong if there had been sufficiently strong local pressure. It might not have succeeded but the application of pressure would have meant a greater political role be played by the people of Hong Kong.

With Britain largely, if not completely, removed from the power equation after June 1997, the people of Hong Kong will lose a buffer between themselves and Beijing in the power game. The local people may wish to consider adopting a policy of firmly asking for what they want without being provocative, particularly over matters sensitive to the Chinese leadership in Beijing. The greatest scope of political autonomy can be achieved by the Hong Kong people making the most of China's policy of maximum flexibility without being seen to try to violate its rigid framework.

---

[79] Lau Siu-kai, "Institutions without Leaders," pp. 197 and 203.

3

Executive and Legislature: Institutional Design, Electoral Dynamics and the Management of Conflicts in the Hong Kong Transition

Li Pang-kwong

Introduction

Amid the surge in the number of new democracies around the world since the 1980s, studies of democratic transition have been flooding the fields of comparative politics and third world development.[1] Among this literature,

---

[1] Scott Mainwaring and Timothy R. Scully (eds.), *Building Democratic Institutions: Party Systems in Latin America* (Stanford, California: Stanford University Press, 1995); Alfred Stepan and Cindy Skach, "Constitutional Frameworks and Democratic Consolidation: Parliamentarianism versus Presidentialism," *World Politics*, Vol. 46 (1993), pp. 1–22; G. Bingham Powell, Jr., "Constitutional Design and Citizen Electoral Control," *Journal of Theoretical Politics*, Vol. 1 (1989), pp. 107–30; Matthew Soberg Shugart and John M. Carey, *Presidents and Assemblies: Constitutional Design and Electoral Dynamics* (Cambridge: Cambridge University Press, 1992); Samuel P. Huntington, *The Third Wave: Democratization in the Late Twentieth Century* (Norman and London: University of Oklahoma Press, 1991); Giovanni Sartori, *Comparative Constitutional Engineering: An Inquiry into Structures, Incentives and Outcomes* (Hampshire: Macmillan, 1994); Scott Mainwaring, "Presidentialism, Multipartism, and Democracy: The Difficult Combination," *Comparative Political Studies*, Vol. 26, No. 2 (1993), pp. 198–228; Fred W. Riggs, "The Survival of Presidentialism in American: Para-constitutional Practices," *International Political Science Review*, Vol. 9 (1988), pp. 247–78.

one will note that institutional arrangements and design have been emphasized by several scholars as playing a significant role in building up the
new political order and therefore would contribute to successful democratic
transition. Putting it in more specific terms, what kinds of regime type
(presidential, parliamentary or hybrid system) would be more conducive to
the stability of a newly established polity? What kinds of electoral and party
systems would work more harmoniously with the chosen regime type?
What kinds of representation system could help to reflect the relative
strength of social forces and contribute to consensus-building? How low
should the institutional threshold be so as to accommodate as many social
forces, which want to have political representation, as possible? Or how
high should it be so as not to discriminate against some minor forces? What
kinds of voting system would be best for bringing voters' preferences into
the decision-making process?

Although Hong Kong will not follow the usual path of decolonization
to become an independent state, the transition from a British colony to a
Special Administrative Region of the People's Republic of China does
involve some kind of institutional reform and restructuring. The need for
institutional reforms stems from (1) the change of political status after
1997: from a colony to an integrated part of a sovereign state, and (2)
China's promises to let "Hong Kong people governing Hong Kong" under
the parameter of "one country, two systems." The dual transition of
sovereignty and regime has a profound impact upon the colonial political
structure and order, and this in turn gives rise to a new political market, in
which partisan alignment, de-alignment and realignment have taken place.

Faced with this tremendous transformation, the designing of a new
institution that has the capability to cope with the turbulence of realignment
of political forces is significant and critical to the political stability of Hong
Kong and the legitimacy of the emerging political order. This chapter,
therefore, aims to explore the dynamic relationships between as well as the
institutional designs of the executive and the legislature in the post-1997
Hong Kong and to examine the institutional arrangements in terms of their
capacity for conflict resolution and management.

Constitutional Engineering

It is very easy to detect the "drastic" institutional changes that have been
laid down in the Sino-British Joint Declaration (JD) and the Basic Law.
What I mean by "drastic" here is in the sense that elections have replaced

the appointment system in returning the chief executive (governor) and all members of the legislature in twelve years' time.

"Drastic" or not is in the eye of the beholder. For those people who advocate democratic government would argue that the reforms of the Victorian colonial political structure have been delayed for a long period of time. In addition, they argue, Hong Kong possesses the necessary socio-economic conditions that would facilitate the development of democratic government. But, for those people who have reservations about the pace of the political reforms, they would argue that the reforms in such a short period of time and in such a "drastic" pace would jeopardize the stability and prosperity of Hong Kong.

No matter how the proponents and opponents argue their case, the reality is that the foundation of the colonial political order has been eroded and this would give rise to a new political order. The various political forces within and beyond Hong Kong would try to shape the emerging political order to their favour. As a result, the direction and pace of the change would be a sensitive and an explosive issue. Therefore, access to the constitution-making process is a vital step in shaping the emerging constitutional order.

The "subjective dimension" of the constitution-making process is the aspiration and values that the participants want to materialize as well as the consensus or compromise that they have come to terms. Therefore, one scholar notes that,

> Constitutions are man-made designs. These designs reflect the constitution-makers' values, their expectations of the consequences of various arrangements, their often laboriously negotiated compromises.[2]

If most of the significant forces are included in the constitution-making process, the resulting constitutional framework would be a lasting one. If not, it will face possible challenges from the excluded forces. At this juncture, the objective dimension of constitution-making comes into play.

The meaning of "objective dimension" is: whether the new constitutional framework can successfully provide an open and fairer political arena in which various political forces can represent their constituencies to compete for power and to resolve inter-constituency's differences and conflicts.

---

[2] G. Bingham Powell, Jr., *Contemporary Democracies: Participation, Stability, and Violence* (Mass. and London: Harvard University Press, 1982), p. 66.

Therefore, the capability of conflict resolution is one of the most important indicators to see whether the emerging constitutional framework is legitimized or not. As R. Kent Weaver suggests,

> Successful conflict management in a democratic society does not mean that there is no conflict, but rather that conflict is resolved in a way that all parties accept as legitimate, even if the outcome is not particularly to their liking.[3]

The failure of conflict management is said to be reflected in the following three ways: the suppression of political competition (*de jure* and *de facto*), political instability resulted from violent and disruptive conflict, and regime instability.[4]

The matching between the "subjective" and the "objective" dimensions of the constitution-making process is indispensable for a political community. Needless to say, we are not hoping for a total matching for there is no such thing in reality. Instead, what we can look for is the shorter the distance between the "subjective" and the "objective," the better the chance the emerging constitutional framework can survive.

Accompanying the erosion of the British colonial political order is the need to reframe the political institutions under which a new political order will emerge. China, as the sovereign state of Hong Kong after 1997, is holding the trump card in shaping the constitutional framework of the Hong Kong Special Administrative Region (HKSAR). Although the British Government has a role to play in that process, one may doubt about how decisive its say would be.

It is widely believed that China plans to have as little political reform as possible. That means the "executive-led" government will serve as the basic model in designing the post-1997 political institutions. But, for better or for worse, the replacement of the appointment system by elections in returning the chief executive and all members of the legislature has worked to undermine the very foundation of the "executive-led" government and

---

[3] R. Kent Weaver, "Political Institutions and Canada's Constitutional Crisis," in *The Collapse of Canada?*, edited by R. Kent Weaver (Washington, D.C.: Brookings, 1992), p. 9.

[4] Richard Gunther and Anthony Mughan, "Political Institutions and Cleavage Management," in *Do Institutions Matter? Government Capabilities in the United States and Abroad*, edited by R. Kent Weaver and Bert A. Rockman (Washington, D.C.: Brookings, 1993), pp. 273–74.

would likely transform the role of the legislature from a submissive to an assertive one. From China's point of view, potential conflicts between the chief executive and the legislature could be contained by tailoring an institutional framework under which a fragmented legislature would emerge. By doing so, the "executive-led" government could function as before.

Access to the constitution-making process is vital in the sense that its participants would have the prerogatives to mould the new rules of the political game and thus their rights and interests would be protected. For those sectors who are lucky enough to have their representatives in the process, their views and interests are more easily being articulated; for those sectors who find no representative in the process, their rights have to rely on the attitude of the participants. The control of entry into the constitution-making process is therefore highly political and manipulative.

The Framing of the Post-1997 Constitutional Parameter

In the period leading to the Sino-British Joint Declaration, the formal players were highly restricted to the Chinese and the British Governments. The Chinese side had reiterated that they opposed the idea of "three-legged stool" for the then negotiations were held between sovereign states and there was no role for the Government and people of Hong Kong to play. Moreover, China claimed to represent the views and interests of Hong Kong people in the negotiations. Although the British Government tried in the initial period to include local representatives from the Hong Kong Government (led by the then Governor, Edward Youde), it met with strong opposition from China. The Governor and officials from the Hong Kong Government joined the negotiation as members of the British delegation. Although the British Government claimed to consult the Executive Council (Exco) members after each round of negotiation, the way the Exco members had been recruited limited their representation in relation to the whole community. In a formal sense, only the Chinese and the British Governments were involved in the negotiations over the transfer of sovereignty of Hong Kong and the detailed arrangements contained in the subsequent Sino-British Joint Declaration (initialled in December 1984). The exclusion of Hong Kong people from the negotiations has stimulated a sense of powerlessness in response to the fact that they cannot control their fate.

For the British, an honourable withdrawal from Hong Kong was probably the second best option after China flatly rejected the validity of the three "unequal" treaties and the idea of exchanging sovereignty with British continued administration after 1997. What the British negotiators could aim for was to persuade the Chinese Government to agree to a set of principles based upon which the pre-1997 order could be maintained and safeguarded.

As far as the institutions of the executive and the legislature are concerned, the two governments agreed to the following terms laid down in the JD's Section I of Annex I:

> The chief executive of the Hong Kong Special Administrative Region shall be selected by election or through consultation held locally and appointed by the Central People's Government.... The Legislature of the Hong Kong Special Administrative Region shall be constituted by elections. The executive authorities shall abide by the law and shall be accountable to the legislature.

Although the word "elections" is not clearly defined and may be subject to different interpretation, the nature of the relationship between the Governor (the Chief Executive in the HKSAR) and the legislature has undergone drastic transformation. In twelve years' time, the political structure of Hong Kong would be transformed from an appointed governor and legislature to an elected chief executive and legislature. More important is the "spill-over" effect on the operation of the whole political system and the way of governance. It seems that the effect of the introduction of elections into the political system has been underestimated. Retrospectively speaking, although Hook has regarded the changes (the introduction of popular elections at the district level) in the early 1980s as "change within tradition,"[5] the subsequent introduction of popular elections to the Legislative Council (Legco) and the related structural changes seem highly logical and possible because of the British need to prepare for the "unusual" decolonization process.

In terms of constitution-making, the relevant clauses in the JD would have an effect on the drafting of the Basic Law (the mini-constitution of Hong Kong after 1997). China has to transform the promises in the JD into an enforceable constitutional law. Needless to say, China will hold the upper hand in interpreting and transforming the promises into binding constitutional laws. Shifting from international negotiations to domestic constitution-making, China has taken the driving seat in steering the direction of constitutional change under the parameter of the JD.

---

[5] See Brian Hook, "The Government of Hong Kong: Change within Tradition," *China Quarterly*, Vol. 95 (1983), pp. 491–511.

From Political Principles to Institutional Arrangements

From the beginning, China has been the single powerful force in controlling access to the drafting of the Basic Law and its ideas on the design of the future political framework have therefore become the dominant view. By allocating differential seat ratio to different sectors, China could monitor which social or political forces would have more say in the drafting process. In fact, the Basic Law Drafting Committee (BLDC) was formed in 1985 with a total of 59 members. Of whom, 23 were from Hong Kong and these Hong Kong members have been overwhelmingly drawn from the business and industrial sectors. Although the Basic Law Consultation Committee (BLCC) had a wider representation and was formed to solicit opinions, its influence was limited by its advisory role. Opinions were encouraged to be expressed, but the real decision was made by the drafters, not the ones who were being consulted or expressing opinions.

The politics of appointment would set the parameter of the constitutional discussion and more important was the contribution of the majority members of the drafting committee to the final shape and content of the constitution. In theory, the drafting committee members had to consider all views and proposals put forward before them. But, at the end of the day, their own views or interests prevailed and the final decision was made by the count of number.

Through the appointment system, China could keep the initiative in its own hand. This is not to suggest that China could do anything it likes, but it possesses the necessary resources to mobilize support for what it wants and to build up opposition to what it does not want.

The final product of the constitutional framework, as stipulated in the Basic Law, has reflected both the "cautious" attitude of the Chinese Government and the "conservative" approach of the business community towards democratization. As Kuan Hsin-chi notes, the Basic Law is "a pact between the Chinese government and the business and industrial elites in Hong Kong."[6] But the more important thing is whether the emerging constitutional framework has the capacity to resolve conflicts. Before going into discussion on this aspect, let me introduce the role of and relationships between the executive and the legislature, as stipulated in the Basic Law.

---

[6] Kuan Hsin-chi, "Power Dependence and Democratic Transition: The Case of Hong Kong," *China Quarterly*, Vol. 128 (1991), p. 785.

The Chief Executive (CE) of the HKSAR is no longer returned by appointment, but through consultation, nomination or election held locally. The responsibility for selecting the CE is vested in the Selection Committee (Election Committee in and after the second term) of 400 (800 in and after the second term). The Selection or Election Committee is composed of four pre-defined functional sectors: industrial, commercial and financial; professional; labour, social services and religious groups; and political figures (Hong Kong deputies to the National People's Congress (NPC), Hong Kong representatives to the National Committee of the Chinese People's Political Consultative Conference (CPPCC), and Legco members, and etc.). Each group has a quota of 100 (200 in and after the second term).

The CE is assisted by an appointed Executive Council in policy-making. The members of the Exco shall be appointed by the CE and shall be drawn from "the principal officials of the executive authorities, members of the Legislative Council and public figures." (Article 55)

If there is a need to change the selection or election method of the CE, the earliest year of putting amendment into effect is 2007 and shall be subject to the following procedures:

1. endorsement of a 2/3 majority of the Legco;
2. the consent of the CE; and
3. be reported to the Standing Committee of the NPC for approval. (Annex 1 of the Basic Law)

The legislature is composed of members returned by different election methods in the first three terms. The methods and proportion of members returned by each method are summarized in Table 1.

Although the CE and the Legco members both have the rights to initiate bills, the latter cannot move any bills that have an effect on "public expenditure or political system or government operation." Furthermore, the

Table 1: The Composition of the Post-1997 Legislature

	Functional constituency	Geographical constituency	Election committee	Total
1997	30 (50.0%)	20 (33.3%)	10 (16.6%)	60 (100%)
1999	30 (50.0%)	24 (40.0%)	6 (10.0%)	60 (100%)
2003	30 (50.0%)	30 (50.0%)	0 (00.0%)	60 (100%)

Legco members have to seek the CE's written approval before they can move any bills that are related to government policies. (Article 74)

The influence and power of the Legco are further kept under control by instituting a separate vote count mechanism under which all motions, bills and amendments to government bills introduced by Legco members should have the majority support from "each of the two groups of members present." These two groups are: members returned by functional constituencies; and members returned by geographical constituencies and by the Election Committee.

The institution of the separate vote count mechanism has the merit of moderating a radical change of policy direction by imposing a higher threshold of approval and is, thus, conducive to an integrated executive leadership and a higher degree of policy continuity. This will have the effect of maintaining the status quo. But the limitation is its effect of limiting the chance of the minority, but popular, view to become the Legco majority view. Any political forces which want to block the bills or motions initiated by individual Legco members could do so by having only 16 votes. In fact, this threshold is low enough to defeat all initiatives taken by individual Legco members and would therefore contribute to a weak legislature.

Like the CE, amendments to the composition of the legislature and the voting procedure of passing bills and motions are subject to procedures similar to those of the CE, except for the requirement of seeking approval from the Standing Committee of the NPC. (Annex 2)

Apart from the above institutional arrangements aimed at containing the emergence of a fully-fledged legislature, the "executive-led" governing model is further maintained by the provisions that the CE can dissolve the legislature if the former refuses to accept bills passed by the legislature twice or the legislature withholds its approval of the government budget or other important bills. (Articles 49 and 50)

Although the CE has to resign when the new constituted legislature passes the same bill or withholds their approval again, the legislature will find it very difficult to have a two-thirds majority on a particular issue or bill. Why is this so? It is due to the methods of returning Legco members and the resultant fragmented legislature, and to the decision-making procedures the legislature has to follow.

The segmented methods of returning Legco members by functional constituency, geographical constituency and election committee have the effect of limiting the chance of having a legislature with a clear majority voice, especially an opposition one. First of all, the functional constituency commands half of the Legco seats up to 2007 and that proportion will probably be maintained for a while even after 2007. One of the reasons advanced to justify the adoption of functional constituency elections is to provide those functional groups which have contributed a lot to the "success" of Hong Kong with a certain level of representation in the legislature. But the diffuse nature of functional groups has rendered it difficult for any coalition-building effort because of a more direct constituency linkage and a more easily identifiable sectoral interests. In addition, their close relationship with the establishment not only subjects them to tremendous executive pressure but also makes them prime lobbying targets of the government.

Secondly, the members returned through election committee have a pro-status quo tendency by default. It is because the constituency demarcation has followed, more or less, those of the functional constituency.

Lastly, although the members returned by geographic constituency have a better chance of building a voting bloc within the legislature, they so often fall into ideological clashes or have different views and judgements over social welfare and political reforms.

From Institutional Arrangements to Rule-making Procedures

According to the Decision[7] adopted by the NPC on 4 April 1990, the Preparatory Committee:

> shall be composed of mainland members and of Hong Kong members who shall constitute not less than 50 per cent of its members. Its chairman and members shall be appointed by the Standing Committee of the National People's Congress. (Article 2)

From the membership list of the Preparatory Committee, one can note that most of the appointees come from the business, commercial and financial sectors. The underprivileged are greatly under-represented in the Committee.

In August 1996, the Preparatory Committee (established in January 1996) passed the policy document on the Formation Method of the

---

[7] "The Decision of the National People's Congress on the Method for the Formation of the First Government and the First Legislative Council of the Hong Kong Special Administrative Region" can be found in *The Basic Law of the Hong Kong Special Administrative Region of the People's Republic of China* (Hong Kong: The Consultative Committee for the Basic Law, 1990), pp. 65–67.

Selection Committee which has been charged with selecting the first Chief Executive of the HKSAR and the Provisional Legislature.[8] The latter job is not mentioned in the Basic Law, but was added to the Selection Committee's responsibilities by the Preparatory Committee which is empowered by a resolution of the Standing Committee of the NPC in August 1994. This last-minute adjustment was due to the failure of the Sino-British negotiations over the 1994/95 electoral arrangements in 1994 which signified the overturn of the "through train."

As stated in Articles 2 and 5 of the Formation Method, the 400-member Selection Committee shall be returned by four pre-defined groups and each group has a quota of 100. Those who want to apply for a candidacy are free to choose which group he or she wants to apply to (except the group for political figures). The application has to be made through a registered association or organization. The full list of applications is first screened by the Preparatory Committee members and each of them shall then recommend 100 candidates for each group (except the group for political figures). Considering all the members' recommendations, the Presidium of the Preparatory Committee shall recommend at least 120 candidates for each group and forward the short-listed candidates to the Preparatory Committee members to vote on. No reason will be given to those applicants who do not have the recommendation of the Presidium. Each member is then allowed to vote on up to 100 candidates in each group and the top 100 candidates having the highest votes in each group will be declared elected.

The group for political figures is subject to another procedure. All the Hong Kong representatives to the NPC who are permanent residents of Hong Kong (26 in number) will automatically become members of the Selection Committee. The Hong Kong representatives to the CPPCC have to elect among themselves to fill up 40 seats. The rest of the seats (34) will be open to nomination from any registered associations and from the Preparatory Committee members. The election rule is the same as those of the first three groups.

The Preparatory Committee also passed the methods of returning the CE and the Provisional Legislature in October 1996.[9] It is stipulated that those who are interested in running for the CE election have to apply to

---

[8] The full text of the formation method of the first HKSAR Selection Committee can be found in *Wen Wei Po*, 11 August 1996, p. A4.

[9] For the relevant documents, see *Wen Wei Po*, 6 October 1996, pp. A1 & A6.

the Presidium of the Preparatory Committee and the latter will examine the applicants' eligibility. For those who are confirmed as being eligible, they have to seek at least 50 Selection Committee members' nominations so as to be qualified as a candidate for the CE post. The double ballot is adopted if the leading candidate fails to receive the majority support of the Selection Committee members.

As for the Provisional Legislature, each potential candidate is required to have the nomination of 10 Selection Committee members, and each Selection Committee member, in turn, shall not nominate more than 5 candidates. Similar to the nomination procedure of the CE, the eligibility of the potential candidates has to be confirmed by the Presidium of the Preparatory Committee. Simple majority is adopted as the decision rule and each Selection Committee member is allowed to vote for up to 60 candidates.

As described in previous sections and summarized in Table 2, access to both the constitution-making process and the political positions charged with rule-making power for the institutions of the HKSAR is highly moderated by China. Through appointment, Beijing can easily shape the membership of the Preparatory Committee. Although the Selection Committee is open for nomination, the Presidium of the Preparatory Committee

Table 2: Access to the Constitution-making and Decision-making
Processes by the General Public

	Methods of recruitment	Public access
Sino-British Joint Declaration	Delegation	Highly restricted
Basic Law Drafting Committee	Appointment	Restricted
Preliminary Committee of the Preparatory Committee	Appointment	Restricted
Preparatory Committee	Appointment	Restricted
Selection Committee	Nomination & appointment	Restricted
Chief Executive	Consultation/Nomination/ Election	Restricted
Provisional Legislature	Nomination & election	Less restricted
Legislature (Functional constituencies)	Nomination & election	Less restricted
Legislature (Election committee)	Nomination & election	Less restricted
Legislature (Geographic constituencies)	Nomination & popular Election	Least restricted

has been empowered to screen the candidates' list. It is therefore widely believed that only those who can pass the "trust" test can successfully be selected as members of the Preparatory and Selection Committees, and the members of the latter are subsequently empowered to select the CE and the Provisional Legislature. It is quite clear that the Chinese Government is in a strong position in defining the role and the relative strength of the participants in the constitution- and rule-making processes.

As a result, the colonial governing philosophy does find a new form in the HKSAR, with an elected but out-of-reach CE and a fragmented legislature. These institutional arrangements are made possible through the high institutional threshold of accessing the CE, the departmentalized methods of returning Legco members, and the installation of multi-veto points in the decision-making procedures of the legislature. Two major, but related, effects resulted: the insulation of political figures who are responsible for policy-making from citizen control and their insensitivity to social demands and conflicts.

Election Dynamics and Cleavage System

Elections have been regarded as an instrument to detect the presence of social conflicts and their intensity. The conflicts, or what we call cleavages for those conflicts which are durable and have political significance, that find political or electoral expression may serve as a dividing line that cuts across the electorate and as a mobilizing basis that helps the political groups or parties to fight the election battle. The popular elections held since the 1980s have demonstrated that those political groups or parties that represent the grassroots or the underprivileged have received majority electoral support.

As noted earlier, the major conflicts, in terms of the pace of democratization, during the constitution-making process in the late 1980s are the role of the legislature and its relations with the executive, the proportion of directly elected seats in the legislature, the decision-making procedures in the legislature and so on. China and the conservative elites want to maintain the political status quo as far as possible, while the democrats prefer a democratic reform to the colonial governing structure.

At the electorate level, the voters seem to align along the cleavage lines of centre-periphery and consumption. The continued salience of these two cleavages would contribute to the dominance of the democrats in popular elections, in terms of vote share, not seat share. It is suggested that the raw support is better calculated on the basis of vote share than seat share because the latter is more sensitive to the kind of election system that will be adopted.

The centre-periphery cleavage is defined as:

> the clash of the "centre" dominant Chinese Government with the "periphery" constituted unit(s) of Hong Kong over the pace of democratization and the degree of autonomy enjoyed by the latter after 1997.[10]

It also reflects the long-term historic distrust between the Communist Chinese Government and the people of Hong Kong in general. Given that the restoration of Hong Kong sovereignty to Chinese Government is inevitable, some kinds of institutional protection have been sought by the emerging middle class to protect their existing way of life. These include an open and democratic government, a high degree of autonomy after 1997, and the rule of law. On the other hand, the Chinese Government does promise what the middle class want to have, but there is a credibility gap between what it agrees in principle and what it really does in the constitution-making process and the resultant executive-dominance governing model.

Those people, groups or parties who share or articulate these values and viewpoints, or fight to see them in place, could be classified as "pro-periphery." Those who do not share these values and see no reason to antagonize the Chinese Government over the pace of democratization and the related institutional reforms could be termed as "pro-centre."

The application of the consumption cleavage concept in explaining vote choice was first developed by Patrick Dunleavy in the late 1970s.[11]

---

[10] Li Pang-kwong, "1995 Legislative Council Direct Election: A Political Cleavage Approach," in *The 1995 Legislative Council Elections in Hong Kong*, edited by Kuan Hsin-chi, Lau Siu-kai, Louie Kin-sheun and Wong Ka-ying (Hong Kong: The Hong Kong Institute of Asia-Pacific Studies, The Chinese University of Hong Kong, 1996), p. 251.

[11] Patrick Dunleavy, "The Urban Basis of Political Alignment: Social Class, Domestic Property Ownership, and State Intervention in Consumption Processes," *British Journal of Political Science*, Vol. 9 (1979), pp. 409–43; "The Political Implications of Sectoral Cleavages and the Growth of State Employment: Part 1, The Analysis of Production Cleavages," *Political Studies*, Vol. 28 (1980), pp. 364–83; "The Political Implications of Sectoral Cleavages and the Growth of State Employment: Part 2, Cleavage Structure and Political Alignment," *Political Studies*, Vol. 28 (1980), pp. 527–49.

His line of reasoning is that: accompanying the state expansion is the state intervention into the consumption process; sectoral cleavages (collective vs. individualized consumption) then emerge and cross-cut the existing class cleavages. Any change in policy direction will be rejected by the affected sector(s) and any move to privatize the collective consumption goods will cause shifts in electoral support. He further differentiates the collective and individualized forms of consumption in the following three "politically significant ways":

(a) Collective consumption in advanced capitalist societies is typically concerned with services provided by the state apparatus, ...

(b) ... individuals' location in these consumption processes is no longer directly determined by market forces....

(c) Collective consumption processes create an inter-subjective basis for the development of political action....[12]

In the context of Hong Kong, the consumption cleavage denotes the contraction of the Hong Kong state through the adoption of a privatization policy. The expansion of the social services programmes in the 1970s was made possible by the government's high land price policy. That policy has allowed the government to continue the traditional low tax policy while at the same time to expand its programmes in housing, education, health care, and so on. The state distanced itself from these resource-sucking programmes because of the sudden drop of land revenue as a result of the political uncertainty in the late 1970s and early 1980s. In order to keep tax low enough so as to compete with other developing countries, a government budget cut is a logical result. Under such circumstances, the privatization of some government services is deemed desirable, especially the provision of public housing and cheap health care services. Although the government uses the pretext of "cost recovery" and "user pay," the effect of moving the financial burden back to the user is the same as that of the privatization policy.

For those people who have a collective mode of consumption, they may reject the privatization policy and, therefore, logically support those groups or parties with the same orientation in popular elections. They may be termed as "pro-collective consumption." For those people who have an individualized consumption, they may accept the privatization policy

---

[12] Patrick Dunleavy, "The Urban Basis of Political Alignment," p. 418.

and, therefore, vote for those groups or parties which share the same attitude with them in popular elections. They may be regarded as "pro-individualized consumption."

The above-mentioned twin cleavages of centre-periphery and consumption are believed to be salient in the 1995 Legco direct elections.[13] As sketched in Figure 1, the democrats seem to draw their majority support from those voters who held a pro-periphery attitude and have a collective mode of consumption. Given that the existing three major political forces (democrats, leftists and conservatives) did not compete in all constituencies in 1995 and the effect of proportional representation, adopted for the first HKSAR Legislature's geographical constituency elections to be held in 1998, upon vote share of these political forces has not yet known, whether the democrats can maintain their electoral support in post-1997 Legco popular elections is called into doubt.

However, what I would argue here is the continued salience of the twin cleavages of centre-periphery and consumption in the first few popular elections after 1997. It is because once the cleavages gain prominence, they are quite durable. It is sure that cleavage transformation is possible, but it would happen in a rather slow and gradual manner. If other things being equal, the partisan alignment along the twin cleavage lines is highly

Figure 1: A Sketch of the Electoral Market of Hong Kong in 1995

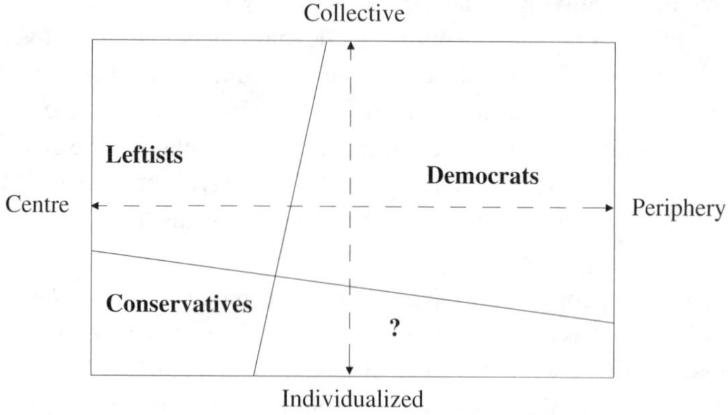

---

[13] For details, see Li Pang-kwong, "1995 Legislative Council Direct Election," pp. 245–73.

possible. As a result, the democrats may likely gain the majority support in terms of vote share in the first few popular elections after 1997.

The Post-1997 Constitutional Order and Conflict Management

Conflicts may be different in nature and take different forms. The minimum requirement that a political community needs to survive is the spread of "we-group" feeling among members, based upon which the sense of nationhood is built.[14] Therefore, if there is conflict over national identity, political instability would then follow. The typical example is Northern Ireland. The nationhood (statehood) crisis can be regarded as the basic challenge to the very survival of a political community.

Less critical, but it does not mean that it is not important and significant, in threatening the survival of a political community is the conflict over the kind of regime that would be constituted. Regime is defined as:

> ... that part of the political system which determines how and under what conditions and limitations the power of the state is exercised.... [R]egime embody the norms and principles of the political organization of the state, which are set out in the rules and procedures within which governments operate.[15]

The conflict over regime type is a reflection of the way members of that community diverged on the basic principles of organizing the polity and of dispersing political power and social resources.

Under the broad political framework, members may further have conflicts over how to transform the accepted principles into corresponding

---

[14] Conceptually, there are differences between "state" and "nation." I make no attempt to differentiate them in this chapter. For a simple definition of the two words, see Vernon Bogdanor (ed.), *The Blackwell Encyclopaedia of Political Institutions* (Oxford: Basil Blackwell, 1987), pp. 380–81. The word "nation" is defined as "a named human community with a myth of common ancestry, historical memories and standardized mass culture, possessing a single territory, division of labour and legal rights for all members," and the word "state" is defined as "a set of public institutions, autonomous of other institutions, differentiated, centralized and possessing the monopoly of coercion and extraction in a demarcated and recognized territory."

[15] Stephanie Lawson, "Conceptual Issues in the Comparative Study of Regime Change and Democratization," *Comparative Politics*, Vol. 25 (1993), p. 187.

institutional rules and decision-making procedures (institutional arrangements). That means there may be more than one way to operate the same
principles. As Krasner rightly points out:

> Principles and norms provide the basic defining characteristics of a regime. There
> may be many rules and decision-making procedures that are consistent with
> the same principles and norms. Changes in rules and decision-making procedures
> are changes within regimes, provided that principles and norms are unaltered.[16]

Therefore, the conflicts over the rules and decision-making procedures can
be regarded as "changes within regime" and do not necessarily relate to
the conflicts over the regime type itself. The latter conflict can be regarded
as "regime change" which will touch upon the fundamental principles of
the regime.

Conflicts over public policy may be located at the lowest level of
political conflicts. Compared with conflicts over institutional arrangements,
policy conflicts are narrower in scope and more specific in content. As long
as the conflict resolution mechanisms (decision-making procedures) are
effective, policy conflict may not transform into a higher level of political
conflicts.

In considering whether cross-level, either upward or downward,
transformation of conflicts would be developed, the nature of the conflicts
may have a role to play. If the conflict is categorized as an "encapsulat-
ing" one, the possibility of a downward cross-level transformation of conflicts may be higher, and vice versa. Figure 2 illustrates those relationships
graphically.

The concept of "encapsulated conflicts" is borrowed from Amitai
Etzioni. He refers "encapsulation" to "the process by which conflicts are

Figure 2: The Typology of Political Conflicts

	Encapsulation	Non-encapsulation
State		
Regime		
Rule		
Policy		

---

[16] Stephen D. Krasner (ed.), *International Regimes* (Ithaca: Cornell University
Press, 1983), p. 3.

modified in such a way that they become limited by rules." Etzioni indicates that encapsulation "does not require that the conflict be resolved or extinguished but only that the range of expression be curbed" and "hostile parties are more readily 'encapsulated' than pacified."[17]

As noted earlier, one of the functions of a constitution is to provide a legitimate channel for conflict management or resolution. Although the nature and scope of conflicts vary across societies, the way these conflicts are being resolved does have a tremendous impact on the political order and stability of a society. The effectiveness of the channel to settle conflicts depends on whether the conflicting parties regard the existing institutional arrangements as just and legitimate. That kind of feeling or judgement, in turn, depends on firstly, how high the institutional threshold of allowing the political elites, groups or parties to represent their perceived social conflicts into the resolution process if they see fit (the lower the better, but not that low as this will overload the process) and secondly, how effectively the conflicts are being resolved within the existing institutional arrangements.

In the context of Hong Kong, even though the democrats or any other political forces have received the majority support in the popular polls, they are highly unlikely to become the majority force in the whole legislature, not to speak of in the election of the CE. The reason is simple. More than half of the Legco seats are not returned by popular elections (half in 2003). Even when a majority party emerges in popular elections, this party is most likely a minority party in the whole legislature. Moreover, the institutional arrangements between the executive and the legislature are not structured in such a way as to strengthen citizen control or public accountability of those who are involved in decision-making. The blocking of the popular will, if any, by institutional barriers has, in one way or the other, provided the basis of further reinforcing the existing cleavages system and the related partisan alignment. The underprivileged will sooner or later transform the policy conflicts into rule conflicts.

For illustrative purposes, Figure 3 is constructed to chart the political orientations of Legco members returned by functional constituencies, election committee, and geographic constituencies. Scenarios (I) and (IV) reflect that the Legco members have shared a common view or have arrived

---

[17] Amitai Etzioni, "On Self-encapsulating Conflicts," *Journal of Conflict Resolution*, Vol. 8 (1964), pp. 242–43.

Figure 3: The Dynamics within the Legco

**Geographic
constituency**

	(I) Agree	(II) Disagree
Election committee & functional constituency	Agree	Agree
	(III) Agree	(IV) Disagree
	Disagree	Disagree

at a consensus on a particular issue. If this is the case, it would pose a tremendous pressure on the executive to act and the popular views are more likely to have effect on subsequent executive decision- or policy-making. Scenarios (II) and (III) indicate that there is a conflicting view among Legco members and the Legco would become divisive on that particular issue. If this is the case, the executive could have more room in manoeuvring the decision-making.

Given the segmented methods of returning Legco members and the different basis of interests representation and articulation, a fragmented legislature is highly possible. Therefore, scenarios (II) and (III) are likely to happen more often than scenarios (I) and (IV).

If we further consider the number of seats in each category, a majority in favour of the business and professional interests apparently emerges. One of the effects is that the gap between the majority view of the Legco and the popular views may become wider and therefore, the conflicts between them may be escalated.

If the cleavage system is added to the above discussion, the conflicts between the majority Legco view and the popular views become even clearer. As shown in Figure 4, the Legco majority view (established interests) is likely to adopt a pro-centre and pro-individualized consumption attitude (scenarios I and III), while the non-established (supposedly representing the popular views) tends to favour a pro-periphery and pro-collective consumption orientation (scenarios II and IV).

The separate origin and survival of the executive and the legislature

Figure 4: The Twin Cleavages and the Legco

Legislature

	Established	Non-established
	(I)	(II)
Centre- Periphery	Centre (conservative & leftists)	Periphery (democrats)
Cleavage	(III)	(IV)
Consumption	Individualized (conservatives)	Collective (democrats & leftists)

will raise the issue of which institution is representing the popular views. In a typical presidential system, both the executive and the legislature are returned by popular elections or by electoral college comprised of popularly elected members. So, there is not much problem. On the other hand, in a typical parliamentary system, the legislature is supposedly representing the popular views and the executive relies on the confidence of the legislature. The issue of representing popular views is therefore not an issue at all. But in the case of Hong Kong, the issue of representing the popular views is quite complicated. Based upon the institutional arrangements stipulated in the Basic Law, neither the executive nor the legislature could, on procedural grounds, claim that it is representing the popular views. Strictly speaking, only those elected in popular elections could qualify themselves as speaking for the popular views.

If this is the case, the popularly elected representatives would tend to challenge those representatives returned by other forms of election. Supported by the voters, these popularly elected representatives will demand an increase in the proportion of popularly elected seats. This in turn would entail opposition from those Legco members who are returned by functional constituencies and the election committee. The conflicts would not be so easily resolved because of the zero-sum nature of the change of the seat proportions.

The way the CE is being elected has prevented him/her from moving too close to the popular views. The rather small constituency and the close, interdependent relations within the constituency have to be responsible for that. The room for manoeuvre is not as large as that of the popularly elected CE. The dominance of the established interests in the decision-making process and the suppression of the popular views in the Legco would further force the voters to vote for the groups or parties that represent the grassroots.

The conflicts mentioned above seem to be clustered around the rule and policy levels and the conflicting parties are judged to have been encapsulated. If these judgements are correct, the pressing task at this moment is to redesign the institutional arrangements of the executive and the legislature in such a way as to contain the conflicts effectively and to ward off the possible development towards non-encapsulation.

Concluding Remarks — Alternative Arrangements

The fragmentation of the Legco, the dominance of established interests in the Legco, the distortion of popular views in the decision-making process, the insulation of the CE from popular election and the resultant weakening of public accountability of the CE may all work to antagonize and polarize the existing conflicts (as reflected in popular elections) which have, in turn, de-legitimized the newly installed conflict resolution mechanism.

Which direction will the adjustment proceed if needed? (In this chapter, I will only touch on the adjustment within the Basic Law's parameter. The alternative design for the post-1997 political institutions will need another paper to deal with.) My suggestions are as follows:

Policy Co-option

This method requires the CE and the executive to grant access to those related or interested parties to the policy-making process by policy area. The CE or the executive is obliged not only to consult those who are being identified in a particular policy network, but also to try to draw the common denominator among them. Because of its informal nature, its successful operation depends highly on the "will and skill" of the CE and the executive.

Institutional Co-option

In order to compensate for the high institutional threshold of entry of the

CE and the resultant gap between the established and the non-established interests in the decision-making process, it would be better to appoint some popularly elected Legco members to the Exco. The expected effects are to strengthen the grassroots' views or interests in the policy deliberation process, and to facilitate the emergence of elite consensus and integration.

Although Legco members have been identified as one of the potential sources of appointing Exco members (Article 55 of the Basic Law), reservations about appointing those Legco members who have political affiliation have been expressed. Judging from the past two Legco popular elections, nearly all the winners have party affiliation. It will, therefore, defeat the original idea of co-option if those Legco members who are popularly elected and have party affiliation are excluded from the Exco.

The appointment of those popularly elected Legco members to the Exco may put pressure on the CE and the Exco members to make compromises, but the resultant deals are very likely be the median option in the spectrum of policy choices.

Abolition of Separate Vote Count Mechanism

The high institutional threshold imposed by the separate vote count mechanism to adopt Legco individual bills or motions is designed in such a way as to counter the surge of the non-established interests in the Legco decision-making process. But this mechanism also works to the disadvantage of the established interests. It is because only 16 votes can effectively block any individual bills or motions from passage. The abolition or lowering of the threshold may ease the tension within the Legco and more important, may help reflect the societal preferences in a more proportional way.

Readjusting the Proportion of Functional Constituency and Geographical Constituency Seats

As stated in the Basic Law, the Legco members will be eventually returned by "universal suffrage." (Article 68) If this is going to happen, the earlier the time to make that adjustment, the lesser the conflicts will be. A timely and gradual manner of introducing the adjustment would help prevent the polarization of political forces within the Legco. It is because firstly, the non-established interests may expect a growing role in the Legco, so its frustration may thus be lessened; and secondly, the adjustment will bring pressure on the established interests to join the popular elections and, therefore, their policy stance will be dictated by the logic of the electoral market.

Returning the CE through Popular Election

How to make the CE accountable to the public is a perennial question. However, as stated in the Basic Law, the "ultimate aim is the selection of the Chief Executive by universal suffrage upon nomination by a broadly representative nominating committee in accordance with democratic procedures." (Article 45) The designers' logic is clear. By balancing the non-established interests, "a broadly representative nominating committee" is used to screen the potential candidates and subject them to popular election later. If implemented, this will bring the CE under periodic popular electoral pressure and thus, keep the CE in touch institutionally with the wider spectrum of interests. Although the method of organizing the "broadly representative nominating committee" has not been worked out at this moment, it is preferable not to set a high threshold of entry. Otherwise, the purpose of popular election will be defeated. Moreover, the earlier the time to return the CE through popular election, the better the chance to keep the conflicts at the policy level.

Given that no political institutions could remain intact in an age of rapid and dynamic changes, institutional reforms are always needed and desirable so as to enhance its capacity of coping with the emerging social conflicts or to fine-tune the existing mechanism with growing effectiveness. It is true that whether to carry out reform is a political and partisan decision, but the effectiveness of the institutions in resolving conflicts and the justifications of reforms could be evaluated on more objective grounds as well as subject to a rigorous academic examination.

Bibliography

Burton, John W. "Conflict Resolution as a Political Philosophy." In *Conflict Resolution Theory and Practice: Integration and Application*, edited by Dennis J. D. Sandole and Hugo van der Merwe, pp. 55–64. Manchester and New York: Manchester University Press, 1993.

Dunleavy, Patrick. "The Urban Basis of Political Alignment: Social Class, Domestic Property Ownership, and State Intervention in Consumption Processes." *British Journal of Political Science*, Vol. 9 (1979), pp. 409–43.

———. "The Political Implications of Sectoral Cleavages and the Growth of State Employment: Part 1, The Analysis of Production Cleavages." *Political Studies*, Vol. 28 (1980), pp. 364–83.

———. "The Political Implications of Sectoral Cleavages and the Growth of State Employment: Part 2, Cleavage Structure and Political Alignment." *Political Studies*, Vol. 28 (1980), pp. 527–49.

Etzioni, Amitai. "On Self-encapsulating Conflicts." *Journal of Conflict Resolution*, Vol. 8 (1964), pp. 242–55.

Gunther, Richard and Anthony Mughan. "Political Institutions and Cleavage Management." In *Do Institutions Matter? Government Capabilities in the United States and Abroad*, edited by R. Kent Weaver and Bert A. Rockman, pp. 272–301. Washington, D.C.: Brookings, 1993.

Hook, Brian. "The Government of Hong Kong: Change within Tradition." *China Quarterly*, Vol. 95 (1983), pp. 491–511.

Huntington, Samuel P. *The Third Wave: Democratization in the Late Twentieth Century*. Norman and London: University of Oklahoma Press, 1991.

Krasner, Stephen D., ed. *International Regimes*. Ithaca: Cornell University Press, 1983.

Kuan Hsin-chi. "Power Dependence and Democratic Transition: The Case of Hong Kong." *China Quarterly*, Vol. 128 (1991), pp. 774–93.

Lawson, Stephanie. "Conceptual Issues in the Comparative Study of Regime Change and Democratization." *Comparative Politics*, Vol. 25 (1993), pp. 183–205.

Li Pang-kwong. "Elections, Politicians, and Electoral Politics." In *The Other Hong Kong Report 1995*, edited by S. Y. L. Cheung and S. M. H. Sze, pp. 51–66. Hong Kong: The Chinese University Press, 1995.

———. "1995 Legislative Council Direct Election: A Political Cleavage Approach." In *The 1995 Legislative Council Elections in Hong Kong*, edited by Kuan Hsin-chi, Lau Siu-kai, Louie Kin-sheun and Wong Ka-ying, pp. 245–73. Hong Kong: The Hong Kong Institute of Asia-Pacific Studies, The Chinese University of Hong Kong, 1996.

——— and David Newman. "Give and Take: Electoral Politics in Transitional Hong Kong." *Asian Perspective*, Vol. 21, No. 1 (1997), pp. 213–32.

Lijphart, Arend, Ronald Rogowski and R. Kent Weaver. "Separation of Powers and Cleavage Management." In *Do Institutions Matter? Government Capabilities in the United States and Abroad*, edited by R. Kent Weaver and Bert A. Rockman, pp. 302–44. Washington, D.C.: Brookings, 1993.

Mainwaring, Scott. "Presidentialism, Multipartism, and Democracy: The Difficult Combination." *Comparative Political Studies*, Vol. 26, No. 2 (1993), pp. 198–228.

——— and Timothy R. Scully, eds. *Building Democratic Institutions: Party Systems in Latin America*. Stanford, California: Stanford University Press, 1995.

Powell, G. Bingham, Jr. *Contemporary Democracies: Participation, Stability, and Violence*. Mass. and London: Harvard University Press, 1982.

———. "Constitutional Design and Citizen Electoral Control." *Journal of Theoretical Politics*, Vol. 1 (1989), pp. 107–30.

Riggs, Fred W. "The Survival of Presidentialism in America: Para-constitutional Practices." *International Political Science Review*, Vol. 9 (1988), pp. 247–78.

Sartori, Giovanni. *Comparative Constitutional Engineering: An Inquiry into Structures, Incentives and Outcomes*. Hampshire: Macmillan, 1994.

Shugart, Matthew Soberg and John M. Carey. *Presidents and Assemblies: Constitutional Design and Electoral Dynamics*. Cambridge: Cambridge University Press, 1992.

Stepan, Alfred and Cindy Skach. "Constitutional Frameworks and Democratic Consolidation: Parliamentarianism versus Presidentialism." *World Politics*, Vol. 46 (1993), pp. 1–22.

Weaver, R. Kent. "Political Institutions and Canada's Constitutional Crisis." In *The Collapse of Canada?*, edited by R. Kent Weaver, pp. 7–75. Washington, D.C.: Brookings 1992.

4

The Transition of Bureaucratic Authority: The Political Role of the Senior Civil Service in the Post-1997 Governance of Hong Kong[1]

Cheung Bing-leung, Anthony

Introduction

Hong Kong is in a process of transition towards becoming a Special Administrative Region (SAR) of China on 1 July 1997. That process began when the Chinese and British Governments signed a Joint Declaration formally recognizing China's resumption of sovereignty over Hong Kong in 1997. Under the Joint Declaration Hong Kong is supposed to enjoy a high degree of autonomy from the Chinese Central Government on the basis of "Hong Kong people governing Hong Kong." For a while after 1984 there was wide expectation that the reconstitution of political order before and after British departure was to implement a democratic system of governance. At least that was what the then emerging pro-democracy forces in Hong Kong were hoping and campaigning for.

---

[1] Part of this book chapter consists of arguments and discussion which appear first in this author's article "Rebureaucratization of Politics in Hong Kong: Prospect after 1997," *Asian Survey*, Vol. 37, No. 8 (August 1997), pp. 720–37.

Just prior to the signing of the Sino-British Joint Declaration, the British administration introduced representative government for the first time in Hong Kong's colonial history, promising firstly indirect elections to the previously wholly appointed Legislative Council by 1985 and thereafter gradual direct elections on popular franchise.[2] The British move marked the beginning of a process of decolonization with an aim to return the power of government to a system "firmly rooted in Hong Kong."[3] The Chinese Government, on the other hand, considering the British move unilateral, strongly opposed the scheme which it accused of pre-empting the Basic Law, the new constitution that China was about to draft for the future Hong Kong SAR. The Sino-British tug-of-war over the reconstitution of political order for Hong Kong, first centred on whether direct elections to the Legislative Council should be introduced in 1988, was to last for nearly a decade. It came to a climax in 1992–1994 when disagreements on Governor Christopher Patten's electoral reform proposals resulted in China dumping the "through train" arrangements previously agreed with Britain, and going alone with setting up alternative political institutions after the 1997 take-over, including a provisional legislature selected by a 400-member Selection Committee to replace the more democratically elected Legislative Council of 1995.

Much discussion about the period of political transition after 1984 has centred on the electoral arrangements for forming the legislature and for producing the Chief Executive of the SAR. There is an unwarranted neglect of the role of the civil service bureaucracy — particularly the senior civil service — which has been the backbone of the British colonial administration in Hong Kong.[4] This chapter examines the evolution of the role of the senior civil service and argues that despite the change of sovereignty and the imposition by China of a new political order on Hong Kong, the administrative bureaucracy is likely to remain the most powerful political institution. Hong Kong after 1997 seems destined to become another

---

[2] Hong Kong Government, *Green Paper: The Further Development of Representative Government in Hong Kong* (Hong Kong: Government Printer 1984).

[3] *Ibid.*, para. 7(a).

[4] For the purpose of this chapter and for the reasons to be elaborated in the course of discussion, attention is focused on the administrative class which virtually runs the government.

bureaucratic polity which may marginalize, if not "suppress," popular politics as its colonial predecessor.

Hong Kong's System of Governance and the Gradual Transformation of Bureaucratic Authority

In appearance the system of governance in Hong Kong under British colonial rule has changed little for the past 150 years. In practice it has undergone considerable reorganizations resulting in the alteration of some basic institutional "rules" and practices and in the gradual transformation of bureaucratic authority.

This system had been variously described as "an administrative state"[5] and "bureaucratic polity."[6] These descriptions all pointed to the fact that the government was dominated by administrator-bureaucrats who at the same time governed as well as administered in the absence of accountable politics. Such a system has only begun to change very recently with the development of some form of representative government[7] in preparation for the political transition to 1997. Despite the introduction of elected members to the Legislative Council (indirect elections and functional constituency elections in 1985 and some directly elected seats in 1991), political powers have remained firmly within the administration, in the hands of policy administrators in the Government Secretariat. This is in contrast to the pattern of development identified by Aberbach, Putnam and Rockman[8] in Western democracies, where top bureaucrats were seen to have grown in power and influence, not only in the formulation of policy but increasingly in the brokerage and articulation of interests, functions which conventionally were regarded as within the exclusive province of elected

---

[5] P. Harris, *Hong Kong: A Study in Bureaucratic Politics* (Hong Kong: Heinemann Asia, 1978), pp. 53–61.

[6] S. K. Lau, *Society and Politics in Hong Kong* (Hong Kong: The Chinese University Press, 1982), pp. 26–29.

[7] Hong Kong Government, *White Paper: The Further Development of Representative Government in Hong Kong* (Hong Kong: Government Printer, 1984); *White Paper: The Development of Representative Government: The Way Ahead* (Hong Kong: Government Printer, 1988).

[8] J. D. Aberbach, R. D. Putnam and B. A. Rockman, *Bureaucrats and Politics in Western Democracies* (Cambridge, Mass.: Harvard University Press, 1981).

politicians. Hong Kong is on the reverse path, with the bureaucrats monop-
olizing such political functions until very lately when newly emerging local
politicians begin to demand a share of powers.

How to cope with societal "politics" has always been a key preoccupation of the administrative elite — the concern in the past was how to
accommodate politics and yet to maintain administrative domination in
government. From the 1980s onwards, because of the 1997 question, a new
dimension has been added, namely that of decolonization. From the departing British administration's point of view, decolonization within the Hong
Kong context refers to the transfer of the powers of governance to the local
community, not only for the sake of democratization itself, but also to avoid
letting the Communist Chinese Government and its appointed governing
agents in Hong Kong to inherit all the autocratic powers of the former
British governor and his mandarins.

How the colonial administrative elite has governed can broadly be
divided into three rather distinct phases: the period up to the late 1960s
when Hong Kong was governed as a typical British colony and "indirect
rule" was the dominant ruling ideology;[9] the era of administrative reforms
since the 1970s in response to the legitimation crisis; and the attempts at
decolonization from the 1980s onwards.

1841–1968: Indirect Rule, Synarchy and the Administerization of Politics

Much of the way Hong Kong is being governed is shaped by the fact that
it is a colony. In constitutional terms the Hong Kong Government followed
the footsteps of other British colonies when the British Government took
over the territory from Qing China in 1841 after the Opium War. The
governance of the territory was put into the custody of the Governor

---

[9] Indirect rule was a typical approach in most British colonies, see Henrika
Kulick, *The Imperial Bureaucrat: The Colonial Administrative Service in the
Gold Coast 1920–1939* (Stanford, California: Hoover Institution Press, 1979).
Lord Lugard, a former governor of Hong Kong, was a strong advocate of indirect
rule, see F. J. D. Lugard, *The Dual Mandate of British Tropical Africa*, 5th edition
(London: Cass, 1965); *Political Memoranda: Revision of the Instructions to Politi-
cal Officers on Subjects Chiefly Political and Administrative, 1913–1918*, 3rd
edition (International Specialized Book Service, 1970).

appointed by the Crown upon advice of the Secretary of State in London. The Governor made policies and major administrative decisions on the advice of the Executive Council, and made local laws with the advice and consent of the Legislative Council. In practice the Governor could act as an autocratic ruler as he was given overriding powers within the colony and had effective control over the two Councils until most recently.[10]

However, Hong Kong was unlike typical British colonies in that it was founded originally as a military, diplomatic and trading station, not as a settlement.[11] Strategic considerations would have demanded a greater degree of imperial control than would be normal in other British colonies. In practice such administrative absolutism was constrained by a style of indirect rule. From the very beginning the British administration had adopted a policy of economic as well as political *laissez-faire*. The colonial government operated over a very restricted field covering little more than the maintenance of law and order and the raising of taxes to meet the cost of the civil establishment and necessary public works. The local Chinese population was virtually left alone, to be under their own Chinese law and customs and looked after in their welfare by their own community leaders.[12]

Social acquiescence of colonial rule was attributed by Lau[13] to the cultural ingredients of "utilitarianistic familism" and a "minimally-integrated

---

[10] The membership of the Executive and Legislative Councils comprised "official" members (who were top civil servants) and "unofficial" members appointed by the Governor. The officials, who had to vote with the government, formed the majority of the Executive Council until 1966 and that of the Legislative Council until 1977. Elected members were only introduced to the Legislative Council (24 out of 57) in October 1985. The Executive Council has remained wholly appointed.

[11] G. B. Endacott, *Government and People in Hong Kong, 1841–1862: A Constitutional History* (Hong Kong: Hong Kong University Press, 1964), p. 25.

[12] Until 1968, the Secretary for Chinese Affairs was the only top colonial official designated within the government to deal with the Chinese population and to act as the link with Chinese community leaders. The leased New Territories of the colony were administered by district officers as in other British colonies, who acted at the same time as the civil authority, the land authority and the local magistrate. After the 1967 riots, the Secretary for Chinese Affairs was retitled Secretary for Home Affairs (in 1968).

[13] S. K. Lau, *Society and Politics in Hong Kong*.

socio-political system" within the Chinese community, resulting in the availability of social "resource networks" which helped to meet the needs of the
lower strata and prevent their grievances and claims from becoming overt
political demands. Miners[14] similarly argued that Hong Kong's early political tranquillity was a result of the paternalistic authoritarian nature of the
colonial government which the Chinese population had been culturally accustomed to as well as the latter's refugee mentality. Such kind of cultural
explanations were however not shared by Rear[15] who suggested it was the
Chinese population's sense of political impotence ("an acceptance of the
inevitable necessity of British rule") that had rendered it apathetic.

What resulted was a system in which popular participation and politics
were discouraged, if not outrightly suppressed. Indirect rule means the
colonial administration was out of reach of the ordinary people. The senior
administrators (essentially British officers), directed by the Governor, ruled
the territory on behalf of the British Crown and were only subject to limited
check and balance by the appointed unofficial members of the Executive
and Legislative Councils. Endacott described the system positively as
"government by discussion" whereby interested opinion was consulted
continuously before any important government decision.[16] The critical
question is, however, what counted as interested opinion. Certainly indigenous Chinese were excluded from mainstream government except for
the few Chinese community leaders who made it to government advisory
bodies and the two Councils. Ambrose King tended to agree with Endacott
and described the process of colonial governance as "administrative absorption of politics" by which "the government co-opts the political forces,
often represented by elite groups, into an administrative decision-making
body, thus achieving some level of elite integration."[17] He supplemented
his thesis with the concept of "synarchy" by which he referred to the

---

[14] N. Miners, "Hong Kong: A Case Study in Political Stability," *The Journal
of Commonwealth and Comparative Politics*, Vol. 13, No. 1 (March 1975), pp.
26–39.

[15] J. Rear, "One Brand of Politics," in *Hong Kong: The Industrial Colony*,
edited by K. Hopkins (Hong Kong: Oxford University Press, 1971).

[16] G. B. Endacott, *Government and People in Hong Kong*, p. 229.

[17] Ambrose King, "Administrative Absorption of Politics in Hong Kong:
Emphasis on the Grass Roots Level," in *Social Life and Development in Hong
Kong*, edited by A. Y. C. King and R. P. L. Lee (Hong Kong: The Chinese
University Press, 1981), p. 130.

sharing of power by both British rulers (the colonial officials) and non-British, predominantly Chinese, local leaders through formal as well as informal interactions, so as to evolve a form of elite consensual government. This interpretation of the "administerization" of politics[18] has long been recognized as the key to the understanding of colonial governance in Hong Kong.

It can be said that British rule in Hong Kong up to the late 1960s followed the traditional form of colonial administration. Senior civil bureaucrats, mainly administrative class officers or "cadet officers" as they were known in the early days,[19] acted as "political officers"[20] to keep full control over the indigenous population with the assistance of co-opted local Chinese leaders.

1968–1984: The Legitimacy Crisis and the Reform of the Bureaucracy

Both King and Lau had tried to account for the status quo in Hong Kong's colonial system of governance, one relying more on an administrative-political explanation and the other emphasizing socio-cultural factors. In a more recent account, Scott[21] identified the legitimacy crisis as an important factor in Hong Kong's political development. He argued that Hong Kong's political history had been punctuated by many crises, most notably the 1967 riots, which were crises over consent, in which the colonial government's claim to the right to rule was challenged.[22] The legitimacy at stake was

---

[18] *Ibid.*, p. 133.

[19] The Administrative Class was instituted locally only in 1960 to replace a previous cadet scheme started in 1861 through which young recruits obtained from Britain by competitive examination were groomed for high administrative posts within the colonial civil service. Its officers formed a nascent administrative elite, operating as "a minuscule band of officials with the same values and from the same social backgrounds." See H. J. Lethbridge, *Hong Kong: Stability and Change* (Hong Kong: Oxford University Press, 1978), p. 32.

[20] F. J. D. Lugard, *Political Memoranda*.

[21] I. Scott, *Political Change and the Crisis of Legitimacy in Hong Kong* (Hong Kong: Oxford University Press, 1989).

[22] Even King agreed that the riots were symptoms of mal-integration between the elite and the masses in the rapidly urbanizing city of Hong Kong. See Ambrose King, "Administrative Absorption of Politics in Hong Kong," p. 136.

only somewhat sustained by the governed after it had followed a corporatist strategy from the 1970s onwards, departing clearly from the previous "hands-off," minimally-integrated approach towards a relatively more pro-active style of political management, involving greater state intervention and supply of public services.[23] The post-1967 reforms included more significantly the extension of "administrative absorption" to the grassroots level, the McKinsey modernization of the colonial government machinery in 1974, the anti-corruption reform of the 1970s and the introduction of district administration in 1980.

The first step towards extending administrative absorption was in the form of setting up City District Offices (CDOs) in the aftermath of the 1967 riots. The CDO scheme was significant not in altering the existing distribution of power, but rather in serving as "the foundation for a new basis of legitimacy for the continued existence of a colonial regime whose senior officials were increasingly conscious that the territory was subject to political vicissitudes of a volatile China."[24] By reaching out to the people at the local level, in order to both explain government intentions to the community and sound out popular sentiments and opinions, the colonial government had for the first time broken the traditional tenet of governance which was "exclusionary" and dependent on an approach of indirect rule. From then onwards, the government had tried to become a government of the people, though it was not and would not be a government by the people.[25] Young, local Chinese administrative officers were recruited to be city district officers as they were better able to communicate with local people in their own language.

---

[23] Though Scott's analysis was criticized by Wong and Lui for under-exploring the "society" dimension of legitimacy — i.e. "the way in which 'legitimacy' is being 'socially constructed' by the ruled population," it was instrumental in bringing out the legitimacy question as a major factor of political change in Hong Kong. About Wong and Lui's viewpoint, see T. W. P. Wong and T. L. Lui, *From One Brand of Politics to One Brand of Political Culture*, Occasional Paper No. 10 (Hong Kong: Hong Kong Institute of Asia-Pacific Studies, The Chinese University of Hong Kong, 1992) p. 18.

[24] I. Scott, *Political Change and the Crisis of Legitimacy.* p. 125.

[25] As the Deputy Secretary for Home Affairs argued in April 1969 at a teach-in organized by the Current Affairs Committee of the University of Hong Kong Students' Union:

The District Administration (DA) Scheme was announced in June 1980[26] and adopted in the following year. It involved the setting up of two types of new district-level institutions: "district boards" which were to be partially directly elected on universal franchise and partially appointed,[27] to advise the government on any matters which may affect the well-being of those residing or working in the district; and "district management committees" which were formalized inter-departmental committees at the district level to act as a focal point for coordination of various governmental activities and services and for improving government responsiveness to local community needs. The official explanation for introducing district administration put it as an outcome of the natural evolution of Hong Kong's unique systems of representation, participation and consultation,[28] which could be dated back to the district office system and elected rural committees in the New Territories, and more recently to the CDO scheme in the urban areas. However, the DA scheme had carried both a political reform agenda and an administrative reform agenda.

After the visit by the then Governor, Sir Murray MacLehose, to Beijing in March 1979 to meet Chinese leader Deng Xiaoping, the British government realized that China intended to take back Hong Kong in 1997 when

---

We have no general elections for the central government and yet the general trends of government policy conform to the wishes of the mass of the people ... The Government here through formal councils, committees and boards, through reading the press, through informal contacts with individuals and groups, in high station and low, has its antennae turned constantly to public wishes in a thousand fields of our administration ... Our methods can certainly be improved, our thoughts thrown wider open, but we do have the essential ingredients of a democracy which has produced a general understanding of the people by the government and the government by the people ... (quoted in Rear, 1971).

[26] Hong Kong Government, *Green Paper: A Pattern of District Administration in Hong Kong* (Hong Kong: Government Printer, 1980).

[27] Initially only one-third of the members were elected; the rest were government officials and appointed unofficial members. From 1985 District Boards comprised only unofficial members with two-thirds elected and one-third appointed. Appointed seats were abolished under the new electoral arrangements implemented in 1994.

[28] D. Aker-Jones, "A Perspective of District Administration," speech at the New Asia College Assembly, 17 February 1984 (Hong Kong: City and New Territories Administration, Hong Kong Government).

the lease of the New Territories expired and had to prepare for the eventual negotiations with China over the future of the territory. The lack of any representative institutions would render difficult any British position to claim to negotiate on behalf of the interests of the local population. Being only advisory in power and yet partially elected in composition, district boards would not seriously challenge the colonial government but would be able to tap some degree of popular support and participation in line with the government's political agenda. Administratively, district management committees, chaired by upgraded district officers, followed the path of the "corporate revolution" in the United Kingdom during the 1970s[29] in terms of facilitating a more structured system of corporate management and coordination of government services at the local level. As the legitimacy of the government depended increasingly on its performance, bureaucratic expansion was unavoidable and had created problems of administrative overload at the centre and insufficient monitoring of lower-level bureaucratic performance. By subjecting local departmental officials to mild local pressure from the new district advisory machinery, it was hoped that the problem of bureaucratic control of lower-level officials within the bureaucracy could be partially solved.[30]

Major administrative innovation took place in the mid-1970s in what are known as the McKinsey reforms, implemented upon acceptance of the McKinsey consultants' report[31] on reforming the central government machinery. The main purposes of the McKinsey reforms were, firstly, to streamline government coordination of policy formulation and resource control through the establishment of high-level "Secretaries" in the Government Secretariat, directly below the Chief Secretary and Financial Secretary to oversee departments; and secondly, to introduce more

---

[29] R. J. Haynes, *Organization Theory and Local Government* (London: George Allen and Unwin, 1980), Chapter 3.

[30] S. K. Lau, "Local Administrative Reform in Hong Kong: Promises and Limitation," *Asian Survey*, Vol. 22, No. 9 (September 1982), pp. 858–73.

[31] McKinsey & Co., *The Machinery of Government: A New Framework for Expanding Services* (Hong Kong: Government Printer, 1973). For discussion of the McKinsey reforms, see N. Miners, *The Government and Politics of Hong Kong*, 5th edition (Hong Kong: Oxford University Press, 1991), pp. 88–91, and P. Harris, *Hong Kong: A Study in Bureaucracy and Politics* (Hong Kong: Macmillan, 1988), pp. 135–41.

systematic programme planning and resource allocation processes following the rationalist "global" fashion at the time. As far as the senior administrative civil servants were concerned, the McKinsey changes could be conceived as some form of "ministerialization."[32] Wettenhall had examined how the independence of colonies had brought about the need to introduce new institutions such as ministries and the cabinet. The evolution of the colonial government structure took various "modes" of ministerialization whereby the former secretariat divisions simply became new ministries or ministerial secretariats. The full integration of departments within the ministries was not always an early feature of independence, though eventually ministers would achieve control over departments that came within their portfolios. In Hong Kong independence was not on the agenda; however, the administrative reforms of the 1970s had a very strong connotation of modernization representing an attempt to "re-invent" the government administration so as to remove its colonial wrappings as far as practicable. As such, the McKinsey reorganization of the Government Secretariat in effect facilitated the evolution of a cabinet of some kind — the only distinction being that this cabinet would not be a "political" one composed of politicians, but would remain in the hands of administrative officers who are increasingly expected to act and operate as ministers and ministerial staff. While the Hong Kong Government had shied away from political reforms in the aftermath of the 1967 riots, those reform measures which were since implemented served to give the administrative elite a more politicized posture with which to better face up to the external political challenges and turbulences.

Another feature of this period of bureaucratic reforms is the rise of professional civil servants (like medical doctors, engineers, social service professionals, planners, law and order enforcement professionals) in line with the rapid expansion of government services and interventions during the 1970s and 1980s. Administrative class officers remained to be the backbone of government leadership and to dominate key posts in departments and the Government Secretariat. However professional civil servants

---

[32] R. L. Wettenhall, "Modes of Ministerialization. Part I: Towards a Typology — The Australian Experience," *Public Administration*, Vol. 54, No. 1 (Spring 1976), pp. 1–20; "Modes of Ministerialization. Part II: From Colony to State in the Twentieth Century," *Public Administration*, Vol. 54, No. 4 (Winter 1976), pp. 425–51.

began to assert their power within more professionally oriented departments (such as Trade and Industry, Medical and Health, Public Works) and the generalist/specialist cleavage had become a significant aspect of intra-bureaucratic conflict, adding fuel to the already contentious mode of Secretariat-department interaction.[33]

The nature of the senior civil service during the era of bureaucratic reforms and modernization was seen to have departed substantially from the traditional colonial administrative mode. On the one hand, there had been a clear attempt to modernize and professionalize the civil service. More emphasis had since been placed on training and rational management. "Professional" power in specialist departments was increasingly recognized. On the other hand, senior civil servants, mainly the administrative elite, had become more "political" in their role orientation. In the absence of professional politicians in Hong Kong's system of governance, administrative officers took up the role of political officers representing the government and winning support for the government. They formed the *de facto* "government party." At the same time, they acted more and more like ministers and junior ministers in policy formulation and coordination.

1980s: Aborted Attempts at Decolonization

The legitimacy crisis identified by Scott[34] in theory could have been averted by more fundamental political reforms, but the colonial government had chosen not to pursue that route until the 1980s when the future of Hong Kong was to be negotiated with China. The most significant aim of decolonization was to install "a system of government the authority for which is firmly rooted in Hong Kong, which is able to represent authoritatively the views of the people of Hong Kong, and which is more directly accountable to the people of Hong Kong."[35] The political reform proposals first

---

[33] I. Scott, "Generalists and Specialists," in *The Hong Kong Civil Service and Its Future*, edited by I. Scott and J. P. Burns (Hong Kong: Oxford University Press, 1988).

[34] I. Scott, *Political Change and the Crisis of Legitimacy in Hong Kong.*

[35] Hong Kong Government, *White Paper: The Further Development of Representative Government in Hong Kong*, para. 2.

set out in the July 1984 Green Paper[36] on representative government, apart from calling for direct and indirect elections to the Legislative Council, also advocated that the majority of appointed unofficial members of the Executive Council should be replaced progressively by members elected by the Legislative Council, a clear sign of moving towards some kind of Westminster system. Both the direct election component for the Legislative Council and the partially elected Executive Council proposal were abruptly dropped in the White Paper of November 1984. After the review of the development of representative government, the Government decided, against strong popular demands, that direct election to the Legislative Council would not take place in 1988 as previously hinted but had to be postponed to 1991 after the Basic Law for the future Hong Kong SAR was promulgated by China.[37]

Whether or not the real reason for failing to implement constitutional changes was China's opposition to introducing into Hong Kong party politics and elections along Western lines, as alleged by the British Government,[38] the point remains that for a long time political options were ruled out by the colonial administration as a solution to its legitimacy difficulties, and administrative reforms became the only feasible answers to those difficulties. Constraints on political reforms in Hong Kong within the transitional period since 1984 were argued by Lau[39] to have resulted from Hong Kong's unique constitutional development path which was supposed to lead to "decolonization without independence." The impossibility of ultimate independence had even before 1982 (when Sino-British negotiations began over the future of the territory) precluded the transfer of the Westminster model to Hong Kong or the need to prepare for it. The only

---

[36] Hong Kong Government, *Green Paper: The Further Development of Representative Government in Hong Kong*.

[37] Hong Kong Government, *White Paper: The Development of Representative Government: The Way Ahead*.

[38] British Government, *White Paper: Representative Government in Hong Kong*, presented to the Parliament by the Secretary of State for Foreign and Commonwealth Affairs, 24 February 1994 (Hong Kong: Government Printer, 1994).

[39] S. K. Lau, *Decolonization without Independence: The Unfinished Political Reforms of the Hong Kong Government*, Occasional Paper No. 19 (Hong Kong: Centre for Hong Kong Studies, The Chinese University of Hong Kong, 1987).

significant proposals for reform in the postwar period (in 1946 and 1966 respectively) came at the level of municipal councils, but even those moderate reforms were eventually rejected.[40] Lau suggested that the failure of such limited political reforms was largely because of the fear of opposition from China and of infiltration by pro-Communist elements into government institutions. After the signing of the Sino-British Joint Declaration which promised Hong Kong's return to Chinese sovereignty, the absence of the prospect of independence loomed even larger as a constraint on fundamental political reforms, since the successor regime would increasingly view any significant political change with suspicious eyes. The political reality was that Chinese leaders would not like to see Hong Kong being turned into a fully democratic entity which would contrast too strongly with the highly controlled polity in mainland China. As China's presence and dominance in the local political system expanded, any major constitutional reforms initiated by the departing colonial government would be short-lived and replaced by another executive-centred system of government bent on "re-centralization" and "re-dependence on the bureaucracy."[41] What Lau has omitted is the reluctance of the administrative elite to give up its predominant powers within the existing political system voluntarily and to accept a back-seat role like neutral civil servants elsewhere.

The year 1988 marked the end of the first attempt by the British Government to decolonize Hong Kong in the wake of the Sino-British Joint Declaration. Afterwards, the British Government concentrated on co-operating with and influencing the Chinese Government in the drafting of the Basic Law. As the former chief of the New China News Agency Hong Kong Branch Xu Jiatun recalled in his memoirs,[42] every letter in the Basic Law had British input. A second round of decolonization attempt, more with an eye to shore up Hong Kong's political system against future Chinese central interference, was to be launched in 1992 when Christopher

---

[40] S. Y. S. Tsang, *Democracy Shelved: Great Britain, China, and Attempts at Constitutional Reform in Hong Kong, 1945–1952* (Hong Kong: Oxford University Press, 1988); N. Miners, *The Government and Politics of Hong Kong*, 1st edition (Hong Kong: Oxford University Press, 1975), Chapter 15.

[41] S. K. Lau, *Decolonization without Independence*, p. 39.

[42] Xu Jiatun, *Xu Jiatun's Hong Kong Memoirs* (Hong Kong: The United Daily Press, 1993), pp. 154–55. The New China News Agency Hong Kong Branch is China's *de facto* representative office in Hong Kong.

Patten took up the governorship of Hong Kong. Apart from any possible undisclosed British strategic considerations, the internal political environment within Hong Kong had undergone drastic changes since the late 1980s which might have partly contributed towards the British shift in policy towards China over the Hong Kong question. In the aftermath of the 1989 Tiananmen crackdown on the pro-democracy movement in China and the resultant restlessness among the local population, the Hong Kong Government (while still under the former Governor David Wilson who was considered to be reconciliatory towards China) saw the need to introduce a Bill of Rights in 1990 which for the first time recognized civil and political rights of Hong Kong residents. Political parties began to emerge in the early 1990s and took the lead in various levels of local elections.[43]

With the arrival of Patten, new initiatives in both the administrative and political fronts were launched. His political reform proposals sought to strengthen the directly elected elements within the legislature without openly exceeding the perimeters set by the letters of the Basic Law, apparently trying not to upset the "through train" arrangement already agreed about the transition of the legislature. The election to the nine new functional-constituency seats were to be based on universal franchise of the working population and the election committee which returned ten seats was to be formed by elected district board members. In administrative reforms, the Governor introduced performance pledges for all government departments and public agencies, along the lines of the U.K. Citizen's Charter;[44] annual policy progress reports and policy commitments by all Policy Secretaries who have to directly face public monitoring of their policy performance; and a Code of Access to Information. Senior civil servants, particularly those in the policy branches of the Government Secretariat, also had to explain government policies and address matters of public concern in open meetings of the Legislative Council panels. Patten set an example in this form of public accountability by introducing the Governor's Question Time in the Legislative Council.

---

[43] P. K. Li, "Elections, Politicians, and Electoral Politics," in *The Other Hong Kong Report 1995*, edited by S. Y. L. Cheung and S. M. H. Sze (Hong Kong: The Chinese University Press, 1995).

[44] See discussion in A. B. L. Cheung, "Performance Pledges — Power to the Consumer or a Quagmire in Public Service Legitimation?" *International Journal of Public Administration*, Vol. 19, No. 2 (February 1996).

The civil service under Patten had seen two clear developments which by and large were not inconsistent with the reform logic first triggered by the McKinsey reforms in the 1970s. First, it continued to become more professionalized and modernized, or to put it in the latest *reformspeak*, "managerialized." The whole of the civil service and its associated public sector was undergoing changes in structure and processes under the 1989 Public Sector Reform,[45] the aim of which was to transform civil servants from administrators into better and more efficient managers. However, as this author has argued elsewhere,[46] Hong Kong's public sector reforms were not motivated so much by the standard global claims about suppressing Big Government and improving efficiency or coping with the fiscal crisis, as by institutional needs to manage macro-political changes. Public sector reform is a means to "re-manage" the changing realities of both the external and internal environments of the administrative elite, in order to restore legitimacy for the public services concerned. A shift towards the micro-economic notion of efficiency in service as advocated in the new public management orientation would help to depoliticize performance evaluation of public service, thus reducing the impact of pressure for greater political accountability from elected politicians and the population at large. To posit public sector reforms in such a context does not, of course, preclude factors such as a genuine concern among senior civil service administrators for enhancing administrative capacity and managerial competence or influence from global trends of new public management that have been seen to have partly induced movements of administrative change in other countries. However the argument in the case of Hong Kong is that such "managerial" reasons are insufficient in explaining a bureaucratically driven reform process. Besides the need to strengthen administrative capacity to cope with new demands from internal and external constituencies should also be examined against a background of rapid social and political change of the 1980s which had exposed the legitimacy problem of the colonial bureaucracy. In this sense, managerial reforms aimed at

---

[45] A. B. L. Cheung, "Public Sector Reform in Hong Kong: Perspectives and Problems," *Asian Journal of Public Administration*, Vol. 14, No. 2 (December 1992).

[46] A. B. L. Cheung, "Efficiency as the Rhetoric: Public Sector Reform in Hong Kong Explained," *International Review of Administrative Sciences*, Vol. 62, No. 1 (March 1996).

improvements in efficiency and competency are part of a larger attempt at relegitimating the public bureaucratic power.[47] Depoliticization of the civil service activities through managerialization could also help to replace politics with efficiency as the main if not the sole criterion to evaluate institutional performance. The new logic would be a useful tactical means to keep away politics from China during the political transition.

Second, public sector reform has operated as a new political management strategy to manage intra-bureaucratic conflicts, between policy branches and executive departments and between the administrative class and professional civil servants. The paramountcy of the administrative class in terms of policy and resource-control functions is to be secured in exchange for greater managerial autonomy and micro-budgetary powers to be given to departmental managers. In a way, the new civil service configuration consists of two distinct layers, the policy management layer dominated by administrative power and the policy execution layer gradually dominated by departmental professional power. This duality is likely to persist beyond 1997.

The Transition of Bureaucratic Power: Mixed Motives and Agendas

While Patten had been instrumental in making both the political and administrative processes more transparent and accountable in the final days of British rule, his controversial political reform package led to a serious confrontation with the Chinese Government, which insisted that the reforms were in contravention with the Basic Law and previous Sino-British agreements.[48] As a result, China had made it clear that the original "through train" arrangements to facilitate continuity of Hong Kong's political institutions after the change of sovereignty in 1997 would now come to an end. A provisional legislature selected by an exclusive group of four hundred members in the form of a Selection Committee was set up in 1997, which would rewrite the election rules. The same Selection Committee had

---

[47] A. B. L. Cheung, "Public Sector Reform and the Re-legitimation of Public Bureaucratic Power: The Case of Hong Kong," *The International Journal of Public Sector Management*, Vol. 9, Nos. 5/6 (1996).

[48] K. K. Leung, "The Basic Law and the Problem of Political Transition," in *The Other Hong Kong Report 1995*, edited by S. Y. L. Cheung and S. M. H. Sze.

also selected Tung Chee-hwa as the first Chief Executive of the Hong Kong SAR in December 1996. The question of continuity of the senior civil servants has yet to be fully settled, given China's demand for their political loyalty and the rising exodus of senior officials,[49] although the appointment by Tung in February 1997 of all serving Secretary-rank officials in the previous Hong Kong Government (with the exception of Jeremy Matthews, the Attorney General who was not able to meet the Basic Law criterion requiring all principal officials to be Chinese nationals) to the new SAR Government with the same portfolios has helped to restore some confidence among senior civil servants who have been nervous about being politically victimized for their past association with the Patten administration.

Because of China's suspicions about a British conspiracy upon retreat from Hong Kong and the emergence of local democratic politics[50] very often critical of Chinese policies, and more importantly because of the Chinese leaders' preference to retain a bureaucratically controlled Hong Kong (in much the same way as Hong Kong used to be governed during the more typical British colonial days), it is becoming clearer that the Chinese Government would take active steps to halt, if not outrightly reverse, the whole process of political democratization and administrative opening-up belatedly started by the British Government. Two endogenous factors might also have served to reinforce China's determination to derail most of Patten's reforms. First, the major business interests would like to seize the opportunity of British departure to gain a stronger say over public policies. They regard elected local politicians as mostly anti-business and too pro-welfare and pro-grassroots. A return to the kind of politics by

---

[49] A. B. L. Cheung, "The Civil Service in Transition," in *The Other Hong Kong Report 1996*, edited by M. K. Nyaw and S. M. Li (Hong Kong: The Chinese University Press, 1996).

[50] Some local observers were of the view that China had a fundamental ideological opposition to democracy in Hong Kong. King commented in the mid-1980s that "the PRC Government was indeed of the belief that the development of representative government was a conspiracy of *min-chu k'ang-kung* ('民主抗共', using democracy to resist communism); it was not intended to preserve the characteristics of capitalism, instead, it was to transform Hong Kong into a 'separate political entity', a city-state of its own, subject to no constraints from the Central People's Government." See A. Y. C. King, "The Hong Kong Talks and Hong Kong Politics," *Issues and Studies*, Vol. 26, No. 6 (June 1986).

"appointment" would safeguard the domination of the SAR Government by business and professional elites, a feature which used to characterize the colonial administration. Second, while senior civil servants have yet to pass the political loyalty test imposed by Beijing after the change-over, 1997 also represents an opportunity for them to strengthen their hold on government administration since it is quite obvious that China opts for another form of bureaucratic polity in post-1997 Hong Kong either in the classical Hong Kong model or as a variant of the Singapore model. It is not accidental that a video produced by the Association of Former Senior Civil Servants in February 1997 to show the operation of Hong Kong's civil service system has conveyed in no unclear terms the message that civil servants (meaning senior administrators) should best be left to their own to run the government efficiently and smoothly. Both the business and senior civil service interests would gain in power over the SAR by displacing newly emergent politicians and political parties and the two would converge on the need to marginalize electoral politics.

Major Political Actors and Their Agendas

A change of sovereignty brings about a process of reconstitution of political order and a reconfiguration of institutional power. In the case of Hong Kong colonial administrative authority was repeatedly under challenges from newly emerging local forces and rising public demands ever since the late 1960s. From 1980s onwards China has entered the scene of political turbulence for the Hong Kong Government. Because of the political transition, business interests which used to coalesce around the colonial authority have gradually sought to realign themselves with the successor regime, i.e. China and its agents in Hong Kong. A China-centred governing coalition is in formation which has displaced the previous Britain-centred governing coalition.

In the course of political transition, old and new political actors in the Hong Kong scene have their own different agendas which however have one objective in common, that is to subdue bureaucratic power for the sake of their separate interest. The British Government tried to continue with bureaucratic rule until the last days of colonial rule, but in the process and in view of changed political realities had to play up the political neutrality of the civil service so as not to allow other powers to capture the civil servants. Besides, a localized and seemingly independent civil service could be portrayed as proof of the British Government returning the power of government to the local population. The Chinese Government, on the other hand, has been working in the reverse direction, that is to take over the civil service and to turn it into the loyal instrument of SAR rule under the oversight of Beijing. What China seeks is a governing agent and the civil service which had done its job so efficiently under the British political masters is considered most suitable for the new but similar role under the Chinese sovereign. Essentially, China's mind is set on continued bureaucratic rule with only a change of flag and target of political loyalty.

Locally in Hong Kong, the big business elites see the weakening of British rule and the eventual departure of the British as a great historical opportunity for them to further assert their power and influence. While most of them had advocated retaining British administration or British presence during the Sino-British negotiations of the early 1980s, once the 1984 Sino-British Joint Declaration was signed, they immediately turned their attention to forging a new alliance with the Chinese Government which, of course, was happy to co-opt them in a process of what can be described as "political absorption of economics"[51] (i.e. through appointing big business notables onto China's National and lower-level People's Congresses, the People's Political Consultative Conferences, the Basic Law Drafting and Consultative Committees, the SAR Preliminary Working Committee and Preparatory Committee, and as China's Hong Kong Affairs Advisers). On the other hand, newly emerging elected politicians, particularly pro-democratic forces, are demanding a say in the way the government is being run, on the basis of their popular mandate gained through elections. To them, political reform is not just constitutional change *per se*, to suit Hong Kong's new post-1997 status, but also an important process of redistribution of political power, from the business and professional elite sectors to the less endowed middle-class and working class. In the course of political reform, elected politicians demand the same form of political accountability from the civil servants as that which exists in established democracies. Even though elected legislators do not govern, the fact that there is no longer any appointed seat in the Legislative Council now would mean that the administration has sometimes to do the bidding of the legislature if government bills are to be passed and financial appropriations are to be obtained.

---

[51] A. Y. C. King, "The Hong Kong Talks and Hong Kong Politics."

In face of the offensive from China, the business and professional elites, and elected politicians, and not being free entirely from the oversight of the British Governor, the senior civil service had worked under various political constraints during the final days of political transition. Bureaucratic authority is definitely not as unbounded now as before in the old colonial days. The pressure is particularly felt by the administrative class who until recently formed the "government" with the Governor and governed the territory by way of co-optation and consultation. The senior professional civil servants, though anxious about their professional power, have not felt their pride shattered to the same degree, partly because they are very often not at the most forefront of the conflict and partly because they used to be working under the administrative class and had not accumulated so much institutional power.

However the fact that there are competing bids to share power with the administrative bureaucracy and that these competing actors do not agree with one another in their overall political agenda has turned out to favour the senior civil servants. It has been pointed out above that China has always preferred Hong Kong's "executive-led system" which literally implies government by civil servants, so long as these civil servants are politically loyal to Beijing. The New China News Agency Hong Kong Branch Director Zhou Nan made the point, when interviewed by *Time* magazine in June 1996, that even if a political party managed to secure a majority of seats in the legislature it had no right to form a government.[52] China's stance is not based so much on the constitutional nicety of the Basic Law which provides for separation of powers between the executive and legislature as on a fundamental distrust of political parties which could only gain entry into organs of political power through legislative elections. Such anti-politics sentiments were fully articulated within the China-appointed SAR Preparatory Committee which decided in July 1996 that candidates for the post of Chief Executive could not be a member of a political party.

The Impact of Sino-British Conflict

In fact, during the heyday of Sino-British cooperation after the signing of

---

[52] Zhou Nan, "The Pearl Will Shine Brighter," interview by *Time* magazine, 1 July 1996.

the Joint Declaration, it was China's intention to eventually appoint a civil servant (or ex-civil servant) to be the first SAR Chief Executive so as to strengthen the executive-led system, partly on the ground that it has been British practice to appoint a British civil servant as the Governor of Hong Kong, but more importantly in order to keep the Chief Executive from being embroiled in party politics or business interests. In the name of enabling the Chief Executive to be above-politics, such considerations of China in effect served to continue with Hong Kong's "brand of politics"[53] so prevalent in its colonial days. Speaking to U.S.-based ABC News in May 1996, Lu Ping, Director of the Hong Kong and Macau Affairs Office of China's State Council, confirmed rumours that the first Chief Executive could have been chosen as early as 1994 if it were not for the Sino-British conflict over political reforms.[54] "We also even thought of having a vice-governor, a Chinese vice-governor before July 1, 1997 so that by July 1, this vice-governor could be Chief Executive," he was quoted as saying.[55] Both the Chinese and British Governments were apparently looking to the top echelon of the civil service for a suitable candidate for the Chief Executive post. Apart from providing continuity and stability, such a choice would have served to emphasize the independence and impartiality over sectoral interests of the post-holder.

The Sino-British conflict started after Patten's arrival spoiled the original plan. China was determined to prevent the British Government from having any say over the appointment of the Chief Executive. Since Chinese leaders appeared to be unable or unwilling to pick someone from among top officials within the existing senior civil service (such as Anson Chan, the then Chief Secretary) who would be suspected of having been "Pattenized," they were forced by circumstances to consider potential candidates from within the ranks of business leaders in Hong Kong; hence the rumour that Tung Chee-hwa, a shipping tycoon well-connected to leaders in China and Taiwan, was the hand-picked choice of the Beijing leadership.

---

[53] J. Rear, "One Brand of Politics."

[54] C. Yeung, "Beijing's Search for a Face That Fits," *Sunday Morning Post*, 8 September 1996.

[55] *Ibid.*

Political Window for Bureaucratic Polity of Another Kind

Without delving into the issue of selecting the Chief Executive, suffice it to say that in China's thinking, the strategy for taking back Hong Kong has always been premised on the assumption that the senior civil service would remain the most important pillar of SAR governance, and given the present disarray of the local political scene and the suppression of bottom-up electoral politics, probably the only pillar left. Hence the senior civil service as a power group has in no way fallen into political disgrace but has in fact come out from the Sino-British conflict relatively untainted by its close association with Patten's controversial policies. The difficult position faced by the Chinese Government and the limited range of political choices available to it suggest that the Hong Kong administrative elite would have a considerable amount of bargaining power *vis-à-vis* the future sovereign government over the running of the SAR. Indeed, it is an open secret that China has accepted that one of the preconditions in the selection of the SAR Chief Executive is that this person must be acceptable, *inter alia*, to the civil service — in practice, the administrative elite. Thus, although the administrative elite was unable to grasp the highest office of the SAR Government for its member, it managed to secure a second-best solution, i.e. a leadership team on which it has an institutional say. During the 1980s, when the future of Hong Kong after 1997 was still being negotiated between the two sovereign governments, administrative officers in the Hong Kong Government were already tossing with the notion of "Hong Kong bureaucrats governing Hong Kong" (*gangguan zhigang*). It seems now that the ultimate scenario is not too far off from what they had set out to achieve.

After all the hiccups and debates about decolonization, representative government and democratization over the past decade, the governance of Hong Kong has come back to square one — sustaining a form of bureaucratic polity of another kind with the support of China and the connivance of the business and professional elites. However, this prospect does not necessarily mean that local politics will accordingly be assigned to the political wilderness. For one thing, elections and legislative politics have already become part of the political system and will remain so. The senior civil service together with the Chief Executive will not be able to ignore elected politicians and their political parties entirely. The local population will also try to demand political accountability from the SAR Government through those politicians and parties who, as such, would have an active role to play as an "Opposition." Furthermore, it would not be of benefit to the administrative elite if it were to be left on its own to deal with the Central Government in Beijing. To maintain its unbeatable position in SAR governance, the ideal scenario is for it to exploit Central Government support to suppress local challenges to its position and at the same time to be able to defer to the need to consult and obtain consent from local business, professional and party-political elites when there are occasional demands from the Central Government which they may find it difficult to accept without a fight.

China's "dependence" on the administrative civil servants to govern the SAR, however, needs to be properly qualified. Despite repeated remarks by senior Chinese officials praising the high quality of Hong Kong's civil service, the Chinese Government is apparently still obsessed with fear that senior local bureaucrats might try to defy China's political dictate. What China has looked for is a bureaucracy which can act as the Central Government's governing agent in much the same way as it did in the old British colonial days. While on the one hand trying to protect the civil service from challenge by local politics through the suppression of political democratization and the sidelining of elected politicians, in the name of preserving Hong Kong's so-called "executive-led" features, China has on the other hand attempted to tighten its political control of the civil service. A kind of China-centred politicization is to gradually displace local politicization. Such a prospect generates all the more a need for the senior civil service not to cut itself entirely from the local politicians and their "support."

Prospect in the Tung Era

Under British colonial rule it was the civil service bureaucracy essentially running the government. With the change of sovereignty, top civil servants are still keen to keep their administrative power largely intact. Some of them have resented the high-profile leadership (and at times intervention) of Governor Patten during the late transition period. Patten was blamed for unduly politicizing government administration as well as the role of civil servants. The notion of civil service neutrality and arguments against "politicizing" the civil service are being turned into near-myths by some top civil servants to justify their continued monopoly of governmental power.

The new Chief Executive Tung Chee-hwa had campaigned on a platform of depoliticization, asking, for example, "Is our civil service too bogged down in the politics of our legislative process? Should they be devoting more time and energy to the formulation and efficient implementation of policies?",[56] thus seemingly playing to the music of those senior civil servants frustrated by Patten and the legislative politics of the 1990s. However, Tung has also claimed that he would exercise "strong leadership" and suggested that the non-civil service members of his Executive Council would play a more prominent political role by promoting government policies. A vocal and assertive Executive Council team would certainly provide an important bulwark to counterbalance the power and influence of the senior civil service. Although all previous Secretary-rank officials and heads of designated departments/agencies have been retained by Tung to serve in the same posts of the new SAR Government, the worst fear of top civil servants is that Tung would exercise his authority of appointment indulgently. Tung can make top government appointments increasingly more conditional on policy terms. He can bring in non-civil servants to take up principal official posts (as in the case of Elsie Leung, a lawyer sitting in China's National People's Congress as a Hong Kong delegate, who became Secretary for Justice to fill the Attorney General vacancy left by Jeremy Matthews). There is no reason to believe that Tung will definitely not pursue a kind of ministerial system with all Secretary posts, or at least the three key ones, namely the Chief Secretary, Financial Secretary and Secretary for Justice, being turned into political appointments. One cannot imagine a strong Chief Executive giving up his crucial power of appointment if he is keen to place his own mark on the administration. In the immediate post-1997 period, Anson Chan as the incumbent Chief Secretary (retitled Chief Secretary for Administration in SAR nomenclature) will play the role of representing and safeguarding the interests of the civil service bureaucracy transited from the previous British colonial era. However, as and when Chan retires, that would be an opportunity for Tung to decide if he prefers to bring in a loyalist to head and subdue his inherited civil service.

A possible Tung era scenario may therefore see a see-saw game in power sharing between the Chief Executive and his senior civil service. However, one needs to bear in mind that without a clear popular mandate from Hong Kong and in lack of a firm local political power base (not

---

[56] Tung Chee-hwa, *Building a 21st Century Hong Kong Together*, 22 October 1996 (Hong Kong: np.), p. 5.

being linked to any political party), Tung has to strive hard in his early years of administration to deliver effective government so as to build up his authority. In so doing he must rely on the support and cooperation of his top civil servants and cannot afford to alienate them. Like its counterparts elsewhere, the Hong Kong SAR senior civil service will try to capture the new Chief Executive. It is too early to suggest that a strong leadership by Tung would necessarily mean a demise of public bureaucratic power in any substantive sense.

Despite the desire of senior civil servants to maintain their administrative power under a paradigm of "depoliticization," such a hope may prove to be wishful thinking. Apart from local politics to be articulated through elections and legislative bargaining, the senior civil service has to learn to live with politics coming from the Chief Executive (of a kind different from previous British Governors) and from the Chinese Central Government, not to mention a strong political coalition of local interests allied to Beijing and always ready to seek the latter's intervention. To keep its dominant position within SAR governance, the senior civil service will need to cultivate its own linkage with Central Government authorities and various local political forces and not let itself be marginalized.

Conclusion

This chapter argues that historically the administrative elite had enjoyed unchallenged authority in the governance of Hong Kong as a British colony, although it had to share some of its powers with the local elites and had to secure the latter's consent and support through an elaborate system of appointments and administrative co-optation. With the erosion of colonial authority, the administrative elite was subject to more and more challenges to its power, both locally and from China. Administrative modernization of the civil service and the gradual opening up of the government since the 1970s represented attempts to restore some form of legitimacy through efficient and responsive institutional performance. The post-1984 political transition has, however, brought about uncertainties with respect to both the institutional rules of the future SAR political structure as well as to the role of the senior civil service. For a while, particularly under the British rhetoric of developing representative government fuelled by strong local demands for democratization, there seemed to be the possibility of the civil service relegated to becoming an instrumental, politically neutral administrative arm of an elected government. Such possibility, considered remote even when it was contemplated in the less constrained climate of the 1980s, has now definitely proved to be unattainable, in view of China's clear preference for an executive-led system with the civil service in charge and of the underdevelopment of party politics. Although big business has enjoyed much political clout in influencing the thinking of both sovereign governments, and will likely continue to sustain such clout after 1997, the fact that there are intra-business rivalries and popular distrust of the self-interest of business leaders would mean that China would be reluctant to lean too much to the side of the business elites.

In the Chinese Central Government's tactics of striking a delicate balance among various competing local forces and of ensuring top-down control, a new bureaucratic polity to some degree checked-and-balanced by a local legislature representing major stakeholders of Hong Kong but with an unquestioned executive-led ethos will probably be seen to be the best possible mode of SAR governance. Ironically, it is its lack of any substantial social power base within the local scene (unlike the business elites or political parties) which gives the administrative elite of the civil service its most appealing "right to govern" in the eyes of Chinese leaders.

Bibliography

Aberbach, J. D., R. D. Putnam and B. A. Rockman. *Bureaucrats and Politics in Western Democracies*. Cambridge, Mass.: Harvard University Press, 1981.

Akers-Jones, D. "A Perspective of District Administration." Speech at the New Asia College Assembly, 17 February 1984. Hong Kong: City and New Territories Administration, Hong Kong Government.

British Government. *White Paper: Representative Government in Hong Kong*. Presented to the Parliament by the Secretary of State for Foreign and Commonwealth Affairs, 24 February 1994. Hong Kong: Government Printer, 1994.

Cheung Bing-leung, Anthony. "Public Sector Reform in Hong Kong: Perspectives and Problems." *Asian Journal of Public Administration*, Vol. 14, No. 2 (December 1992), pp. 115–48.

———. "Performance Pledges — Power to the Consumer or a Quagmire in Public Service Legitimation?" *International Journal of Public Administration*, Vol. 19, No. 2 (February 1996), pp. 233–60.

———. "Efficiency as the Rhetoric: Public Sector Reform in Hong Kong Explained." *International Review of Administrative Sciences*, Vol. 62, No. 1 (March 1996), pp. 31–47.

————. "The Civil Service in Transition." In *The Other Hong Kong Report 1996*, edited by M. K. Nyaw and S. M. Li, pp. 67–87. Hong Kong: The Chinese University Press, 1996.

————. "Public Sector Reform and the Re-legitimation of Public Bureaucratic Power: The Case of Hong Kong." *The International Journal of Public Sector Management*, Vol. 9, Nos. 5/6 (1996), pp. 37–50.

Endacott, G. B. *Government and People in Hong Kong, 1841–1962: A Constitutional History*. Hong Kong: Hong Kong University Press, 1964.

Finance Branch (Hong Kong Government). *Public Sector Reform*. February 1989, Hong Kong.

Harris, P. *Hong Kong: A Study in Bureaucratic Politics*. Hong Kong: Heinemann Asia, 1978.

————. *Hong Kong: A Study in Bureaucracy and Politics*. Hong Kong: Macmillan, 1988.

Haynes, R. J. *Organization Theory and Local Government*. London: George Allen and Unwin, 1980.

Hong Kong Government. *Green Paper: A Pattern of District Administration in Hong Kong*. Hong Kong: Government Printer, 1980.

————. *Green Paper: The Further Development of Representative Government in Hong Kong*. Hong Kong: Government Printer, 1984.

————. *White Paper: The Further Development of Representative Government in Hong Kong*. Hong Kong: Government Printer, 1984.

————. *White Paper: The Development of Representative Government: The Way Ahead*. Hong Kong: Government Printer, 1988.

King, Ambrose Y. C. "Administrative Absorption of Politics in Hong Kong: Emphasis on the Grass Roots Level." In *Social Life and Development in Hong Kong*, edited by A. Y. C. King and R. P. L. Lee, pp. 127–46. Hong Kong: The Chinese University Press, 1981.

————. "The Hong Kong Talks and Hong Kong Politics." *Issues and Studies*, Vol. 22, No. 6 (June 1986), pp. 52–75.

Kulick, H. *The Imperial Bureaucrat: The Colonial Administrative Service in the Gold Coast 1920–1939*. Stanford, California: Hoover Institution Press, 1979.

Lau Siu-kai. *Society and Politics in Hong Kong*. Hong Kong: The Chinese University Press, 1982.

————. "Local Administrative Reform in Hong Kong: Promises and Limitations." *Asian Survey*, Vol. 22, No. 9 (September 1982), pp. 858–73.

————. *Decolonization without Independence: The Unfinished Political Reforms of the Hong Kong Government*. Occasional Paper No. 19. Hong Kong: Centre for Hong Kong Studies, The Chinese University of Hong Kong, 1987.

Lethbridge, H. J. *Hong Kong: Stability and Change*. Hong Kong: Oxford University Press, 1978.

Leung, K. K. "The Basic Law and the Problem of Political Transition." In *The Other Hong Kong Report 1995*, edited by S. Y. L. Cheung and S. M. H. Sze, pp. 33–50. Hong Kong: The Chinese University Press, 1995.

Li Pang-kwong. "Elections, Politicians, and Electoral Politics." In *The Other Hong Kong Report 1995*, edited by S. Y. L. Cheung and S. M. H. Sze, pp. 51–66. Hong Kong: The Chinese University Press, 1995.

Lugard, F. J. D. *The Dual Mandate of British Tropical Africa*. 5th edition. London: Cass, 1965.

——— . *Political Memoranda: Revision of the Instructions to Political Officers on Subjects Chiefly Political and Administrative, 1913–1918*. 3rd edition. International Specialized Book Service, 1970.

McKinsey & Co. *The Machinery of Government: A New Framework for Expanding Services*. Hong Kong: Government Printer, 1973.

Miners, N. *The Government and Politics of Hong Kong*. 1st edition. Hong Kong: Oxford University Press, 1975.

——— . "Hong Kong: A Case Study in Political Stability." *The Journal of Commonwealth and Comparative Politics*, Vol. 13, No. 1 (March 1975), pp. 26–39.

——— . *The Government and Politics of Hong Kong*. 5th edition. Hong Kong: Oxford University Press, 1991.

Rear, J. "One Brand of Politics." In *Hong Kong: The Industrial Colony*, edited by K. Hopkins, pp. 55–139. Hong Kong: Oxford University Press, 1971.

Scott, I. "Generalists and Specialists." In *The Hong Kong Civil Service and Its Future*, edited by I. Scott and J. P. Burns, pp. 17–49. Hong Kong: Oxford University Press, 1988.

——— . *Political Change and the Crisis of Legitimacy in Hong Kong*. Hong Kong: Oxford University Press, 1989.

The Sino-British Joint Declaration on the Question of Hong Kong [Joint Declaration of the Government of the United Kingdom of Great Britain and Northern Ireland and the Government of the People's Republic of China on the Question of Hong Kong], September, 1984. Hong Kong: Government Printer.

Tsang Yiu-sang, Steve. *Democracy Shelved: Great Britain, China, and Attempts at Constitutional Reform in Hong Kong, 1945–1952*. Hong Kong: Oxford University Press, 1988.

Tung Chee-hwa. *Building a 21st Century Hong Kong Together*. 22 October 1996. Hong Kong.

Wettenhall, R. L. "Modes of Ministerialization. Part I: Towards a Typology — The Australian Experience." *Public Administration*, Vol. 54, No. 1 (Spring 1976), pp. 1–20.

——— . "Modes of Ministerialization. Part II: From Colony to State in the Twentieth Century." *Public Administration*, Vol. 54, No. 4 (Winter 1976), pp. 425–51.

Wong, Thomas W. P. and Lui Tai-lok. *From One Brand of Politics to One Brand of Political Culture.* Occasional Paper No. 10. Hong Kong: Hong Kong Institute of Asia-Pacific Studies, The Chinese University of Hong Kong, 1992.

Xu Jiatun. *Xu Jiatun's Hong Kong Memoirs.* Hong Kong: The United Daily Press, 1993.

Yeung, C. "Beijing's Search for a Face That Fits." *Sunday Morning Post,* 8 September 1996.

Zhou Nan. "The Pearl Will Shine Brighter." Interview by *Time,* 1 July 1996, pp. 28–29.

5

Fractionalization of the "Party" System in the Hong Kong Transition[1]

K. K. Leung

Introduction

Since the Sino-British talk on the future of Hong Kong began in 1982, a number of political groups have been burgeoning in the once politically indifferent colony. Some of them have consolidated their resources to form "political parties" to run the direct Legislative Council (Legco) election in 1991 and to go on board the controversial "through train" in 1995.

As the political system has always been colonial and "party" politics is still in its embryonic form, Hong Kong is undergoing an extremely high degree of "party" fractionalization. Using an index of fractionalization, this chapter attempts to measure how far seats were evenly distributed among the political groups in the 1991–1992, 1992–1993, 1993–1994 and 1994–1995 Legco sessions. Unlike the colonial government before the 1990s, a rather unstable "coalition" government was discernible in the past four sessions (1991–1995). Rival political camps not only reflected the diverse views of the public in the legislative arena but also aroused dissension in society. Ideological and perhaps social cleavages were taking shape and mobilizations either for or against government policies were frequent. Political instability seems inevitable in the countdown to 1997 and beyond.

According to the Governor's Speech in 1992 and the Basic Law of the Hong Kong Special Administrative Region (SAR) of the People's Republic

---

[1] A full version of this chapter with appendixes is published in *Asian Thought and Society*, Vol. 22, No. 64 (January–April 1997), pp. 18–60.

of China (P.R.C.), the number of directly elected seats in the Hong Kong legislature should increase from 20 (33%) in 1995 to 30 (50%) in 2003. High fractionalization will remain to be seen in the next decade. Whether the "democratic" foundation will be shaken or strengthened is a question to be analysed. The "no-majority-party" system in Hong Kong is unique and worth looking into as there is no appointed members in the Legco. It is predicted that the future government, run by various political groups and "parties," will be deeply divided and unstable unless and until a dominant "party," backed up by the British and/or the Chinese Governments, emerges.

The Framework

The Concept

The definitions of political party, broad or narrow, have always appeared in two extremes in Western literature. A minimal (broad) definition was put forward by Sartori: "A party is any political group that presents at elections, and is capable of placing through elections, candidates for public office."[2] Others offered a narrow sense of the term, defining political party as "an organized group of individuals seeking to seize the power of government."[3] Most Hong Kong political scientists like Louie Kin-sheun, Lau Siu-kai, Jane Lee and Norman Miners adopted a "minimal" definition and described "party" in Hong Kong as "any political group which sponsors candidates at an election."[4]

---

[2] Giovanni Sartori, *Parties and Party Systems: A Framework for Analysis*, Vol. I (Cambridge: Cambridge University Press, 1976), p. 64.

[3] C. C. Rodee, T. J. Anderson and C. Q. Christol, *Introduction to Political Science* (Tokyo: McGraw-Hill, 1967), p. 490.

[4] Louie Kin-sheun, "Political Parties," in *The Other Hong Kong Report 1991*, edited by Y. W. Sung and M. K. Lee (Hong Kong: The Chinese University Press, 1991), pp. 56–58; Lau Siu-kai, *Public Attitude toward Political Parties in Hong Kong* (Hong Kong: Hong Kong Institute of Asia-Pacific Studies, The Chinese University of Hong Kong, 1992), pp. 1–5; Jane Lee, "The Emergence of Party Politics in Hong Kong, 1982–92" (paper presented to the international conference on "25 Years of Social and Economic Development in Hong Kong," organized by the University of Hong Kong, 1992); quotation from Norman Miners, *The Government and Politics of Hong Kong* (Hong Kong: Oxford University Press, 1995), p. 196.

In a survey conducted by Lau in the second half of 1990, it was indicated that the "public acceptance of political parties is at best lukewarm and does not furnish a hospitable environment for the rise of political parties."[5] However, reviewing the political development of Hong Kong in 1991–1992, Louie stated that "political parties have been recognized as part of Hong Kong's political reality by all concerned sectors of the community, including the Chinese and Hong Kong governments."[6] In this respect Lee seems more reserved: "party politics is still at an embryonic stage of development."[7] From the establishment of pressure groups in the 1970s to the formation of "political parties" in the 1990s, we have witnessed the development of *lunzheng tuanti* ("political commentary group"), *canzheng tuanti* ("political participation group") and *zhengtuan* ("political group or political organization").[8] Although various research has been conducted on "party" development in Hong Kong, most Hong Kong scholars admit that political parties exist in the sense of Western democracy. Though sharing this view to a certain extent, the author has the following reservations:

First, the minimal definition demonstrated by Sartori is "by no means a sufficient definition"; it is required "only to dispel *indefiniteness* by indicating what is to be included in, or excluded from, a given class" and it has "neither explanatory nor predictive power."[9] A minimal definition without a framework will easily be reduced to conceptual obscurity.

Second, the word "party" was first adopted at the turn of the 17th century. It was commonly accepted as a sign of free government and the development of parties was usually "bound up with that of democracy, that is to say with the extension of popular suffrage and parliamentary preroga-tives."[10] The origin and growth of parties have two implications: free

---

[5] Lau Siu-kai, *Public Attitude toward Political Parties in Hong Kong*, p. 22.

[6] Louie Kin-sheun, "Politicians, Political Parties and the Legislative Council," in *The Other Hong Kong Report 1992*, edited by Joseph Y. S. Cheng and Paul C. K. Kwong (Hong Kong: The Chinese University Press, 1992), p. 63.

[7] Jane Lee, "The Emergence of Party Politics in Hong Kong, 1982–92," p. 27.

[8] Louie Kin-sheun, "Political Parties," and Jane Lee, "The Emergence of Party Politics in Hong Kong, 1982–92."

[9] G. Sartori, *Parties and Party Systems*, p. 64.

[10] *Ibid.*, pp. 64–65; Maurice Daverger, *Political Parties* (London: Methuen, 1954), p. xxiii.

election and representative government. The meaning of "election" is now broadened to cover free and non-free, parliamentary and non-parliamentary voting activities. "Party," existing even in an undemocratic regime, bears the connotation of "free" election, "representative" legislature and the "ins" (*the* governing party).

Third, Hong Kong is a colonial society. Miners admitted that "it is not possible to acquire power by success in electoral competition" as all the District Boards, Municipal Councils and Legislative Council are only advisory in nature.[11] Lau attributed the objective constraints on "party" development to the limited constitutional power of legislature, the powerful bureaucracy and executive, the semi-dependent character of Hong Kong's politicians and the limited role of the government in social and economic affairs. Summing up, he wrote: "Even though recent political reforms and changes in the political atmosphere have opened up some political space for party formation, objective constraints are such that opportunities for expansive party development will still be quite limited."[12] Not surprisingly, according to Annex II of the Basic Law, only half of the Legco seats will be directly elected until 2007 and consequently neither one "party" nor a coalition of "parties" can *actually* run a "wholly elected" government.

Neither "political party" nor "political group" appears to be an appropriate label. While "political party" does not quite fit in the context of Hong Kong, "political group" offers little or no theoretical construct. Following Sartori's argument, it is found that the term "political fraction" is able to explain Hong Kong's unique political situation: free election without a majority party system before and after 1997.

We should bear in mind that political fraction is not to be confused with faction. Zariski defined factions as "forces which compete for the acquisition of influence over the principal institutions of intra-party government, over the formulation of party policy, and over the selection of party leaders and party nominees for public office."[13] While "faction" carries value judgement (i.e. "what parties are *not*"), "fraction," a neutral term used

---

[11] N. Miners, *The Government and Politics of Hong Kong*, p. 196.

[12] Lau Siu-kai, *Public Attitude toward Political Parties in Hong Kong*, pp. 3–4.

[13] Quoted from Ian McAllister, "Party Adaptation and Factionalism within the Australian Party System," *American Journal of Political Science*, Vol. 35, No. 1 (February 1991), p. 208.

by Sartori, involves "an index of fractionalization [that] need not be confined to party systems and that it may work equally well for party systems *and* party fractions."[14] The implication is explicit: fraction connotes both intra- and inter-group (or party) competitions.

In this chapter, fraction refers to (1) a political group seeking *partial* power in the Hong Kong legislature either alone or in concert with two or more political groups; (2) a political part competing for dominance over others within one political group. The quoted word "party," therefore, is equivalent to political fraction hereafter.

The Index

Rae defined political party system as "the competition between ... [a collection of] parties within a single political regime" and "the whole assortment of interparty rivalries in a single country at any single time."[15] He has worked out two sophisticated measurements of party fractionalization based on the elective party system (shares of votes) and parliamentary party system (shares of seats). Gross criticized Rae's unit of analysis (aggregate vote totals) for its overestimation and Sartori attacked Rae's index as being "oversensitive to the 'bigness' of the first or two first parties," but the former did recognize the "desirable characteristics" of Rae's fractionalization index.[16]

> First, the index forms a continuum from 0 to 1 on which any party system can be placed. Second, it is sensitive both to the number of parties and the relative equality of party shares. Third, it allows one to examine, and thus compare, the party system in different competitive spheres.... A final advantage of the fractionalization index is that it can be generalized to many competitive situations beyond the case of interparty competition. Since the fractionalization index can be used to compare party systems with varying numbers of political parties, it is especially useful to students of comparative politics.

---

[14] G. Sartori, *Parties and Party Systems*, p. 74.

[15] Douglas W. Rae, *The Political Consequences of Electoral Laws* (New Haven: Yale University Press, 1971), p. 47.

[16] Donald A. Gross, "Units of Analysis and Rae's Fractionalization Index," *Comparative Political Studies*, Vol. 14, No. 1 (April 1982), p. 86; G. Sartori, *Parties and Party Systems*, pp. 307–9.

Despite its limitation, Rae's index is used by Ranney to classify democratic party systems.[17] The following is an attempt to make use of the index of fractionalization in parliament (measured in seats) instead of the fractionalization in election (measured in votes) for purpose of analysis. The formula for the fractionalization of seat shares is as follows:[18]

$$F_p = 1 - \left(\sum_{i=1}^{n} Si^2 \right) \qquad \text{Formula 1}$$

where p = party
n = the number of parties
Si = the ith party's decimal share of seats

One extreme of the computation is a one-party system with a score of 0.00 and the other is a multi-party system which can score 1.00 theoretically. In between is a half-half perfect split of a two-party system scoring 0.50.

In Hong Kong, political fractions can be categorized simply according to (1) the method for the formation of the Legco, or (2) the self-claimed political affiliation by Legco members. In the four sessions (1991–1995), the fraction composition in the Legco was: 21 appointed members (35%), 18 directly elected members (30%) and 21 members elected by functional constituencies (35%). Using the revised Formula 2, the score of the three fractions in the Legco is 0.6650 (see Table 1 for computation).

$$F_f = 1 - \left(\sum_{i=1}^{n} Si^2 \right) \qquad \text{Formula 2}$$

where f = fraction
n = the number of fractions
Si = the ith fraction's decimal share of seats

However, this categorization is not particularly useful. First, while most of the appointed members conformed to the government's position, there were always some members who claimed to be independent and acted otherwise. Second, instead of grouping themselves under a democratic

---

[17] Austin Ranney, *Governing: An Introduction to Political Science* (London: Prentice-Hall, 1996), pp. 215–20.
[18] D. W. Rae, *The Political Consequences of Electoral Laws*, p. 62.

Table 1: Computation for the Fractionalization Index, 1991–1995
(According to the Method for the Formation of the Legco)

Fractions	Seats	Si	Si^2	F$_f$
APP	21	0.3500	0.1225	
DE	18	0.3000	0.0900	1 – 0.3350
EFC	21	0.3500	0.1225	
Total	60	1	0.3350	0.6650

Abbreviations: APP = Appointed Members
DE = Directly Elected Members
EFC = Members Elected by Functional Constituencies

camp, directly elected members split into various fractions. Third, members elected by functional constituencies were even more divided: some were pro-government, some belonged to pro-democratic fractions, others independent. With the exception of the appointed members who followed more or less the official line, most Legco members were not equipped with any strong ideological or interest base to keep themselves unified. Therefore, we try to delineate fractions according to members' political affiliation.

This is illustrated in Table 2 in which 10, 11, 12 and 13 fractions can be discerned in the 1991–1992, 1992–1993, 1993–1994 and 1994–1995 sessions respectively. Based on the same Formula 2, the fractionalization indices are: 0.7850 (1991–1992), 0.7899 (1992–1993), 0.7993 (1993–1994) and 0.8420 (1994–1995) (see Tables 3 to 6 for computation). There is only a slight increase (0.057) of fragmentation between the four sessions. Compared with the average scores of twenty-five democratic countries (1977–1988), Hong Kong's fractionalization score is well above average, ranging between Belgium (0.8464) and Italy (0.7357) (Table 7). Unlike these countries which have a long democratic tradition, Hong Kong has just begun to taste the painful experience of fragmentation under the colonial government and its half-hearted democratic reform.

The Competition

Centrifugal or Centripetal

Owing to the high degree of fragmentation in the Hong Kong legislature since the 1991 direct election, political competition is keen especially during the passing of motions and bills.

Table 2: Distribution of Seats in the Legislative Council, 1991–1995

Fractions	1991–1992 N (%)	1992–1993 N (%)	1993–1994 N (%)	1994–1995 N (%)
ADPL	1 (1.67)	1 (1.67)	1 (1.67)	1 (1.67)
ASHK	—	1 (1.67)	1 (1.67)	1 (1.67)
CRC	16 (26.67)	—	—	—
CTU	—	—	—	1 (1.67)
DABHK	—	1 (1.67)	1 (1.67)	1 (1.67)
FTU	1 (1.67)	—	—	—
GOVT	4 (6.67)	4 (6.67)	4 (6.67)	4 (6.67)
HKDF	2 (3.33)	1 (1.67)	1 (1.67)	1 (1.67)
IND	17 (28.33)	18 (30.00)	17 (28.33)	17 (28.33)
LDFHK	—	—	1 (1.67)	1 (1.67)
LP	—	15 (25.00)	15 (25.00)	15 (25.00)
MP	3 (5.00)	4 (6.67)	4 (1.67)	4 (6.67)
NHKA	1 (1.67)	1 (1.67)	1 (1.67)	1 (1.67)
TUC	1 (1.67)	1 (1.67)	1 (1.67)	1 (1.67)
UDHK	14 (23.33)	13 (21.67)	13 (21.67)	12 (20.00)
Total	60 (100)	60 (100)	60 (100)	60 (100)

Abbreviations: ADPL = Association for Democracy and People's Livelihood

ASHK = Association for Stabilizing Hong Kong

CRC = Cooperative Resources Centre

CTU = Confederation of Trade Unions

DABHK = Democratic Alliance for Betterment of Hong Kong

FTU = Federation of Trade Unions

GOVT = Government (the Ex-officio members and the Deputy President)

HKDF = Hong Kong Democratic Foundation

IND = Independent

LDFHK = Liberal Democratic Federation of Hong Kong

LP = Liberal Party

MP = Meeting Point

NHKA = New Hong Kong Alliance

TUC = Trade Union Confederations

UDHK = United Democrats of Hong Kong

Table 3: Computation for the Fractionalization Index, 1991–1992
(According to the Political Affiliation of the Legco Members)

Fractions	Seats	Si	Si^2	F_f
ADPL	1	0.0167	0.0003	
CRC	16	0.2667	0.0711	
FTU	1	0.0167	0.0003	
GOVT	4	0.0667	0.0044	
HKDF	2	0.0333	0.0011	$1 - 0.2150$
IND	17	0.2833	0.0803	
MP	3	0.0500	0.0025	
NHKA	1	0.0167	0.0003	
TUC	1	0.0167	0.0003	
UDHK	14	0.2333	0.0544	
Total	60	1	0.2150	0.7850

Table 4: Computation for the Fractionalization Index, 1992–1993
(According to the Political Affiliation of the Legco Members)

Fractions	Seats	Si	Si^2	F_f
ADPL	1	0.0167	0.0003	
ASHK	1	0.0167	0.0003	
DABHK	1	0.0167	0.0003	
GOVT	4	0.0667	0.0044	
HKDF	1	0.0167	0.0003	
IND	18	0.3000	0.0900	$1-0.2101$
LP	15	0.2500	0.0625	
MP	4	0.0667	0.0044	
NHKA	1	0.0167	0.0003	
TUC	1	0.0167	0.0003	
UDHK	13	0.2167	0.0470	
Total	60	1	0.2101	0.7899

Table 5: Computation for the Fractionalization Index, 1993–1994
(According to the Political Affiliation of the Legco Members)

Fractions	Seats	Si	Si^2	F_f
ADPL	1	0.0167	0.0003	
ASHK	1	0.0167	0.0003	
DABHK	1	0.0167	0.0003	
GOVT	4	0.0667	0.0044	
HKDF	1	0.0167	0.0003	
IND	17	0.2833	0.0803	1 – 0.2007
LDFHK	1	0.0167	0.0003	
LP	15	0.2500	0.0625	
MP	4	0.0667	0.0044	
NHKA	1	0.0167	0.0003	
TUC	1	0.0167	0.0003	
UDHK	1	0.2167	0.0470	
Total	60	1	0.2007	0.7993

Table 6: Computation for the Fractionalization Index, 1994–1995
(According to the Political Affiliation of the Legco Members)

Fractions	Seats	Si	Si^2	F_f
ADPL	1	0.0167	0.0003	
ASHK	1	0.0167	0.0003	
CTU	1	0.0167	0.0003	
DABHK	1	0.0167	0.0003	
GOVT	4	0.0667	0.0044	
HKDF	1	0.0167	0.0003	
IND	17	0.2833	0.0803	1 – 0.1580
LDFHK	1	0.0167	0.0003	
LP	15	0.2500	0.0625	
MP	4	0.0667	0.0044	
NHKA	1	0.0167	0.0003	
TUC	1	0.0167	0.0003	
UDHK	12	0.2000	0.0040	
Total	60	1	0.1580	0.8420

Table 7: Party Fractionalization in 25 Democracies, 1977–1988

Country	Average fractionalization score
Belgium	.8464
Finland	.8340
Denmark	.8138
Switzerland	.8041
Italy	.7357
The Netherlands	.7302
Israel	7299
Portugal	.7191
Norway	.7175
Sweden	.6984
West Germany	.6862
France	.6527
Japan	.6447
Venezuela	.6408
Ireland	.6152
Spain	.6152
India	.5845
Australia	.5812
Austria	.5760
Colombia	.5436
Greece	.5435
United Kingdom	.5348
New Zealand	.4931
Canada	.4839
United States	.4796

Source: Extracted and revised from Austin Ranney, *Governing: An Introduction to Political Science* (London: Prentice-Hall, 1996), p. 217.

In the first Legco session (1991–1992) after the introduction of direct election, the Government lost only on one motion (2.9%) (the motion of the "Court of Final Appeal") out of 34 motions or bills. This later rose to 6 out of 38 (15.8%), 19 out of 86 (22.1%) and 31 out of 151 (20.5%) in the sessions of 1992–1993, 1993–1994 and 1994–1995 sessions respectively. From the above observations, we can say that the "government party" has been losing ground in its control of the presumably executive-led legislature when entering the 1990s. Rivalries between the CRC/LP and UDHK, the ethereal alignment of the fractions and the individual independents, and the emotional appeal to the public concerning controversial policies add up together to stifle the consolidation power of the government.

Three distinct fractions, viz. conservative, liberal and independent can be discernible (Tables 8 and 9) when we examine the voting pattern in the passing of motions and bills. The corresponding fractionalization indices are 0.5228 (1991–1992), 0.6049 (1992–1993), 0.6617 (1993–1994) and 0.6050 (1994–1995) with a maximum increase of 0.1389 (Tables 10 to 13). This is consistent with the political reality in which contention among the fractions in the 1992–1995 sessions was more poignant than ever.

Table 8: Three Distinct Fractions in the Legco, 1991–1993

Fractions	Sub-fractions*	1991–1992 N (%)	1992–1993 N (%)
Conservative	APP-GOVT	4 (6.67)	4 (6.67)
	APP/EFC-CRC/LP	16 (26.67)	15 (25.00)
	APP/EFC-IND	14 (23.33)	11 (18.33)
	EFC-NHKA	1 (1.67)	1 (1.67)
	Sub-Total	35 (58.34)	31 (51.67)
Liberal	DE-ADPL	1 (1.67)	1 (1.67)
	DE-MP	3 (5.00)	4 (6.67)
	DE/EFC-UDHK	14 (23.33)	13 (21.67)
	EFC-HKDF	2 (3.33)	1 (1.67)
	EFC-TUC	1 (1.67)	0 (0.00)
	DE-IND	1 (1.67)	0 (0.00)
	Sub-Total	22 (36.67)	19 (31.67)
Independent	APP-IND	1 (1.67)	1 (1.67)
	DE-ASHK	0 (0.00)	1 (1.67)
	DE-DABHK	—	1 (1.67)
	DE-IND	0 (0.00)	2 (3.33)
	EFC-FTU	1 (1.67)	—
	EFC-TUC	0 (0.00)	1 (1.67)
	EFC-IND	1 (1.67)	4 (6.67)
	Sub-Total	3 (5.01)	10 (16.68)
Grand Total		60 (100)	60 (100)

* Legco members are classified as one of the sub-fractions according to their voting pattern in the passing of motions and bills in the year. Some have shifted their voting pattern in the following year and therefore the numbers of members in sub-fractions are different.

The heated antagonism in the conservative-liberal relationship develops a centrifugal tendency in fraction emulation, that is, from a bipolar to tripolar or even quadripolar (the rise of the pro-China fraction) development. This has no doubt weakened the stability of the Hong Kong legislative system and society as a whole.

Table 9: Three Distinct Fractions in the Legco, 1993–1995

Fractions	Sub-Fractions*	1993–1994 N (%)	1994–1995 N (%)
Conservative	APP-GOVT	4 (6.67)	4 (6.67)
	APP/EFC-CRC/LP	15 (25.00)	16 (26.67)
	APP/IND	4 (6.67)	6 (10.00)
	EFC-NHKA	0 (0.00)	1 (1.67)
	DE-LDFHK	0 (0.00)	1 (1.67)
	EFC-HKDF	0 (0.00)	1 (1.67)
	EFC-TUC	0 (0.00)	1 (1.67)
	Sub-Total	35 (58.34)	31 (51.67)
Liberal	DE-ADPL	1 (1.67)	1 (1.67)
	DE-MP	4 (6.67)	4 (6.67)
	DE/CTU	—	1 (1.67)
	DE/EFC-UDHK	13 (21.67)	12 (20.00)
	EFC-HKDF	1 (1.67)	0 (0.00)
	DE-IND	1 (1.67)	3 (5.00)
	Sub-Total	20 (33.34)	21 (31.01)
Independent	APP-IND	5 (8.33)	2 (3.33)
	DE-ASHK	1 (1.67)	1 (1.67)
	DE-DABHK	1 (1.67)	1 (1.67)
	DE-IND	1 (1.67)	1 (1.67)
	EFC-TUC	1 (1.67)	0 (0.00)
	EFC-IND	6 (10.00)	4 (6.67)
	EFC-NHKA	1 (1.67)	0 (0.00)
	DE-LSDHK	1 (1.67)	0 (0.00)
	Sub-Total	17 (28.35)	9 (15.01)
Grand Total		60 (100)	60 (100)

* Legco members are classified as one of the sub-fractions according to their voting pattern in the passing of motions and bills in the year. Some have shifted their voting pattern in the following year and therefore the numbers of members in sub-fractions are different.

Table 10: Computation for the Fractionalization Index, 1991–1992
(According to the Voting Pattern in the Legco)

Fractions	Seats	Si	Si^2	F_f
Conservative	35	0.5833	0.3402	
Liberal	22	0.3667	0.1345	1 – 0.4772
Independent	3	0.0500	0.0025	
Total	60	1	0.4772	0.5228

Table 11: Computation for the Fractionalization Index, 1992–1993
(According to the Voting Pattern in the Legco)

Fractions	Seats	Si	Si^2	F_f
Conservative	31	0.5167	0.2670	
Liberal	19	0.3167	0.1003	1 – 0.3951
Independent	10	0.1667	0.0278	
Total	60	1	0.3951	0.6049

Table 12: Computation for the Fractionalization Index, 1993–1994
(According to the Voting Pattern in the Legco)

Fractions	Seats	Si	Si^2	F_f
Conservative	23	0.3833	0.1469	
Liberal	20	0.3333	0.1111	1 – 0.3383
Independent	17	0.2833	0.0803	
Total	60	1	0.3383	0.6617

Table 13: Computation for the Fractionalization Index, 1994–1995
(According to the Voting Pattern in the Legco)

Fractions	Seats	Si	Si^2	F_f
Conservative	30	0.5000	0.3383	
Liberal	21	0.3500	0.2500	1 – 0.3950
Independent	9	0.1500	0.0225	
Total	60	1	0.3950	0.6050

Volatility or Stability

On the eve of the 1992–1993 Legco session, three "political parties" — LP, MP and DABHK — were formally established, thus further enfeebled the already unstable legislature in Hong Kong. The capricious alignment and realignment in the Legco only worsened the situation. This volatility was further aggravated by the absence of a strong sense of unity within the legislative fractions: loose internal structure (in ADPL, ASHK, HKDF and NHKA), low level of "party" discipline, frequent accusations between the two leading fractions (LP vs. UDHK), internal conflicts within political fractions (i.e. intra-fraction division), etc. The situation is shifting from a centre-conservative to a centre-liberal coalition and will eventually evolve into a more fragmented and multipolar fraction competition.

Korosenyi[19] has generalized three instability hypotheses for the Hungarian party system:[20]

H1: "The emerging political cleavages are likely to be *ideological oppositions* than interest-specific ones" (formulated by George Schopflin).

H2: "The new parties and the party system do not reflect the political cleavages of the society" (popular among Hungarian political scientists).

H3: "Parties are likely to be more competitive when there are more voters in competition and when the electoral market is more open" (Peter Mair).

It is interesting to test these hypotheses against the Hong Kong situation. First, during the countdown to 1997, more and more political issues are likely to come up and they will usually escalate to a Sino-British diplomatic level. Korosenyi wrote: "In Western Europe the ideological conflicts are surpassed by the economic, material conflicts … , in which it is easier to reach a compromise."[21] On political issues such as the Court of Final Appeal, democratic

---

[19] Many of the ideas are borrowed from Andras Korosenyi's paper to apply onto the case of Hong Kong. See Korosenyi's paper titled "Stable or Fragile Democracy? Political Cleavages and Party System in Hungary," *Government and Opposition*, Vol. 28, No. 1 (Winter 1993), pp. 87–104.

[20] A. Korosenyi, "Stable or Fragile Democracy?" pp. 95–97.

[21] *Ibid.*, p. 96.

reform and the new airport construction project, debates and votings in the Legco are far less "bargainable" than other social and economic matters. And ideological conflicts would easily surface as strategic points for the fractions' wrestling against one another.

Second, the history of the "parties" is too short for Hong Kong voters to develop a strong "party" identification. These parties have difficulty in representing various sectors in society because of their small size. Their under-representation is also reflected by the low electoral turnout rates. And it is not untrue to say that the political climate in Hong Kong is not ripe for a "party" system. As far as the directly elected seats are concerned, it is found that a four-member "party" (MP) can be considered the second largest in the Legco and that the democratic legitimacy of the members elected by functional constituencies is also under question, hence political diversities in society cannot be adequately expressed by a handful of colonial "party" seats in the advisory Legco.

Finally, the surging of "parties" in a short period of four years and the introduction of direct Legco election in Hong Kong mean that voters have to be quickly mobilized with campaign strategies. As a free electoral market has existed for more than ten years and Hong Kong has a huge voting population but limited seats in the Legco for the fractions to scramble, one would anticipate severe political competitions. Fraction rivalries will undermine the stability of society and the cohesiveness of the fractions themselves if there is still an ample market for the "hungry" fractions to manoeuvre. These cleavages will further be exposed in the debates in the legislative circle as the fractions are eager to speak for the people in exchange for future confidence. When the fractions fail to gain an upper hand in the Legco, they appeal to the general but unsophisticated public for support. Society will then be agitated into a state of instability. As Hong Kong shares some of the characteristics of the political cleavages in Hungary, it is fair to say that Hong Kong is also suffering from some sorts of "Hungarian syndromes."

An Evaluation

This chapter attempts to offer another angle to look into the fraction system in Hong Kong. Although the term "political party" is widely accepted in academic and political circles, the author is not satisfied with the common usage of the term without investigating its nature and implication in the light of Hong Kong's unique political (colonial) environment.

When the Hong Kong government initiated direct Legco election in 1991, the design of an approximate one-third proportional distribution of seats (appointed, directly elected and elected by functional constituencies) has actually created a hindrance to the cultivation of a genuine party system in Hong Kong. There may be two reasons for this. First, during the transition period, no dominant group, not even the Hong Kong Government itself, emerges to settle controversies, thus leaving the British Government much say regarding major political issues. Second, the "no-majority-party" legislature will go beyond 1997 and the P.R.C. is likely to face an "ungovernable" legislature.

There is not, and in the near future will not, be sufficient democratic breeding ground for party building. Self-claimed "parties" are burgeoning. They perform party functions like candidate selection, fund raising and campaign propaganda. (Pressure groups also engage in similar activities.) In fact, the gist of the problem lies in the absence of a mechanism of representative government, which includes universal suffrage and a democratically elected legislature. If the so-called "parties" or collection of "parties" cannot control the government, external forces will easily take advantage to fill the gap.

The author does not look upon the term "fraction" as panacea to all the problems. Instead, he tries to demonstrate that "fraction" and "fractionalization" can better reflect the political reality and tries to project a feasible political development for Hong Kong.

What is projected, however, is not so optimistic. Fractionalization is expected to be intense. And a "Big Brother" will always be behind the scene to control the Hong Kong Government before and after 1997.

6

Political Opposition, Co-optation and Democratization: The Case of Hong Kong

Lo Shiu-hing

Introduction

The recent studies on democratization have explored its dynamics, process and consolidation; nonetheless, in the process of democratization, the linkage between the political opposition and an authoritarian regime's attempt at co-opting the opposition is an area at which future research can be directed.[1] The power relationship between the ruling elite and the opposition, according to Samuel Huntington, determines whether the authoritarian regime will experience "transformation" or "replacement" process.[2] If the reform-minded ruling elite were stronger than the opposition, says

---

[1] For a useful review of the recent literature on democratization, see Doh Chull Shin, "On the Third Wave of Democratization: A Synthesis and Evaluation of Recent Theory and Research," *World Politics*, Vol. 47, No. 1 (October 1994), pp. 135–70. In his discussion of the future direction for research on democratization, Gerardo Munck calls for "the need to deal with both actors' choices and the context within which choices are made." He also observes: "Probably the primary factor explaining the shape of emerging institutions, as has been underlined by various authors, is the relative power of the actors involved in the process, the rulers and the opposition." See Gerardo L. Munck, "Democratic Transitions in Comparative Perspective," *Comparative Politics*, Vol. 26, No. 3 (April 1994), pp. 369–70.

[2] Samuel P. Huntington, *The Third Wave of Democratization in the Late Twentieth Century* (Norman: University of Oklahoma Press, 1992), pp. 141–51.

Huntington, then there would be a "transformation" process. In the event that the opposition were stronger than the ruling elite, a "replacement" process would occur. Although Huntington examines the consequences of the ruling elite *vis-à-vis* the opposition, the question of co-optation efforts made by the regime is neglected. Guillermo O'Donnell and Philippe Schmitter observe that the authoritarian regime under the pressure for democratization could deal with the political opposition by using "selective repression, manipulation and co-optation," and that the other possible responses from the regime are to hold elections and to negotiate "pacts" that would propel further political reforms.[3] Yet, focusing on the process of pact-making in democratization, O'Donnell and Schmitter have not elaborated on the relations between the three factions of political opposition they discuss — "maximalists," "minimalists" and "opportunists" — and the regime's efforts at co-optation. The linkage between political opposition and co-optation, as this chapter will show by using Hong Kong's democratizing transition as a case study, is a crucial determinant in the process of democratization.

This chapter will attempt to apply the factions of political opposition as discussed by O'Donnell and Schmitter to the Hong Kong case. According to O'Donnell and Schmitter, during the process of democratization under which the civil society emerges in the form of social groups making demands and exerting pressure on the regime, the political opposition is usually heterogeneous and split into three factions: "maximalists," "minimalists" and "opportunists."[4] Maximalists are those political actors who

---

[3] Guillermo O'Donnell and Philippe Schmitter, *Transitions from Authoritarian Rule: Tentative Conclusions about Uncertain Democracies* (Baltimore: Johns Hopkins University Press, 1986), p. 55. The importance of "pacts" in democratizing transition can be seen in the case of South Africa. See Timothy D. Sisk, *Democratization in South Africa: The Elusive Social Contract* (New Jersey: Princeton University Press, 1995).

[4] O'Donnell and Schmitter, *Transitions from Authoritarian Rule*, p. 55. Similar observation on the factions of political opposition as discussed by O'Donnell and Schmitter had also been made in the case of the former Soviet Union, where the opposition was split into "moral-absolutist," "instrumental-pragmatic" and "anomic-militant" types. See Rudolf L. Tokes, "Varieties of Soviet Dissent: An Overview," in *Dissent in the USSR: Politics, Ideology, and People*, edited by Rudolf L. Tokes (Baltimore: Johns Hopkins University Press, 1975), pp. 13–14.

attempt to maximize the scope and accelerate the pace of democratization, and refuse to make compromise on their principles. O'Donnell and Schmitter do not state clearly whether the maximalists seek to topple the authoritarian regime by force, implying that they may do so. Regardless of whether the maximalists have a propensity to overthrow the existing regime, they can be viewed as the relatively radical elements within the political opposition. Minimalists are those members of the democratic elite who are willing to negotiate with the ruling authorities on the condition that their demands for political changes are satisfied, and they can be regarded as the moderate elements trying their best to oppose the government and the regime within the existing constitutional or legal framework.[5] Opportunists refer to those politicians willing to negotiate with the ruling elite, and to reach political compromise for the sake of achieving democratization, albeit the scope of democratic changes may be relatively narrow. In other words, the opportunists can be regarded as the soft-liners willing to work with the regime for minimal reforms within a limited political space. This chapter will show that not only can these three factions of the political opposition be found in the Hong Kong case, but also each of them has its function in democratization even in the face of co-optation. Co-optation refers to "the process of absorbing new elements into leadership or policy determining structure of an organization as a means of averting threats to its stability or existence."[6]

---

[5] The minimalists briefly described by O'Donnell and Schmitter can be viewed as pro-democracy elements who wish to become, to borrow from Stephanie Lawson, a "constitutional political opposition," which means "a commitment to the right of political dissent within a general consensual framework as to how, and within what limits, that dissent can be legitimately expressed." The constitutional political opposition "does not seek to change or overthrow a regime by force. If it seeks to bring about changes at regime level, it does so only by means of the regime's own rules for change, which are normally expressed in a constitution." See Stephanie Lawson, "Conceptual Issues in the Comparative Study of Regime Change and Democratization," *Comparative Politics*, Vol. 25, No. 2 (January 1993), p. 193.

[6] See Philip Selznick, "Co-optation: A Mechanism for Organizational Stability," in *Reader in Bureaucracy*, edited by R. K. Merton *et al.* (New York: The Free Press, 1952), pp. 135–37. Co-optation is also "brought about by both persuasion and the judicious use of inducement — commonly in the form of an offer of a position at some level of actual or symbolic leadership or participation

The relationship between co-optation and democratization is not neces-sarily a zero-sum one; in the event that only part, not all, of the political opposition is neutralized or paralysed by the ruling elite through co-optation, democratic changes could still occur at a gradual pace and within limited scope. Even if the opportunists were co-opted in the policy-making mechanism, they might have some degree of, albeit limited, influence upon democratization of the authoritarian regime. As long as the minimalists and maximalists are not really neutralized through co-optation, the former could also influence government policy outside the constitutional structure whereas the latter could do so inside the state apparatus. Therefore, there could be a constrained process of democratization unless all the factions of the opposition are politically neutralized and crippled by co-optation.

It is noteworthy that O'Donnell and Schmitter's model of democra-tization is originally designed for cases that regime transition is from an authoritarian to a democratic one. The Hong Kong case appears to be the opposite in the sense that Hong Kong was transformed from a lack of political rights during the colonial era to more political rights enjoyed by citizens in the transition period. Yet, Hong Kong is incorporated into the People's Republic of China (P.R.C.) where the polity is characterized by authoritarianism. In other words, the Hong Kong case is a special one in my application of the O'Donnell and Schmitter's model. It must be emphasized, however, that the maximalist-minimalist-opportunist typology is still very useful to pigeon-hole or comprehend Hong Kong's opposition forces. Political opposition is broadly defined in this chapter as a movement led by politicians or groups that reject the policies of the existing regime. Such a movement embraces various factions, including those who advocate a rapid, moderate or gradual pace of political reforms. Political opposition can also be narrowly defined as "the right to dissent from the views of the government."[7] Regardless of which definition is employed, political

---

in the regime. Such absorption may be used as a means not only of terminating the opposition of particular individuals, but also of exercising control over them as they are socialized into the values of the regime and grow accustomed to the fruits of their membership of the ruling group." See Simon Barraclough, "Co-optation and Elite Accommodation in Malaysian Politics," *Contemporary Southeast Asia*, Vol. 6, No. 3 (December 1984), p. 308.

[7] Robert A. Dahl, "Preface," in *Political Oppositions in Western Democracies*, edited by Robert A. Dahl (New Haven: Yale University Press, 1966), p. xiii.

opposition becomes one of the "three great milestones in the development of democratic institutions" in Western countries, apart from the right to vote and the right to be represented.[8] In many developing countries, however, political oppositions remain relatively fragile and vulnerable to state coercion.[9] The P.R.C., for example, has a weak and a "loyal opposition" seeking to promote political changes within the regime.[10] In the wake of the military suppression of students demonstrators in the Tiananmen Square in June 1989, members of the "loyal" political opposition in the P.R.C. have become increasingly receptive to the view that "only institutional and legal checks on the power of the state and a broader base of support from below could protect them as a whole."[11]

Political opposition is at stake in Hong Kong which has been experiencing democratization triggered by the British rulers and whose sovereignty was resumed by the P.R.C., a socialist and authoritarian regime, on 1 July 1997. Because Hong Kong has become the P.R.C.'s Special Administrative Region, the fate of the local political opposition led by pro-democracy activists is hanging in the balance, given the destiny of their mainland counterparts who either become exiles or are imprisoned by P.R.C. authorities.[12] It is the issue of political opposition in Hong Kong at which this chapter is directed, an issue that is not only crucial to democratization in the territory but can also indicate the degree of autonomy to which the Hong Kong Special Administrative Region (HKSAR) enjoys.

---

[8] *Ibid.*

[9] See, for example, Garry Rodan (ed.), *Political Oppositions in Industrializing Asia* (London: Routledge, 1996).

[10] Merle Goldman, *Sowing the Seeds of Democracy in China: Political Reform in the Deng Xiaoping Era* (Massachusetts: Harvard University Press, 1994), Chapter 1, pp. 20–24. In contrast to China where the civil society and political opposition are relatively weak, Poland envisaged a "reconstitution" of the civil society and a change of the resistance strategy "from dissidence to opposition." See Michael H. Bernhard, *The Origins of Democratization in Poland* (New York: Columbia University Press, 1993), pp. 2–13.

[11] Merle Goldman, *Sowing the Seeds of Democracy in China*, p. 357.

[12] In July 1996, Governor Christopher Patten requested the Canadian government to consider accepting several mainland Chinese political dissidents staying in Hong Kong. In response, P.R.C. officials challenged Britain's efforts to help the dissidents to find sanctuary. See *Sing Tao Daily*, 25 July 1996, p. A16.

Political opposition is hitherto not a major concern of Hong Kong observers who, even if dealing with the question of political opposition, tend to subsume it under the topic of democracy movement.[13] In any case, as this chapter will show, Hong Kong provides very useful empirical evidence to explore the relations between political opposition and co-optation in the democratizing transition.

Hong Kong: A Special Case Study of Political Opposition and Co-optation during Democratization

The rise of political opposition in Hong Kong could be traced back to a gradual growth of the civil society during the 1970s and particularly the 1980s. In order to stabilize and legitimize the colonial regime, the British administrators in Hong Kong have been traditionally relying on co-optation of elites into various consultative bodies and political institutions.[14] Civil society was weak in the 1940s, 1950s and the early half of the 1960s when most of the Hong Kong people, who were immigrants escaping from the P.R.C., had refugee mentality and lacked interest in political participation.[15] Yet, the 1967 Communist riots in Hong Kong could be viewed as a watershed in the development of civil society, for the working class mobilized by fervent supporters of Maoist China attempted to rebel against the colonial regime.[16] The rise of working-class activism was followed by a

---

[13] See, for examples, Joseph Cheng, "The Democracy Movement in Hong Kong," *International Affairs*, Vol. 65, No. 3 (Summer 1989); Alvin So and Ludmilla Kwitko, "The New Middle Class and the Democratic Movement in Hong Kong," *Journal of Contemporary Asia*, Vol. 20, No. 3 (1990); and Alvin So and Sai Hsin May, "Democratization in East Asia in the Late 1980s: Taiwan Breakthrough, Hong Kong Frustration," *Studies in Comparative International Development*, Vol. 28, No. 2 (Summer 1993), pp. 61–80.

[14] See Ambrose King, "Administrative Absorption of Politics in Hong Kong: Emphasis on the Grass Roots Level," *Asian Survey*, Vol. 15, No. 5 (May 1975).

[15] However, it can also be argued that civil society in Hong Kong was stronger than those in other societies like Singapore. At the very least, Hong Kong's interest groups tended to have more autonomy from the state's control than their counterparts in other authoritarian regimes. I am indebted to the referee for this point.

[16] See Ian Scott, "The State and Civil Society in Hong Kong" (paper presented at the conference on Political Development in Taiwan and Hong Kong, held at the University of Hong Kong on 8–9 February 1996).

further activation of the civil society in the 1970s, when social movements composed of numerous pressure groups emerged and influenced the colonial government on a whole range of issues including anti-corruption, the promotion of Chinese (Cantonese) as an official language, and the provision of adequate housing accommodation to the local people.[17] The Sino-British negotiation on Hong Kong in 1982–1984 provided a catalyst for the further growth of civil society in the colony, where the middle-class intelligentsia formed political groups to express their opinions on Hong Kong's future. However, the middle-class activists were politically alienated by Britain and China which dictated the Joint Declaration without consulting the opinions of Hongkongers. The way in which Britain and the P.R.C. handled Hong Kong's political future not only simply plunged the colonial state into "a crisis of legitimacy,"[18] but it also propelled the development of the civil society further. Political alienation led to the determination of middle-class professionals and intelligentsia to form political parties contesting the local direct elections held for the District Boards in the later half of the 1980s and the first direct elections held for the legislature in 1991.[19] The Tiananmen incident in the P.R.C. in June 1989 served as another turning point in, to borrow from the words of O'Donnell and Schmitter, the "explosion of civil society" in Hong Kong.[20] Not only has the political awareness of Hongkongers increased since the incident, but the civil society which is relatively protected by the rule of law under British rule has become far more resilient and aggressive than ever before.

---

[17] For social movements in Hong Kong, see Alvin So and Ludmilla Kwitko, "The Transformation of Urban Movements in Hong Kong, 1970–1990," *Bulletin of Concerned Asian Scholars*, Vol. 24, No. 4 (1992), pp. 32–44.

[18] See Ian Scott, *Political Change and the Crisis of Legitimacy in Hong Kong* (Hong Kong: Oxford University Press, 1989). Also see Ian Scott, "Legitimacy and Its Discontents: Hong Kong and the Reversion to Chinese Sovereignty," *Asian Journal of Political Science*, Vol. 1, No. 1 (June 1993), pp. 55–75.

[19] For the emergence of political parties, see Louie Kin-sheun, "Political Parties," in *The Other Hong Kong Report 1991*, edited by Sung Yun-wing and Lee Ming-kwan (Hong Kong: The Chinese University Press, 1991), pp. 55–75.

[20] For an application of O'Donnell and Schmitter's analytical framework onto the case of Hong Kong, see Lo Shiu-hing, *The Politics of Democratization in Hong Kong* (London: MacMillan Press, 1997).

What is unique in the Hong Kong case is that political opposition has already been under the enormous pressure from co-optation efforts made by the future sovereign after 1 July 1997, the P.R.C., through its united front work (*tong zhan*).[21] After the transition period in Hong Kong began in 1984, the year in which the Sino-British Joint Declaration was initialled, the departing British administrators speeded up political reforms, allowed more citizens to participate in elections, and liberalized the society further through the enactment of a Bill of Rights in 1991.[22] At the same time, however, Hong Kong's political opposition is under tremendous pressure from its overlord, the P.R.C., whose united front work in the territory aims at winning the hearts and minds of Hongkongers, forming a "cross-class coalition government led by the capitalist class," and marginalizing any opposing forces that challenge the legitimacy of either the mainland Chinese regime or the HKSAR government.[23] As a colonial polity experiencing British-led democratization which generated China's counter-reaction or de-democratization, Hong Kong provides a special case study that can illuminate the interaction between the territory's political opposition and the P.R.C.'s efforts at co-optation through united front work.

---

[21] The P.R.C.'s united front work was originated from the Chinese Communist Party (CCP) which attempted to form a temporary alliance with "all elements, classes, and nations against [Japanese] fascism" during the 1930s, including the Kuomintang (Nationalist Party) and the capitalists which were the CCP's enemies. See Tony Saich (ed.), *The Rise to Power of the Chinese Communist Party* (New York: M. E. Sharpe, 1996), Commentary E, p. 658.

[22] Electoral reforms in Hong Kong during the final years of British rule aim at consolidating the authority and legitimacy of the colonial administration. This phenomenon could also be seen in the former British colonies like India. See Low, *Eclipse of Empire*, pp. 148–63.

[23] See Xu Jiatun, *Xu Jiatun Xianggang Huiyilu (Xu Jiatun's Hong Kong Memoirs)* (Taiwan: United Daily News, 1993), Vol. 1, p. 121. Xu, the former director of the New China News Agency in Hong Kong, was politically purged by hard-line P.R.C. leaders after the Tiananmen incident because of his close relations with the former soft-line premier Zhao Ziyang. In 1990, he went to the United States from China. Xu said that since the P.R.C. aimed at preserving economic prosperity in Hong Kong for fifty years after 1997, it would be necessary for the CCP to utilize the local capitalist class to govern Hong Kong, a phenomenon different from the united front work in the mainland.

Conceptually, co-optation can be viewed as one of the essential elements of united front work.[24] United front work is the strategy adopted by the Chinese Communist Party (CCP) to form an alliance with political supporters and enemies in the short run but to "defeat" the enemies in the long run.[25] In the context of Hong Kong, China's united front work has the objectives of neutralizing political opponents, winning more allies, and securing a pro-Beijing administration through the following means: (1) splitting the opposition forces; (2) developing personal friendship with allies; (3) making political appointments to co-opt friends and possibly enemies; (4) organizing informal or formal gatherings with the local elite; (5) launching political propaganda through the pro-Beijing news media; (6) forming a pro-Beijing political party and supporting like-minded interest groups; and (7) clandestinely recruiting underground members for the CCP.[26] The instruments through which united front work achieves its

---

[24] For a more detailed discussion of the similarities and differences between co-optation and united front work, see Benson Wong Wai-kwok, "China's United Front Work in Hong Kong since the 1980s" (unpublished M.Phil thesis, Division of Social Science, The Hong Kong University of Science and Technology, 1996).

[25] In the words of the late CCP leader, Mao Zedong, "the united front and armed struggle are the two fundamental weapons for defeating the enemy." See Mao Zedong, "Introducing the Communist," in *The Rise to Power of the Chinese Communist Party*, edited by Tony Saich (New York: M. E. Sharpe, 1996), p. 912.

[26] In 1992, the formation of the pro-China Democratic Alliance for Betterment of Hong Kong (DAB) can also be viewed as the P.R.C.'s united front work to win the hearts and minds of Hongkongers through the DAB's grassroots work and electoral participation. The birth of the DAB and the recent emergence of some pro-Beijing district associations in Hong Kong, to borrow the words from Chalmers Johnson, can be regarded as "the creation of and use of front organizations and personalities in the target area" — an essential element of the P.R.C.'s united front campaign. See Chalmers Johnson, "The Mousetrapping of Hong Kong: A Game in Which Nobody Wins," *Asian Survey*, Vol. 26, No. 9 (September 1984), p. 897. For the question whether the DAB has autonomy from the P.R.C., see Lo Shiu-hing, "Political Parties in Hong Kong: The Role of the 'Pro-China' Democratic Alliance for the Betterment of Hong Kong," *Asian Journal of Political Science*, Vol. 3, No. 1 (June 1996). For an excellent discussion of organizations in Hong Kong which are under the control and influence of the CCP, see John P. Burns, "The Structure of Communist Party Control in Hong Kong," *Asian Survey*, Vol. 30, No. 8 (August 1990), pp. 749–63.

objectives are much broader than co-optation which, organizationally speaking, tends to rely on formal political appointments into policy-making and consultative mechanisms.[27] But both united front work and co-optation share the common long-term goals of crippling the political opposition and stabilizing the regime in power.

Since 1984, the P.R.C. has launched a massive united front campaign to win the hearts and minds of the Hong Kong capitalists, middle-class professionals, and working-class citizens.[28] A number of prominent business people who encountered financial problems in Hong Kong asked for the support of mainland Chinese government and organizations, such as the Bank of China, in order to rescue their business operations.[29] Some middle-class professionals, like accountants and lawyers, who see China as a potentially lucrative market for their career or business prospects, are vulnerable to the Chinese united front strategy. Workers, whose well-being is in general at stake as unemployment has deteriorated and housing prices have escalated since the early 1990s, find the appeals and activities of the Federation of Trade Unions (FTU) — a pro-Beijing labour organization heavily under the influence of China's united front work — increasingly attractive.[30] As a result, the P.R.C.'s united front work has already made considerable inroads in Hong Kong, successfully raising the number of underground CCP members from 6,200 in 1989 to 11,200 in 1996, and acquiring the tacit or open support of more Hongkongers than ever before.[31]

From a comparative perspective, political opposition in Hong Kong has a background fundamentally different from its counterpart in the former British colonies. In the former British colonies where the political

---

[27] In fact, political appointment of the Hong Kong elite into various consultative and policy-making bodies established by the P.R.C. is a crucial Chinese co-optation strategy, see Lo Shiu-hing, "The Politics of Co-optation in Hong Kong: A Study of the Basic Law Drafting Process," *Asian Journal of Public Administration*, Vol. 14, No. 1 (June 1992), pp. 3–24.

[28] Xu Jiatun in his memoirs stated that the "upper-middle class," the "middle class" and the "middle-lower class" were the targets of China's united front work in Hong Kong. See *Xu Jiatun Xianggang Huiyilu*, Vol. 1, p. 133.

[29] *Ibid.*, pp. 131–32.

[30] Xu revealed that the FTU was "under the leadership of the CCP." See *ibid.*, p. 148.

[31] *The Trend Magazine*, No. 131 (July 1996), p. 6.

opposition, in the event of organizing a party that captured a majority of the seats in national elections, could form a new government during independence. Yet, Hong Kong's political opposition does not enjoy the luxury to become a party in power partly because of the impossibility of becoming independent and partly due to the constraints imposed by the post-1997 constitution, the Basic Law. According to the Basic Law, there will not be a fully directly elected legislature at least until 2007 when a review of political structure will be conducted.[32] From now to at least 2007, even if a political party could win most of the seats in the legislature, it would not be constitutionally empowered to form a ministerial government and then to occupy seats of the top policy-making Executive Council (Exco), members of which are appointed by the Chief Executive in accordance with the Basic Law. Nor will such popularly supported political party be able to choose the Chief Executive, who will be selected by a Selection Committee (the first Chief Executive Tung Chee-hwa was chosen by a 400-member Selection Committee in December 1996).[33] Therefore, in the foreseeable future, Hong Kong's political opposition is destined to be an opposition without the likelihood of capturing the government, let alone the possibility of a rotation of political party in power as in the West.

Factions of Political Opposition in Hong Kong

Political opposition in Hong Kong has already been split into three major groups: "maximalists," "minimalists" and "opportunists," to borrow from the categories of O'Donnell and Schmitter. The maximalists include those "radicals" like legislators Emily Lau Wai-hing, Leung Yiu-chung, Elizabeth Wong Chien Chi-lien, Lee Cheuk-yan, Lau Chin-shek, members of the Ants Alliance, and members of the April the Fifth Action Group.[34]

---

[32] See *The Basic Law of the Hong Kong Special Administrative Region of the People's Republic of China* (*The Basic Law*) (Hong Kong: One Country Two Systems Economic Research Institute, 1992), pp. 58–60.

[33] *Ibid.*, pp. 57–58.

[34] In August 1996, these legislators formed a political group called Frontier which vowed not to compromise on its call for a fully directly elected Legco. See *Hong Kong Economic Journal*, 16 July 1996, p. 1. Leung Yiu-chung even went so far as to claim that he "does not recognize the Basic Law." See *Ming Pao*, 29 July 1996, p. A18. Some members of the Ants Alliance were the former campaign

They do not seek to topple the Hong Kong Government, a phenomenon different from those radicals in cases of "overthrow transition" like the Philippines under Ferdinand Marcos.[35] Yet, a minority of the Hong Kong maximalists is anti-CCP, vowing to fight for democratization in the mainland. They also advocate that the Chief Executive in the HKSAR should be directly elected by all Hongkongers; that the provisional legislature set up by China in 1997 to replace the existing Legislative Council (Legco) does not conform to the Basic Law; and that the Chinese Government should submit an annual report to the United Nations about human rights conditions in Hong Kong after 1997, as with the British practice during the transition period. In 1995–1996, members of the Ants Alliance even attempted to sue the Hong Kong Government for violating the Bill of Rights by maintaining the functional constituency elections held for Legco.[36] Although the Ants Alliance failed to win the court case, its action demonstrated the use of legal channels to voice political grievances. At the same time, these maximalists often dare to take to the streets, using protests, mass rallies and petitions against the policies of both the Hong Kong Government and China. The mixture of legal means and street tactics is a hallmark of political participation of the Hong Kong maximalists.

The maximalists are not homogeneous in their personal background, but they share common perceptions of Britain and China. A minority of maximalists possess foreign passports, like Emily Lau who is a British

---

assistants of Emily Lau in her contest for Legco's direct elections. The April the Fifth Action Group was formed in 1989 and it now has 20 members, including workers, students and teachers. The Group often confronts with the police outside the New China News Agency in Hong Kong. The leader of the Group, Leung Kwok-hung, said that he was psychologically prepared for the possibility of being "arrested" by authorities after 1997. See *Sing Tao Daily*, 7 July 1996, p. B2.

[35] See Mark R. Thompson, "Off the Endangered List: Philippine Democratization in Comparative Perspective," *Comparative Politics*, Vol. 28, No. 2 (June 1996), p. 184.

[36] Functional constituencies are comprised of professional, industrial, and business groups that elect their group representatives to the legislature. The colonial government designed such constituencies for the sake of co-opting the local elite into the state apparatus and legitimizing the dominance of business and professional elite. See Joan Y. H. Leung, "Functional Representation in Hong Kong: Institutionalization and Legitimization of the Business and Professional Elites," *Asian Journal of Public Administration*, Vol. 12, No. 2 (December 1990).

citizen and Elizabeth Wong a New Zealander, while some members of the April the Fifth Action Group proclaim themselves as Trotskyists and critical Marxists. All the maximalists, however, are permanent residents of Hong Kong and identify themselves as Hongkongers fighting for the interests of the populace. Above all, all of them have been politically alienated by the British policies towards Hong Kong, ranging from reaching the Joint Declaration with China without consultation with the Hong Kong people, to the British reluctance of democratizing Hong Kong's colonial polity much earlier and faster. Although the maximalists no longer have any high hope of Britain standing up for the interests of Hongkongers, a minority like Emily Lau and the Ants Alliance do not give up the tactic of lobbying the British Government, nor the strategy of prosecuting the Hong Kong Government at the Privy Council in London. Strictly speaking, with the exception of the April the Fifth Action Group which opposes both the P.R.C. and the Hong Kong Government outside the existing state apparatus, many maximalists like Emily Lau and the Ants Alliance do not abandon the option of becoming the "constitutional political opposition."[37] Because some tend to have political action and views at the borderline between maximalists and minimalists, they could be seen as "minimalist-oriented maximalists," a term that I refer to those maximalist democrats who try to oppose the regime outside the state apparatus without hesitation but who also do not exclude the likelihood of opposing the government within the existing political institutions.

Overall, the maximalists also mistrust the P.R.C. deeply, believing that its officials suppress democratization in Hong Kong. Having dialogue with P.R.C. officials, to the maximalists, is of no use and, at worst, paves the way for co-optation by China. In terms of attitude towards China, the April the Fifth Action Group even goes so far as advocating democratization in the mainland, seeing the year 1997 as an inception, not the end, of their long-term struggle to democratize the socialist regime in the mainland.[38]

---

[37] See Note 5.

[38] The objectives of the Group are to "promote China's democracy movement and realize democratic reunification," "use working-class interest, solidarity and organization as the foundation of democracy movement," and "establish a political and economic system that allows the people to become a master [in China]." See a leaflet prepared by the Group, protested against the P.R.C.'s national day in October 1989, and distributed to ordinary citizens, dated 21 September 1989. The

In a nutshell, the Hong Kong maximalists are a heterogeneous and a loosely organized group whose members have different political ideologies, ranging from liberalism to Marxism, but they all share the common objectives of democratizing Hong Kong to its utmost limit, and of exhausting all the available channels of participation to make their demands known and influence felt by the regime.

A minority of the minimalist-oriented maximalists have become the target of co-optation by the P.R.C., moving towards the line of opportunists. Christine Loh Kung-wai, for example, was a minimalist-oriented maximalist trying to oppose the P.R.C.'s policies towards Hong Kong before and shortly after the direct elections held for the Legco in 1995. After she had won the direct election, her determination to publicly question the role of the underground CCP in Hong Kong during the Legco session in 1995 was a bold action that publicly challenged the P.R.C. Government. Yet, Loh made a sudden U-turn in her attitude towards the P.R.C. in 1996 when she took an initiative to knock the door of the New China News Agency (NCNA) in Hong Kong, hoping to communicate with P.R.C. officials.[39] In response to Loh's move, the NCNA subsequently discussed with her about Hong Kong affairs, a first step towards further communication. While critics remarked that Loh had become an opportunist co-opted by the P.R.C., communication with mainland Chinese officials could also be viewed as a two-way process, not necessarily a unilateral one in which members of political opposition would be co-opted without any impact on

---

Group shares similar objectives with the Hong Kong Alliance in Support of the Patriotic and Democratic Movement in China. But the Alliance tends to be more moderate in its action than the Group, relying on mass rallies rather than on confrontation with police. The Alliance's objectives are to "rehabilitate the [official Chinese verdict on] the Tiananmen incident," "look for the responsibility of the [Tiananmen] massacre," "release pro-democracy prisoners," "terminate one-party dictatorship" and "establish a democratic China." The slogans of the Alliance are no doubt "subversive" from the P.R.C.'s official perspective. See *Sing Tao Daily*, 7 July 1996, p. B2.

[39] In fact, Loh's articles published in newspapers indicated a gradual transformation from frequently emphasizing democracy and human rights in Hong Kong to currently discussing "Asian values" and nationalism in China. See for example Christine Loh, "Sense of Arrogance Would Be Misplaced," *South China Morning Post* (international weekly), 3 August 1996, p. 10.

the P.R.C. policies towards Hong Kong.[40] Loh's attitudinal change towards China could perhaps be seen as a pragmatic move underlying the fact that a minority of the former maximalists no longer regard dialogue with P.R.C. officials as a zero-sum game, which is a hard-line perspective of maximalists, but as a progressive move towards influencing China on Hong Kong affairs. In May 1997, when Loh formed the Citizens Party with a number of her like-minded professionals, they also emphasized the importance of having dialogue with P.R.C. officials, a position that can be regarded as a hallmark of what I call the minimalist-oriented maximalists.

The Hong Kong minimalists embrace most activists of the local democracy movement. For example, members of the Democratic Party (DP), which won a majority of directly elected seats held for the Legco in 1995, are actually moderates trying to have dialogue with Chinese officials and to oppose the policies of the Hong Kong Government within the existing constitutional framework. Nonetheless, some DP leaders, like Martin Lee and Szeto Wah, played a leading role in denouncing the P.R.C. Government as "fascist" during the Tiananmen incident in 1989. Their rhetoric was no doubt a cause for trepidation on the part of P.R.C. authorities, who labelled them as "subversive" elements trying to overthrow the mainland socialist regime. Szeto Wah was and is a leader of the Hong Kong Alliance in Support of the Patriotic and Democracy Movement in China (HKASPDM), an organization which provided assistance to mainland political dissidents who escaped from China shortly after Tiananmen incident.[41] In comparison with the April the Fifth Action Group, the HKASPDM is more minimalist in the sense that some of the HKASPDM's members, who are also DP members simultaneously, tend to oppose the Hong Kong Government preferably within the existing political structure. Yet, the HKASPDM can be regarded as "maximalist-oriented minimalists,"

---

[40] Wang Wenfang, a former NCNA official responsible for Taiwan affairs and now a political commentator sometimes criticizing the P.R.C.'s policies on Hong Kong, asserts that Loh is a member of the "rational democratic faction," not a member of the "irrational" faction led by the Democratic Party. See Wang Wenfang, "Christine Loh's 'Difference'," *Ming Pao*, 26 July 1996, p. E10.

[41] In terms of slogans, the Alliance is as aggressive as the April the Fifth Action Group, but the former's action is moderate and seldom clashes with the police. Some leaders of the Alliance have been "blacklisted" by China, however. For the "blacklist," see *Sing Tao Daily*, 3 July 1996, p. A24.

a term I coin which refers to the fact that while these minimalist democrats are basically the "constitutional political opposition," they do not abandon the use of street protests against Britain, China and the Hong Kong Government. In other words, the alternative of shifting towards the maximalist stance to become an "unconstitutional" or an "illegal" opposition is open to them, particularly if the political space for their survival becomes narrower than ever before.

As long as some DP leaders are labelled by hard-line P.R.C. officials as "subversive" elements in Hong Kong, both sides cannot resume dialogue easily. Meanwhile, P.R.C. officials responsible for Hong Kong affairs and DP leaders tend to have deep mutual distrust. One possibility of breaking the current deadlock is to rely on middlemen, like a member of the Preparatory Committee (set up by China to make transitional arrangements in 1997) Tsui Tze-man, who invited Martin Lee in July 1996 to discuss with him on transitional matters.[42] In response to Tsui's invitation which was probably endorsed by NCNA officials, Lee asked DP vice-chairman Anthony Cheung Bing-leung to accompany him in the meeting with Tsui.[43] Cheung himself was originally a chairperson of Meeting Point, a nationalistic interest group which was set up in the early 1980s and which supported China's resumption of sovereignty over Hong Kong. Yet, as time passed, Meeting Point became more supportive of democratization in Hong Kong, a change that widened its political differences with the P.R.C. In 1994, the decision of Meeting Point to merge with the DP's predecessor, the United

---

[42] *Ming Pao*, 26 July 1996, p. A18. Although Tsui is a pro-Beijing Hongkonger, he originally opposed the P.R.C. Government's handling of student demonstrators in the Tiananmen incident. His prepared speech on global democratization was censored by P.R.C. authorities in 1990, when he attended the meeting of the Chinese People's Political Consultative Conference of which he was a member. See *Oriental Daily*, 25 March 1990, p. 3. Yet, since 1990 he has gradually toned down his reservations about the Tiananmen incident. Therefore the DP leadership regards Tsui as an "opportunist" within the pro-China camp in Hong Kong.

[43] Later, some DP members led by Cheung also met with Lau Siu-kai, a member of the Preparatory Committee and a professor of sociology at The Chinese University of Hong Kong. Lau said that friendly relations between the Chinese Government and the DP would create "a good international image." See *Sing Tao Daily*, 8 August 1996, p. A12.

Democrats of Hong Kong (UDHK) led by Martin Lee and Szeto Wah, infuriated P.R.C. officials who immediately revoked the appointment of Cheung as a member of China's advisors on Hong Kong affairs. Although there were rumours that the NCNA and the State Council's Hong Kong and Macau Affairs Office (HKMAO) had conflicting opinions regarding the cancellation of Cheung's appointment,[44] his move to amalgamate Meeting Point with the UDHK exceeded the limits of political tolerance on the part of hard-line P.R.C. authorities responsible for Hong Kong matters.

Apart from pro-China elites, another intermediary channel for the minimalists to have dialogue with the P.R.C. Government is regular discussion with the Chief Executive, Tung Chee-hwa. Since the Chief Executive election in December 1996, Tung has met with the DP leaders. This channel of discussion needs to be maintained if the minimalists attempt to lobby the P.R.C. Government through Tung over various issues affecting Hong Kong.

Minimalists share similarities and have some differences in comparison with maximalists. They all have a very strong sense of belonging in Hong Kong. Like maximalists, minimalists also believe that Hong Kong's democratization should be pushed to its utmost limit, like having the Chief Executive directly elected by citizens. They decided to hold a street "referendum" allowing Hongkongers to select their Chief Executive in 1997, a decision that was criticized by P.R.C. officials as a "farce."[45] Minimalists and maximalists also hope to have the Basic Law revised in such a way as to give sufficient autonomy to Hong Kong *vis-à-vis* Beijing, but the former fail to put forward a timetable of amending the constitution whereas the latter wish to do so as swiftly as possible. Similar to maximalists, minimalists view the provisional legislature as a body in

---

[44] At that time, the HKMAO tended to favour Cheung, whereas the NCNA disliked him. This situation reoccurred in August 1996, when the HKMAO prepared a list of names, including Cheung, who would be able to participate in the Selection Committee that would choose the Chief Executive and members of the provisional legislature. However, the NCNA rejected the HKMAO's suggestion. See *Sing Tao Daily*, 2 August 1996, p. A16.

[45] See *Hong Kong Economic Journal*, 14 July 1996, p. 1. For the official response from the NCNA and the HKMAO, see *World Journal* (North American Chinese newspaper), 24 July 1996, p. A18.

"violation" of the Basic Law.[46] In terms of their political demands, minimalists and maximalists are more or less the same.

Their differences, however, lie in their means of opposition and attitude towards the P.R.C. In comparison with most maximalists who do not have sufficient financial resources to lobby other Western industrialized countries for political reforms in Hong Kong, minimalist leaders tend to spend more time to lobby foreign states for the territory's democratization and liberalization. To prepare for the post-1997 elections and secure the financial as well as political support from the overseas Chinese who are supportive of the democracy movement in Hong Kong, the minimalists led by the DP have to pay regular visits to the United States and Canada.[47] In doing so, however, the minimalists run the risk of being labelled by P.R.C. officials and pro-China Hong Kong elites as "traitors" selling out the interest of Hong Kong and "internationalizing" the territory's future. Unlike the maximalists who do not hesitate to use street protests but at the same time viewing electoral participation as an option, minimalists (like Anthony Cheung) regard elections, not demonstrations outside the NCNA and especially confrontation with the police, as an effective and a legal mode of political participation. Because the minimalists have been able to capture a majority of directly elected seats held for the local political institutions since the late 1980s, they tend to be far more supportive of the idea to oppose the policies of the Hong Kong and P.R.C. Governments within the existing state apparatus.

Yet, this does not mean that they preclude the likelihood of mobilizing the masses to stage street demonstrations and petitions. The means of

---

[46] See Martin Lee's vow to oppose the provisional legislature, *Ming Pao*, 5 August 1996, p. A19.

[47] Except for Emily Lau who often lobbied Britain and foreign countries for democratization and the protection of human rights in Hong Kong, most maximalists appear to be relatively passive. The minimalists, however, like Martin Lee, went to the United States and Canada to get financial support from the overseas Hong Kong Chinese. See *Ming Pao*, 7 August 1996, p. A1. Christine Loh, previously a maximalist but presently a minimalist moving slowly towards an opportunist line, calls for the Commonwealth countries to maintain "bilateral" and "multilateral non-governmental links" with Hong Kong after 1997. See Loh, "The Commonwealth and Hong Kong," *The Round Table*, No. 338 (April 1996), p. 237.

opposition, to the minimalists, are flexible and contingent upon whether the participatory methods are tolerated by the regime, whether street protests becomes less effective in influencing the government than before, and whether they can infiltrate the state apparatus through elections. Minimalists, mostly DP members, are also psychologically prepared that if any new electoral law were unfavourable to them but beneficial to the pro-China political groups, then they would be forced to resort to street protests as the means of opposition. In short, different alternatives of political opposition are kept open to the minimalists, whose principle is to exert democratizing pressure on the regime legally and effectively.

In terms of the attitude towards China, the minimalists are less hawkish than maximalists and more willing to grasp the opportunities of communication with P.R.C. authorities. However, the minimalists are caught in a dilemma, worrying that such communication would probably undermine the DP's image in the minds of the voters, who could perceive the DP as inconsistent in its principle. Moreover, the minimalists are concerned about the possibility that if there were a *rapprochement* between some of them and P.R.C. officials, the entire DP would be internally split into hard-liners who resist dialogue with China and soft-liners who support it. In July 1996, a political gesture made by the Preparatory Committee's secretariat, which announced that those Hongkongers who supported the Basic Law would be entitled to be members of the Selection Committee (a body that elected the Chief Executive and members of the provisional legislature), was dismissed by the DP on the grounds that the provisional legislature would "breach" the Basic Law. The fear of being co-opted by China's united front work in the short run, and rejected by voters in the long run becomes a determinant reinforcing the DP's distrustful attitude toward P.R.C. officials. Subsequently, it becomes difficult for both sides to reach a consensus on the direction, scope, and pace of Hong Kong's democratization.[48]

---

[48] In reality, the "lack of trust" among political actors has been one of the "barriers" to their search for the further development of Hong Kong's polity. See Kuan Hsin-chi and Lau Siu-kai, "Hong Kong's Search for a Consensus: Barriers and Prospects," in *The Future of Hong Kong: Toward 1997 and Beyond*, edited by Chiu Hungdah, Y. C. Jao, and Wu Yuan-li (New York: Quorum Books, 1987), pp. 97–99.

As a matter of fact, some minimalists were previously maximalists in Hong Kong's democratization, a sign that the local pro-democracy elite has been softening its political stance under the circumstances in which the survival of political dissidents is at stake. Martin Lee, for example, was very critical of the P.R.C.'s "interventionist" policies towards Hong Kong in the later half of the 1980s, including the criticism of Beijing's opposition to the Hong Kong Government's attempt to introduce direct elections to Legco in 1988.[49] However, since the early 1990s he has toned down his criticism of China's "intervention" in Hong Kong affairs, a subtle change reflecting the fact that his political views tend to become more moderate than ever before. He also stepped down from the leadership position of the HKASPDM, another political move symbolizing that he was willing to water down his anti-Communist rhetoric and moderate his action. In reality, the local media also does not cover Lee's political views in the 1990s as widely and frequently as during the later half of the 1980s, a phenomenon attributable partly to the fact that the Hong Kong media does retrain itself to some extent from reporting comments from politicians critical of the P.R.C.,[50] and partly to the pragmatic shift of Lee himself from a critic to a moderate.

It is noteworthy that those maximalist-oriented minimalists, like Szeto Wah, tend to have similar views and action compared with the minimalist-oriented maximalists, like Emily Lau. They are all pro-democracy activists attempting to oppose the regime both inside and outside the regime. Szeto Wah and his supporters are also psychologically prepared for the worst-case scenario in which they would probably be arrested or barred from re-entering Hong Kong once they were out of the territory after 1 July 1997. The basic difference between the maximalist-oriented minimalists (like Szeto Wah) and the minimalist-oriented maximalists (like Emily Lau) is

---

[49] See Martin Lee, *A Collection of Martin Lee's Democratic Comments* (in Chinese) (Hong Kong: Tin Yuan, 1989), pp. 19–22.

[50] Except for the *Apple Daily* which frequently covers stories about the DP, most Chinese newspapers do not have extensive and frequent coverage of the DP. Moreover, the Hong Kong media is actually under the threat of the P.R.C.'s co-optation strategy, see Joseph Man Chan and Lee Chin-chuan, *Mass Media and Political Transition: The Hong Kong Press in China's Orbit* (New York: Guilford Press, 1991), Chapter 3, pp. 38–63.

that while the former adopts a flexible approach to deal with P.R.C. officials and is willing to discuss with them, the latter tends to be uncompromising and view the former as relatively weak. The fact that Emily Lau tends to form an alliance with other democrats, like the Ants Alliance, instead of joining Szeto's DP illustrates a fissure between the two groupings.[51] Also, the fact that Szeto Wah did meet with Tung Chee-hwa and discussed Hong Kong's political issues testified the flexibility on the part of maximalist-oriented minimalists. Although the maximalist-oriented minimalists and the minimalist-oriented maximalists do not hesitate to use street protests and to participate in elections as the opposition strategy, they cannot join together as a political party due to their divergent attitude towards communication with P.R.C. officials.

At the same time, some minimalists, especially those maximalist-oriented ones, are now hardening their political attitude and shifting towards the position of maximalists. The hard-line policy of China towards Hong Kong's political oppositionists, such as the confiscation of the travel documents of several pro-democracy activists who petitioned against the provisional legislature by flying to Beijing from Hong Kong in July 1996, merely alienated the minimalists further. Instead of winning the hearts and minds of the minimalists, the P.R.C.'s hard-line attitude could coerce them into a more maximalist stance.[52] In the wake of the Tiananmen incident, the political preponderance of hard-line P.R.C. officials dealing with Hong

---

[51] During the Sino-British row over Governor Christopher Patten's political reform blueprint in 1993, the Ants Alliance severely criticized the former members of Meeting Point, like Anthony Cheung, for accepting a political reform package that postponed the introduction of direct elections to the entire Legco. The difference here sowed the seeds of a split within the political opposition into minimalists and maximalists. Also, it is noteworthy that Szeto Wah, according to Xu's memoirs, toyed with the idea of joining the CCP in the past. But this was publicly denied by Szeto, who had been a "patriotic" activist opposing the educational policy of the Hong Kong Government in the 1960s and the 1970s. For Xu's claim that Szeto wished to join the CCP, see *Xu Jiatun Xianggang Huiyilu*, Vol. 1, pp. 149–50.

[52] One DP member Tsang Kin-shing, whose travel document to the mainland was confiscated by the P.R.C. authorities, vowed to oppose the provisional legislature by staging a sit-in at the Legco on the midnight of 30 June 1997. See *Sing Tao Daily*, 7 July 1996, p. B1.

Kong affairs rendered China's united front work on the minimalists largely ineffective, and it became a push factor for radicalizing some of them towards confrontation.

Unlike the minimalists and maximalists who are still encountering obstacles to communicate with P.R.C. officials, the opportunists constitute the only faction within Hong Kong's political opposition which is acceptable to hard-line Chinese officials and which becomes a successful target of the united front work. Some opportunists were originally minimalists, like a former DP member Lau Kong-wah who eventually withdrew from the party and switched to the pro-China forces.[53] Opportunists emphasize the usefulness of having dialogue with P.R.C. officials and are willing to work for gradual political changes within the Basic Law. Strictly speaking, the opportunists can be regarded as members of the "loyal" opposition in Hong Kong *vis-à-vis* China. Fung Kin-kee, for example, and his political group named the Association for Democracy and People's Livelihood (ADPL) adopt the position that it is necessary to discuss with P.R.C. officials on Hong Kong affairs. Yet, Fung and the ADPL suffer from a serious image problem that they appear to bow to political pressure from the P.R.C., seeking to maximize political benefits without any critical or independent judgement. In July 1996, Lu Fan-chi, a founding member of the ADPL, decided to withdraw from the political group on the grounds that its political position had been fluctuating without principles.[54] In fact, the ADPL's oscillating image can also be seen in its attitude towards the provisional legislature. After Fung publicly opposed the establishment of the provisional legislature and then following an immediate warning from P.R.C. officials that he might not be allowed to sit in the Selection Committee, the ADPL leader gradually adopted a low public profile in opposing

---

[53] Lau himself formed a political group called the Civic Force, which performed well in the 1994 District Board elections. He tried but failed to defeat Emily Lau in the 1995 Legco elections. The P.R.C. appointed him as China's adviser on Hong Kong affairs, and his visit to the HKMAO in July 1996 was seen as an indication that Chinese officials might appoint him into the forthcoming Selection Committee. See *World Journal*, 1 August 1996, p. A18. A recent example of such opportunists was Chan Choi-hei, who was a former DP member who decided to run for a position in the provisional legislature.

[54] *Ming Pao*, 30 July 1996, p. A18.

the provisional legislature.[55] Moreover, the ADPL considered the likelihood of allowing its members to join the Selection Committee and the provisional legislature, a body to which Fung originally objected.[56] As a result, Fung and his supporters participated in the selection process of members of the provisional legislature, a decision which prompted some ADPL members to withdraw from the group and to form a new political party named the Social Democratic Front in 1997. If political opportunism marks the democratizing transition of Hong Kong where many capitalists and professionals have already shifted their political allegiance from Britain to the P.R.C., the ADPL case represents a typical example of opportunistic elements co-opted and almost neutralized by China's united front work.

China's United Front Work on Hong Kong's Political Opposition

Basically, P.R.C. officials adopt a resistant attitude towards the maximalists and minimalists in Hong Kong. Hard-line P.R.C. officials of the NCNA and the HKMAO do not really distinguish the maximalists from the minimalists, treating all of them as potential co-optation targets with varying degrees of "pro-British," "pro-American" and "pro-Taiwan" sentiments.[57] Given that P.R.C. officials may endorse a number of pro-Beijing middlemen to discuss with the minimalists on the one hand, and that they themselves communicated with some minimalists like Christine Loh on the other, the targets of China's united front work are comprehensive and do not necessarily exclude any Hongkongers opposing P.R.C. policies.

A case in point is the attitude of P.R.C. officials towards the Hong Kong people who oppose the formation of the provisional legislature. In March 1996, the Preparatory Committee (PC) held consultative sessions in Hong Kong and P.R.C. officials from the NCNA and HKMAO listened to the opinions of the local elite. There were four local interest groups opposing the provisional legislature — the Hong Kong Professional Teachers' Union (HKPTU), the Hong Kong Federation of Student Unions (HKFSU),

---

[55] Fung told the Hong Kong media that P.R.C. officials gave him such warning three times. See *Eastweek*, No. 180 (4 April 1996), pp. 68–69.

[56] *Ming Pao*, 30 July 1996, p. A18.

[57] *Xu Jiatun Xianggang Huiyilu*, Vol. 1, p. 122.

the Bar Association (BA), and a loosely organized group of maximalists (some from DP and others from the April the Fifth Action Group). Nevertheless, they all received different reception from P.R.C. authorities. Once the HKPTU held a press conference and declared that it opposed the provisional legislature's formation, its leaders were forbidden by the PC organizers to attend the ensuing consultative session. Two HKFSU leaders, who did not hold any press conference to express their opposition to the provisional legislature but who went to attend the consultative sessions with T-shirts they wore saying that the public opinion in Hong Kong was "raped," were immediately expelled from the consultation venue. The BA, however, was still given a chance to voice its opposition to the provisional legislature in front of HKMAO officials. The loose coalition of democratic activists clashed with police officers violently and burnt truck tyre outside the consultation venue to vent their political anger. Eventually, P.R.C. officials refused to issue some of them the "home return permits" — documents required by the Hong Kong Chinese to visit the mainland.

The varying degrees of treatment received by these interest groups illustrated a number of characteristics of the P.R.C.'s united front work on Hong Kong's political opposition. First and foremost, P.R.C. officials dislike those Hongkongers who deliberately or unintentionally utilize the mass media to express their opposition to China's policies towards Hong Kong. The press conference held by the HKPTU, the public protest in the form of wearing T-shirts denouncing the provisional legislature, and the political action of burning truck tyre in public became an affront to the P.R.C. officials responsible for Hong Kong affairs. From the vantage point of P.R.C. hard-liners, these interest groups should be punished. The repugnant attitude of P.R.C. officials towards the protest strategies of the local political opposition demonstrated their relatively anti-media political culture.

Second, related to the anti-media culture of P.R.C. officials is their perception of what constitutes "radical" or "subversive" tactics employed by Hong Kong's political opposition.[58] Burning truck tyre and the P.R.C.'s

---

[58] Article 23 of the Basic Law says, "The Hong Kong SAR shall enact laws on its own to prohibit any act of treason, secession, sedition, subversion against the Central People's Government, or theft of state secrets, to prohibit foreign political organizations or bodies from conducting political activities in the Region, and to prohibit political organizations or bodies of the Region from establishing ties with foreign political organizations or bodies." See *The Basic Law*, p. 13.

national flag in public, destroying part or all of the Basic Law openly, violently confronting the police in protests and demonstrations, and privately supporting mainland political dissidents constitute actions that could be perceived by P.R.C. officials as "radical" and "subversive." The fact that top HKPTU leaders, like Szeto Wah, were involved with the HKASPDM's activities had already made the union a sore point to the P.R.C.'s hard-line officials. Therefore, the action of HKPTU to announce in public its opposition to the provisional legislature provided a justification for P.R.C. officials to exclude them at once from participating in the PC's consultative sessions.

Third, P.R.C. officials attach importance to the question of face, a cultural phenomenon that to some extent has shaped the boundary of political exclusion or inclusion of Hongkongers. The HKFSU leaders who wore T-shirts denouncing the P.R.C.'s consultative policy was a humiliation to mainland Chinese officials, who believe that students should be nationalistic and should cherish the political space allowed for them to voice their views in a "rational" manner. Thus, the question of face could determine whether or not P.R.C. officials communicate with political oppositionists in Hong Kong. In contrast to the HKFSU, Christine Loh's action of knocking the doors of the NCNA in public was seen as a sign of giving sufficient face to the nationalistically-minded P.R.C. hard-liners, who subsequently made a reciprocal action to discuss with her and tried to co-opt her under the umbrella of united front work.

Fourth, the realm of China's united front work is comprehensive and embraces professional interest groups. Despite the fact that the BA publicly opposed the provisional legislature, P.R.C. officials still permitted its leaders to voice opposing views in Hong Kong and during their visit to Beijing in July 1996. Clearly, wooing the BA for its support of the provisional legislature is politically necessary for P.R.C. officials, who realized that any prolonged opposition from the BA would weaken and undermine the legitimacy of the HKSAR Government after 1997. Hence, during the BA's visit to Beijing in 1996, a mainland legal expert and senior member of the National People's Congress (NPC) assured its leaders that the Hong Kong courts after 1997 would be empowered to decide those issues which would be interpreted by the NPC. While it remains to be seen whether P.R.C. officials could cajole the BA into supporting Beijing's policies towards Hong Kong in the long run, the assurance hopefully aimed at placating the legal profession's anxiety about the HKSAR's autonomy and diluting its opposition to the provisional legislature in the short run.

In fact, P.R.C. officials have slightly been modifying their united front work in Hong Kong since the transition period.[59] As long as Hong Kong is a pluralistic society where middle-class citizens can exercise independent political judgement and expect the mass media not to toe the official line of either the Hong Kong Government or the P.R.C., and where political oppositionists regard their critical attitude towards China as a must to grasp more votes in local elections, P.R.C. authorities find it relatively difficult to win the hearts and minds of the Hong Kong "compatriots."

In other words, P.R.C. officials have been hard-pressed to become more skilful and sophisticated in their political propaganda, promoting China's policies towards Hong Kong not simply in the name of the interests of Hongkongers but also through vigorous methods. For instance, during the Sino-British row over Patten's political reform proposals in 1993, NCNA officials also held a consultative session similar to the Governor's meet-the-public meetings, consulting opinions of local people on the direction of political reform. In 1995, when the PC's predecessor, the Preliminary Working Committee (PWC) — a body established in 1993 to counter Governor Patten's political reform blueprint — proposed that several legislation which had been amended by the Hong Kong Government to keep in line with the Bill of Rights would have to be repealed, there was fierce local opposition to the PWC's decision. In response to criticism from the relatively autonomous media and political oppositionists, P.R.C. officials decided to send mainland legal experts to Hong Kong, explaining the rationale behind the PWC's suggestion. Although critics of the P.R.C.'s united front work could easily dismiss these responses from Chinese officials as purely public relation activities without accepting the opinions of Hongkongers, it cannot be denied that its united front work has been adapted to the Hong Kong circumstances and modified in such a way as to emphasize the promotion and explanation of China's policies. If the united front work has already been modified to a certain extent, this is a progressive move towards democratization in the sense that P.R.C. officials have been learning how to respond to the pluralistic politics of Hong Kong.

---

[59] Xu Jiatun also admitted that during the Basic Law drafting process from 1985 to 1990, the "usual working style" of the mainland Chinese drafters was changed to make compromise with Hong Kong drafters because of the different circumstances in Hong Kong where dissenting opinions were often tolerated. *Xu Jiatun Xianggang Huiyilu*, Vol. 1, p. 166.

However, the extent to which P.R.C. officials adjust their united front work in Hong Kong is also contingent upon whether they are hard-liners, moderates or soft-liners. Following the Tiananmen incident and particularly after the escape of Xu Jiatun, the former NCNA director, from China to the United States in 1990, the hard-liners have been dominating the Chinese policy-making towards Hong Kong.[60] From 1989 to 1996, the top CCP leaders were preoccupied with other domestic, regional and global affairs, like the issues of enhancing Jiang Zemin's political power and handling Taiwan's increasingly pro-independence sentiments.[61] Under these circumstances, Hong Kong did not become a priority in the policy agenda of Beijing's leaders in the early half of the 1990s. As a result, the Beijing leaders delegated considerable power and responsibilities of policy-making and policy implementation to the NCNA and the HKMAO, which however became relatively uncontrolled mainland organs dictating the policies towards Hong Kong at least from 1989 to the period until 1997, when Beijing's leaders increasingly showed their interest in the matters concerning Hong Kong. Although the resumption of the P.R.C.'s sovereignty over Hong Kong in July 1997 was regarded as significant by top Beijing leaders, like Jiang and Li Peng, after the return of Hong Kong's sovereignty to the P.R.C., the officials in the HKMAO would likely remain influential. Arguably, unless the hard-liners in the HKMAO were replaced by moderate or soft-line officials (the NCNA's future remains unclear at the time of

---

[60] Soft-liners were purged in the wake of the Tiananmen incident, like Xu Jiatun who privately communicated with Martin Lee and Szeto Wah shortly after the incident but without informing the central government in Beijing. See *Xu Jiatun Xianggang Huiyilu*, Vol. 2, p. 398. Although some Hong Kong elites expressed their dissatisfaction with the performance of Lu Ping and Zhou Nan to the Chinese Foreign Minister Qian Qichen, Qian replied that Lu and Zhou were very familiar with Hong Kong affairs and that they would remain in their positions until 1999. See *Cheng Ming*, No. 226 (August 1996), pp. 20–21. For the conflicts between hard-line and soft-line P.R.C. officials on Hong Kong affairs, see Lo Shiu-hing, "The Chinese Communist Party Elite's Conflicts over Hong Kong, 1983–1990," *China Information*, Vol. 8, No. 4 (Spring 1994), pp. 1–14.

[61] For Jiang's survival strategy which includes promotion of the interests of the People's Liberation Army, the recruitment of his political associates to the party leadership, and the combat against bureaucratic corruption, see Richard Baum, *Burying Mao: Chinese Politics in the Age of Deng Xiaoping* (New Jersey: Princeton University Press, 1996), pp. 384–85.

writing), the P.R.C.'s united front work tends to be relatively intolerant of the maximalists, generally conservative and rigid about communication with the minimalists, and occasionally threatening towards a minority of opportunists who sometimes oppose P.R.C. policies towards Hong Kong.

Opportunist elements within the political opposition in Hong Kong are not confined to the democrats; they flexibly involve a minority of the pro-China elite critical of Beijing's policies.[62] The attitude of P.R.C. authorities towards these pro-Beijing critics is the same as that towards the opportunists, trying to continue co-opting them while at the same time neutralizing their opposition. The late Dorothy Liu Yiu-chu — a pro-Beijing nationalistic lawyer who was often critical of the Chinese policies towards Hong Kong before she died of cancer in 1997, including the provisional legislature and China's united front work on the former "pro-British" Hong Kong elite — was often an embarrassment to P.R.C. officials. The hard-line Chinese authorities toyed with the idea of not politically appointing her into the Basic Law Drafting Committee in the 1980s and into the PWC after Liu's sudden visit to Taiwan in 1993. Yet, under the general principle of co-opting Hongkongers who either oppose or support China's policies, P.R.C. officials eventually appointed Liu to various consultative mechanisms with a view to neutralizing her opposition. P.R.C. officials, regardless of whether they are hard-line or not, seem to be tolerant of the criticisms and opposition from the pro-Beijing Hong Kong elite, which is probably more faithful to the CCP than the opportunistic elements within the political opposition.

Other pro-Beijing Hongkongers, who seldom oppose Chinese policies and who do not really constitute the political opposition in Hong Kong, are also the target of co-optation and the P.R.C.'s united front work. Business tycoon Li Ka-shing, for example, was opposed to the proposal of restricting the ability of post-1997 Legco members to initiate private members' bills, which will need the endorsement of different types of Legco members elected from direct elections, functional constituencies and the election committee.[63] But realizing the influential role of Li whose view could shape

---

[62] The pro-China elite in Hong Kong is by no means homogeneous and split into many groupings, see Sonny Lo Shiu-hing and Donald Hugh McMillen, "A Profile of the 'Pro-China Hong Kong Elite': Images and Perceptions," *Issues & Studies*, Vol. 31, No. 6 (June 1995), pp. 98–127.

[63] *Xu Jiatun Xianggang Huiyilu*, Vol. 2, pp. 423–24.

the voting decision of other Basic Law drafters, Xu Jiatun attempted to persuade him to support the separate voting mechanism in the final version of the Basic Law.[64] However, HKMAO officials such as Li Hou and Lu Ping refused to yield to the dissenting view of the Hong Kong business tycoon, resulting in seven opposing votes which, according to Xu, might come from Li Ka-shing and his followers.[65] The case of Li's disagreement with the P.R.C. policy showed that some members of the pro-China Hong Kong elite do have their own judgement relatively autonomous of the influence from the tentacles of the P.R.C.'s united front work. If such independent political judgement persists and develops among the pro-China Hong Kong elite, democratization in Hong Kong after 1997 may not be so pessimistic as conventional wisdom assumes.

Conclusion

The case of Hong Kong demonstrates that, in the democratizing transition, the relations between political opposition and P.R.C. officials responsible for co-optation are complicated and dynamic. First and foremost, political oppositionists themselves are dynamic actors and sometimes oscillate between maximalist and minimalist positions, and from minimalist to opportunist stance — phenomena depending on their strategies, principles, the realm of political space for dissent, attitude towards communication with officials responsible for co-optation, and the policy line of co-optation authorities. In Hong Kong, a minority of former maximalists switch to a more moderate and even opportunistic political stance, viewing communication with P.R.C. officials as a political necessity. Independents without any party affiliation, like Christine Loh, tend to be less constrained by political considerations than those minimalists with party affiliation, like Martin Lee whose DP confronts a dilemma in communicating with P.R.C. officials. On the other hand, a minority of minimalists appear to be politicized and alienated by P.R.C.'s hard-line policies towards Hong

---

[64] *Ibid.*, p. 423.

[65] *Ibid.*, p. 424. Li Hou revealed that the British Government, which negotiated with the P.R.C. on the development of political reform in the Basic Law, had no problem with the separate voting mechanism in Legco after 1997. See Cheung Kit-fung *et al.*, *Fifty Years Unchanged?* (in Chinese) (Hong Kong: Tide, 1991), p. 179.

Kong, adopting a more radical or maximalist style, regarding street protests as the effective mode of participation, and seeing communication with P.R.C. officials as basically fruitless. The maximalists, in general, are also politically alienated by the policies formulated and implemented by hard-line P.R.C. officials responsible for Hong Kong affairs. In contrast to either the maximalists or the minimalists, the opportunists (some of them were previously minimalists) within the political opposition are co-opted easily by the P.R.C. in Hong Kong's democratization. The opportunists cherish the limited political space provided by P.R.C. authorities to express dissenting views. Yet, such occasional dissent is not necessarily accepted by hard-line officials who issue warnings to the former when opposing views exceed Beijing's bottom line, which has been interpreted and established by the NCNA and HKMAO officials particularly since the Tiananmen incident.

Second, co-optation authorities themselves tend to adopt different approaches to cope with varying types of political oppositionists. Political oppositionists who are professionals and whose expertise are valued by co-optation authorities tend to have more opportunities to express divergent views than those whose action of publicizing their dissent through the mass media is unacceptable to the ruling elite. In the case of Hong Kong, P.R.C. officials adopt a tolerant attitude towards the BA but a relatively exclusionary approach to the HKPTU, the HKFSU, and those maximalist demonstrators on the streets. Hence, the perception of co-optation authorities and their shifting bottom line of political tolerance directly affect whether members of the opposition could express dissenting views outside or inside the regime.

Third, although political opposition is heterogeneous, fragmented and under the risk of being co-opted, overall it sustains the momentum of democratization, forcing the regime and co-optation authorities to respond to criticisms. In other words, political opposition coexists with co-optation in the long process of democratization. Maximalists could expose the changing bottom line of co-optation officials; minimalists could maintain a certain distance from the regime while at the same time opposing government policies both inside and outside the state apparatus; and opportunists could continue trying to bargain with the governing authorities within the constitutional framework. Since each of the three factions of the political opposition has its own role or function in democratization, on the whole they could contribute to a political culture perhaps more tolerant of criticisms on the part of co-optation officials. The case of Hong Kong demonstrates that P.R.C. officials have already been forced to adjust their style and deal with public criticism in a more transparent and responsive manner than ever before. If democratization also entails an increase in the responsiveness of the ruling elite, the case study of Hong Kong illustrates a gradual and limited development of democratization in which co-optation authorities realize the necessity of responding to criticisms from the political opposition.

In brief, the democratizing transition in Hong Kong provides very useful empirical evidence that can cast a new light on the relationship between different factions of political opposition and co-optation. Although democratization in Hong Kong is necessarily constrained by the P.R.C.'s political development and atmosphere, political opposition in the territory has already produced its own dynamics and propelled limited democratic reforms further. Under the special circumstances of Hong Kong where decolonization did not bring about independence, and where its socialist motherland has been conducting extensive united front work since the transition period, different factions of the political opposition could altogether provide the necessary momentum for gradual democratization in the relatively liberalized and pluralistic capitalist enclave after the postcolonial era. In spite of the efforts made by P.R.C. authorities to co-opt, neutralize, marginalize and undermine Hong Kong's heterogeneous political opposition, the opportunists will still act as a loyal opposition *vis-à-vis* the mainland Chinese regime and the HKSAR Government; the minimalists will continue to try their best to influence the policies of the central government in Beijing and that of the local government in Hong Kong preferably inside and preparedly outside the territory's existing political institutions; and the maximalists will persist in using street protests to test the limits of the ruling elite's political tolerance in the long, tortuous, unpredictable and perhaps painful path of democratization.

7

Development of Civil Society in Hong Kong: Constraints, Problems and Risks

Ip Po-keung

Introduction

This chapter attempts a critical analysis of the development of civil society in Hong Kong. The notion of civil society can be understood as a descriptive-analytical one or as a normative-philosophical one. I adopt a descriptive and analytical notion of civil society in analysing the Hong Kong situation. I begin a preliminary theoretical discussion of the major features of civil society and propose a way to represent different modes of state-society relationships, which helps to identify the modes which Hong Kong civil society has in its short evolution. I suggest that Hong Kong civil society has a strong state element. Its development has been basically state-driven. I introduce the notions of *civil society in itself* and *civil society for itself* as a pair of concepts in characterizing the nature of a civil society. They correspond to what I take as the institutional and consciousness aspects of civil society respectively. Only the institutional aspect is discussed here. Two major institutional features of the civil society: autonomy and legal entitlements of its citizens are used to assess the state of civil society in Hong Kong. The constraints, problems and risks in connection with these aspects are discussed.

Preliminary Theoretical Exploration

Civil societies come in with a variety of forms and histories. The concept of civil society varies according to different philosophical orientations and theoretical commitments. Liberal contractarians and Marxist communitarians have different visions of civil society. Different political and cultural traditions also help shape the forms and dynamics of civil society in its relationship to the state. Capitalistic democracies breed one type of civil society. Authoritarian or totalitarian regimes nurture a different type of civil society. Despite certain common characteristics among disparate civil societies, some degrees of differences with respect to individual characteristics among civil societies are to be expected. Similar to the concept of democracy, one can say that there are different democracies, or perhaps different degrees of democracies. Likewise, in this chapter we see civil societies as displaying differences in their degree of civility. Instead of assuming a monolithic notion of civil society, this chapter sees a spectrum of civil societies while having some commonalties display different grades of civility.[1]

Civil society can be interpreted broadly as a domain of non-state social activities which are voluntary and public. Some use the notion of public space or public sphere to name it.[2] Whether public sphere or public space can be completely devoid of state elements itself is subject to debate. Whether civil society need to be necessarily non-state in nature is also a subject for further inquiry.

In another context, Chamberlain summarizes three ways to view civil society: (1) civil society is seen as the product of a "revolutionary moment," a sudden formation of a united front comprising disparate social elements; (2) civil society is seen as a recently emergent "counter-elite structure," confined mainly to urban intellectuals and students; and (3) civil society is

---

[1] John A. Hall, *Civil Society: Theory, History, Comparison* (Cambridge: Polity Press, 1995); Meera Chandhoke, *State and Civil Society: Explorations in Political Theory* (New Delhi: Sage, 1995); A. Seligman, *The Idea of Civil Society* (New York: The Free Press, 1992); John Keane, *Democracy and Civil Society* (London and New York: Verso, 1988); P. K. Ip, "Civil Society — The Liberal Conception," in *Human Rights and the Development of Civil Society*, edited by S. W. Man and C. F. Cheung (Hong Kong: Hong Kong Humanity Press, 1996), in Chinese.

[2] Mary B. Rankin, "The Origins of a Chinese Public Sphere: Local Elites and Community Affairs in the Late Imperial Period," *Etudes Chinoises*, Vol. 9, No. 2 (1990); W. T. Rowe, "The Public Sphere in Modern China," *Modern China*, Vol. 16, No. 3 (1990); W. T. Rowe, "The Problem of 'Civil Society' in Late Imperial China," *Modern China*, Vol. 19, No. 2 (1993).

conceived as a phenomenon which has its deep historical root, now after years of forcible suppression, re-emerging itself after a long historical evolution.[3]

What are the major factors that constitute a civil society? In current discussion of the subject, one characterization proposed by Mouzelis seems to capture some common understanding of the concept. A civil society should possess three basic features:[4]

1. the existence of rule-of-law conditions that effectively protect citizens from the arbitrary exercise of state power;
2. the existence of strongly organized non-state interest groups, capable of checking eventual abuses of power by those in power;
3. the existence of a balanced pluralism among civil society interests so that none can establish absolute dominance.

An alternative definition takes civil society as "the independent self-organization of society, the constituent parts of which voluntarily engage in public activity to pursue individual, group or national interests within the context of a legally-defined state-society relationship."[5]

Along the lines suggested, Scott summarizes three major features of civil society.[6] Firstly, the existence of *legal institutions* whereby the powers of the sovereign or the state are constrained and the rights and freedoms of citizens are established.[7] The second feature is *social pluralism*, which is closely connected with the growth of the capitalism. The third feature is

---

[3] H. B. Chamberlain, "On the Search for Civil Society in China," *Modern China*, Vol. 19, No. 4 (1993), p. 220.

[4] Nicos Mouzelis, "Modernity, Late Development and Civil Society," in *Civil Society: Theory, History, Comparison*, edited by John A. Hall (Cambridge: Polity Press, 1995), pp. 225–26.

[5] Quoted from Ian Scott, "The State and Civil Society in Hong Kong" (paper presented at the International Conference on Political Development in Taiwan and Hong Kong, co-sponsored by the Centre of Asian Studies, The University of Hong Kong and Institute for National Policy Research, Taipei, 8–9 February 1996).

[6] Ian Scott, *ibid.*, p. 1.

[7] The scope of the legal entitlement was subsequently widened through the evolution of civil society. The protection of rights and freedoms of the citizens was more entrenched and well established in the subsequent development of the civil societies. This aspect of entrenchment of rights and liberties of citizens manifested more prominently in mature liberal democracies.

autonomy from state interference. The degree displayed by these three features can be used to indicate the vibrancy of civil society.

For our purposes, we broadly agree that civil society possesses these three major features. However, these features may not exist at the same time at the historical development of civil societies. The relationship among these features is a subject too complex to be discussed here. Whether social pluralism occurred at the same time as the other two or as a result or cause of either of them or both is an empirical question which need not to be addressed here. This chapter takes autonomy from state interference and legal entitlements to protect the rights and liberties of citizens as the two aspects to examine the state of the development of civil society in Hong Kong.

State-Civil Society Relationships

Civil societies can be categorized in a variety of ways, depending on what criteria are used. Two criteria are proposed here to delineate civil societies using the state-society relationships. The first criterion uses the *state control* to differentiate different civil societies. There are civil societies with strong state control and there are those with weak state control. The first criterion reflects a top-down (state) perspective. The other criterion, in contrast, employs a bottom-up perspective. It uses *society's quest for autonomy* as a way to categorize civil society. From this perspective, civil societies can have strong and weak quest for autonomy. Figure 1 can be used to categorize civil societies.

In Figure 1, we can see that society can vary with regard to the degree of state control. Though I use High and Low to characterize this aspect of state activities towards society, in reality, the degree of control should be seen as sitting on a continuum rather than a discrete compartmentalized

Figure 1: State-Society Relationships

	Low	High	
STATE CONTROL	Low/Low (CS-I)	Low/High (CS-II)	Low
	High/Low (CS-III)	High/High (CS-IV)	High

SOCIETY'S QUEST FOR AUTONOMY

fashion. Regarding the criterion society's quest for autonomy, again, there are degrees of the quest and that it should likewise be seen as lying on a continuum with regard to its strength of quest. The first criterion basically focuses on the act of state. The second criterion focuses on the society's actions. The four compartments represent different combinations of state control and social quest for autonomy, represented by four types of civil societies: CS-I, CS-II, CS-III and CS-IV respectively.

Civil society CS-IV depicts a situation where there is high state control and high social quest for autonomy. The tensions and conflicts between state and society are frequent and intense. On the other hand, in civil society CS-I, when the state control and the social request for autonomy are both low, it is unlikely to have a friction-ridden state-society relationship. In CS-III where the state control is high and the quest for autonomy is low, conflict and friction may occur, but may often be of a sporadic nature which may not develop into major conflicts and confrontations. In the CS-II where the control is low and the quest for autonomy is high, society may through its polity strengthen more of its freedoms and liberties through legal and other political processes. The end result will be a typical liberal democracy where the state is under the constant and effective supervision of society and there is great accountability of the state to society. The legitimacy of the state is based on the society's approval and consent. Civil society is clearly superior to state in the sense of defining and legitimizing its powers and functions as well as the logic of its activities.[8]

---

[8] According to Scott, "when there is tension between state and society, resulting from either a crisis of legitimacy over political arrangements or a growth in social pluralism associated with rapid economic growth, or both, the regime in power will use state institutions to propagate its own vision of civil society in the interests of maintaining the status quo and its own control.... When an accommodation pertains between state and society — when legal entitlements are recognized, social pluralism is tolerated and autonomy is accepted, however restricted this recognition, toleration and acceptance may be — there is no particular need for the regime in power to embark upon the reinvention of society or community. It is when there is a perceived, implicit or overt, external or internal, challenge to the existing order that regimes using state institutions become inclined to look for new bases for the continuing exercise of power through the creation of an often mythical image of a society." See Ian Scott, "The State and Civil Society in Hong Kong," p. 2.

Modes of Civil Society in Hong Kong

In the case of Hong Kong, civil society, if it exists at all, has always had a strong state element. In fact, the formation and development of the civil society, especially in the late 1970s to the 1980s, displayed clear state design and initiatives. In other words, the state through its initiatives and intervention provided the basis for the emergence of civil society in Hong Kong. Therefore, the development of civil society was basically state-driven. In the late 1980s, after the signing of the Sino-British Joint Declaration and the subsequent passing of the Basic Law, China has become the other major player in shaping Hong Kong civil society and defining its direction. Using the matrix categories to characterize civil society in Hong Kong, civil society in Hong Kong has taken various modes in its short developmental history. As will be clear as we move along, the pre-1960s was dominated by CS-I which has low state control and low quest for autonomy. Perhaps one should be aware that though the colonial state was strong, its control of society was low, despite it had at its disposal an arsenal of draconian laws which were effective in suppressing any dissent and revolt. From the 1970s through the 1980s to the early 1990s, Hong Kong was beginning to move towards a CS-II type of civil society as a result of democratization and the institutionalizing of the rights and liberties for the citizens. Looking ahead, civil society may move into CS-IV, depending very much on how the future democratic arrangement of the Special Administrative Region (SAR) will be, despite the promise of a high degree of autonomy. By then, it may be under a strong state control and strong social quest for autonomy situation, if the current quest for autonomy can be sustained. In pre-1997 situation, the colonial state though strong, is under the supervision of the state of Great Britain, which is basically a liberal democracy with its long tradition of controlling the state's excess and arbitrary power and its respect for rights and liberties of citizens. Therefore, though the colonial state is strong, Hong Kong, unlike other authoritarian or totalitarian societies, has been a highly free society with little state interference. Thus, it may be fair to say that there is a certain anomaly in the sense that a strong state still allows a lot of freedoms and autonomy for its citizens. However, after the change of sovereignty in 1997, the continuation of this strong state and free society combination is uncertain. The state will no doubt be strong after 1997. However, whether the existing freedoms and rights will continue to be tolerated, or whether more rights and liberties will be developed and established are equally uncertain.

This chapter takes the view that civil society need not be completely non-state. It is a domain of public activities whereby the state may take part, not necessarily directly but by providing the necessary basis for the development of the voluntary public activities. In what follows, it will become clear that the Hong Kong civil society has displayed and will display different types of state-society relationships in its developmental process. But the underlying structure has been a strong state initiative and participation, especially in the political area.

Emergence of Civil Society in Hong Kong

Before the mid-1960s, civil society in Hong Kong, if it existed at all, was small, diffused, submerged and weak. The major players were rich Chinese merchant elites who represented the philanthropic organizations, including the Po Leung Kuk and the Tung Wah Group of Hospitals. They voluntarily undertook charitable activities which included helping the sick, the poor, orphans and the women who were under the risk of being kidnapped and sold as prostitutes. These charitable activities continued throughout late nineteen century to the early twentieth century, obviously with the blessings of the colonial state. Of course, the Chinese merchant elites, apart from doing these philanthropic public services, also had their political agenda. Through these organizations and activities, they were able to form alliances to defend their interests against the colonial state as well as other European merchants. It was through these organizations that they had the opportunities to come together to carry out these quasi-political activities under the watchful eyes of the colonial government. Though limited in scope, these voluntary non-state activities in effect signified a sustained and persistent effort of private citizens undertaking responsibilities which obviously belonged to the public domain.[9] These activities indeed were very similar to those undertaken by local people under the leadership of the rich merchant elites in local regions in China from the Ming and Qing dynasties.[10] The

---

[9] Henry Lethbridge, *Hong Kong: Stability and Change* (Hong Kong: Oxford University Press, 1978); W. K. Chan, *The Making of Hong Kong Society: Three Studies of Class Formation in Early Hong Kong* (Oxford: Clarendon Press, 1991); E. Y. K. Sinn, *Power and Charity: The Early History of the Tung Wah Hospital, Hong Kong* (Hong Kong: Oxford University Press, 1992).

[10] M. B. Rankin, "The Origins of a Chinese Public Sphere."

existence of this diffused and rudimentary civil society not only did not pose any threat to the state, but provided social support to those in need, and thus was tolerated and welcomed by the state. The state was strong but minimal. Civil society was small, underdeveloped, and largely non-political.

The colonial state of Hong Kong did not face a significant challenge to its position from the weak and underdeveloped civil society in the first one hundred and thirty years of its existence. Civil Society began to emerge from 1968 to 1989, largely as a result of the state's initiatives. After the 1966–1967 riots, the state was forced to rethink the state-society relationships. The concern of the state was to seek a way to legitimize its governability.

Based on the recommendations of the Commission on the Kowloon riots in 1966, the government initiated some major policy changes which culminated in a gradual but fundamental change of the relationship between the state and society. The extension of legal entitlements was one of the most noticeable. Social pluralism was further enhanced by the other legal provisions. The continuation to absorb the business and professional elites into the government ensured stability and smooth governance. New institutions were set up to allow participation in local affairs. The central power of decision-making was still under firm control of the state. The Legislative Council was occupied by appointed members and government officials. The Executive Council, which in effect was then as it is now, a cabinet of the governor, was never a body for election. Election of the Legislative Council was not allowed until 1984.[11]

The state recognized the urgent need to build up a sense of citizenship and community. The most explicit attempt in this direction was the set of reformist policies initiated by the Governor Sir Murray MacLehose.[12] The

---

[11] Ian Scott, "The State and Civil Society in Hong Kong," p. 3.

[12] MacLehose in a major speech delivered in 1972 to the Legislative Council, provided the backdrop for the reformist policies during his tenure, "the inadequacy and scarcity of housing and all that this implies and the harsh situations that result from it, is one of the major and constant sources of friction between the Government and the population. It offends our humanity, our civic pride and our political good sense." Quoted from Ian Scott, "The State and Civil Society in Hong Kong," p. 9.

setting up of civic organizations in connection with the promotion of cleanness and fighting crimes were prime examples. Mutual aid committees were set up in residential areas to help fight crime and maintain law and order. City District Offices were instituted to serve as a bridge between the government and the public. In the rural area, the Heung Yee Kuk still played a prominent role in voicing the village concerns to the government.

The major focus of the reform was primarily in the social and economic areas. The state saw it as vital that if the livelihood of the people was to be improved, conflict and dissatisfaction would be minimized. It was through the improvement of people's livelihood that the state hoped that a more stable and governable situation could be achieved. In a way, the state in the 1970s did achieve substantive results in these areas. Massive public housing projects were completed, and cultural and recreational facilities were improved. Corruption was under control with the setting up of the Independent Commission Against Corruption (ICAC). As the physical environment and the material conditions of the society began to improve, these set the stage for the development in society of a sense of community the territory had never experienced before. Through these belongingness enhancement activities, the idea that Hong Kong being a society distinctively different from that of mainland China was beginning to take root in the community. With their newly acquired wealth, people in Hong Kong began to develop a sense of local identity which they never so distinctively felt to have before. People began to take pride in their Hongkongness. Hong Kong society no doubt was strongly Chinese, yet it was also uniquely Hong Kong. People also began to construct a new image of the society and of themselves as its citizens in a new way. Hong Kong civil society in the late 1970s began to emerge with its growing wealth and socio-economic development.

As the civil society grew, it became apparent that to continue to confine political participation in the local and district levels could not meet the aspiring democratic needs of the people. People wanted to have more say in running their affairs. Pressure groups and activist organizations, though still a small minority in the community, were critical of the state and its policies, especially on the question of restricting political participation. Despite the existence of these small but vocal groups, Hong Kong people by and large remained apathetic. However, the growing dissatisfaction of the political process apparently forced the state to take some actions in response. A Standing Committee on Pressure Groups was set up in 1979 to this effect. In a report in April 1980, it recommended a new relationship between state and civil society. The recommended state-society relationships are:[13]

1. Government should not be complacent over its achievements but should keep its programmes up-to-date and refined to meet the rising expectations of the community;

2. Government publicity, both aggressive hard-sell and more subtle soft-sell, must continue to play a vital part in explaining policies and programmes, to build up a permanent background of an effective but humane Government;

3. Departments should deal directly and quickly with pressure groups ... [they should] avoid over-reacting and deliberate confrontation; whilst requests for information and interviews should be entertained as far as possible;

4. Departments should ... be prepared to refute inaccurate or biased public statements and ... be prepared to be aggressive;

5. Consideration should be given by Departments most affected by pressure groups to appoint a senior officer to deal specifically with them;

6. Pressure group activities should also be met by an intensification of Government community building efforts, and by selectively enlisting individuals from the groups to Government advisory boards and committees ... ;

7. Closer contacts with student bodies and tertiary educational institutions should be built up ....

It seemed that this revised mode of state-society relationship provided one of the bases of the reformist policies.

The Prescribed Image of Hong Kong by the State

The struggle of Hong Kong civil society against the state has never been overt, confrontational and massive. This was mainly because the civil society, as pointed out earlier, was small and underdeveloped as a result of a careful state design and act. Indeed, the actual development of civil society was basically state-driven, beginning in the 1970s. The direction of

---

[13] Ian Scott, "The State and Civil Society in Hong Kong," pp. 11–12.

its development was to follow the blueprint defined by the state. It involved a prescribed image of society and its citizens. Basically, the state wished the civil society to be moderately democratic. The bottom line was to maintain the stability of the government which would be basically executive-led. A fully democratic government was conceived to be not in the best interests of Hong Kong. Limited participation in the Legislative Council was to be allowed. District as well as Urban and Regional Councils could be fully elected. In other words, the state wanted to shape Hong Kong into a society whose main interests would be predominantly business and economics. Simply put, it would be a capitalistic society with limited democracy. It was through the constitutional and legal design, especially in the political area, that helped to define the "bounds" of the possible development of the civil society. In the end, the state was largely successful in achieving this goal.

This state-prescribed image of the society was apparently welcomed by the Chinese Government. Hong Kong society will remain the same for fifty years after the change of sovereignty, modelling on the non-political capitalistic model. The Sino-British Joint Declaration and the Basic Law in effect constituted the basic legal and constitutional framework within which Hong Kong civil society is allowed to develop and to operate. Underlying the relevant provisions of the Basic Law was an image of society and citizenship that both the Chinese and British Governments have prescribed to the future Hong Kong SAR. The prescribed image of the Hong Kong society, which is basically a continuation of the pre-mid-1960s colonial state's image of society, will be like this. The basic structure of the polity is to remain unchanged. It has to be an executive-led government with a limited number of elected seats in the Legislative Council. Hong Kong society is to remain an economic society with a restricted and tame democracy which is accountable to the Beijing authority. A fully democratic government with related democratic institutions is the least that the Chinese Government wants for the future SAR. It is worth noting here that in the making of both the Joint Declaration and the Basic Law, it was the joint effort of the Chinese and British Governments which systematically disallowed any substantial participation of the Hong Kong Government and its people in the process. The people of Hong Kong were never a major player in the making of these two critical arrangements which defined their fate. Indeed, the making of the Joint Declaration and the Basic Law was another good example of the state-driven nature of civil society development. This time, of course, it involved the future sovereign, the Chinese state. It is clear that both the constitutional and legal framework and the derived image of society were the result of the deliberate acts of design of both the Chinese and British states.

The Bill of Rights which was passed in the Legislature will be repealed after the hand-over, as the Chinese Government does not see this as in line with the Basic Law. Lurking behind the vehement objection to the Bill of Rights apparently lies the deep distrust of the British Government's intention. In the eyes of the Chinese Government, the introduction of the Bill of Rights was intended to subvert Hong Kong society: to politicize the once non-political society and hence make it less governable. The Director of Hong Kong and Macau Affairs Office Lu Ping's earlier remark on 6 May 1996 that Hong Kong should not become a political society was particularly revealing here. It clearly reflected a vision of society that the Chinese authorities prefer for Hong Kong. This perhaps confirms some critics' comment that the Chinese state's intention is to have Hong Kong to remain a Chinese "colony" after the change of sovereignty.

Hong Kong in Transformation since the 1970s

Hong Kong has been going through a gradual and perhaps irreversible transformation in the past decades. Replacing the fading immigrant-refugee mentality was a gradual recognition and self-awareness of the Hong Kong identity. The community has become more conscious of its unique identity as compared with its counterpart across the border. It has continued to grow into a more pluralistic, tolerant and open society. The people are becoming more educated and well-off. Hong Kong is becoming a wealthy society with an increasingly vocal and right-conscious middle class. The economy is slowly shifting from a manufacturing to a service one. This trend will continue in the years ahead. With the manufacturing sector of the economy rapidly moving to the vast hinterland, especially the Pearl River Delta region, the economies of Hong Kong and China are becoming more and more interdependent with each other. Such interdependence and economic integration have quickly rendered the once benign isolation from China a thing of the past. The success which was once hinged on this isolation is now depending on closer engagement. Indeed, this has been the trend set and the strategy adopted by the versatile and highly adaptive manufacturers of this tiny colony since the early 1980s.

With the rapid integration of the two economies, the economic policy of positive non-interventionism is becoming more and more obsolete.

Some form of interventionist policy has been called for from both the business and manufacturing as well as the labour sectors. But what form of an interventionist policy should Hong Kong take remains to be determined. With the serious questioning of the positive non-interventionist policy, the whole governing ideology is under serious scrutiny as well.

In the political arena, the advent of wealth has helped to create in a more right-conscious and well-educated populace rising social and political expectations. The bygone years of elite consensus politics is becoming ill-equipped to meet the growing needs of political expectation and participation. The transformation of the economy has effectively brought in its wake concomitant social and political transformation. The image that Hong Kong is a society whose only concern is material prosperity has been shown to be too superficial to do justice to the reality of Hong Kong society.[14] Accompanying its economic growth, Hong Kong has been undergoing political, social and cultural growth and transformation which it has never experienced in its entire history.[15]

It is the political growth and development in the form of democratization that has added an important dimension to the growth of Hong Kong civil society. As well as developing the non-sovereign autonomy, a topic which will be elaborated later, social and political autonomies may be seen as the further development and enhancement of the overall autonomy. With China becoming more and more influential in interpreting the bounds of the Hong Kong's autonomy framed by the Joint Declaration and the Basic

---

[14] According to two veteran Hong Kong Studies scholars, Hong Kong in the 1980s has assumed its uniqueness as a society. It displayed several features:
1. There was a high level of trust in Hong Kong and more emphasis was placed on personal freedom and civil liberties;
2. Hong Kong Chinese were more tolerant of conflict;
3. The economy was clearly differentiated from the polity and capitalism had been fully embraced;
4. Hong Kong Chinese were less fearful of the government and even expect fair treatment from it.

See S. K. Lau and H. C. Kuan, *The Ethos of the Hong Kong Chinese* (Hong Kong: The Chinese University Press, 1988).

[15] B. K. P. Leung and T. Y. C. Wong, *25 Years of Social and Economic Development in Hong Kong* (Hong Kong: Centre of Asian Studies, 1994); Brian Hook, "Political Change in Hong Kong," *The China Quarterly*, Vol. 136 (1993).

Law, the question to be asked is: to what extent can Hong Kong develop its social and/or political autonomy within the framework set by the Joint Declaration and the Basic Law?

Economically, Hong Kong is sophisticated and advanced. Politically, it is conservative and backward. The increasing tension developed as a result of the mismatch between the economy and the polity exposes many deficiencies of the antiquated political system. The traditional elite consensus system and selected consultation have become ineffective in addressing the issues of wider political participation and representation, among other things.

As the change of the sovereignty is approaching, the gradual erosion of the political authorities of the government is apparent. On several occasions, the government has been subject to serious challenges unprecedented in its one hundred and fifty years of governance. The power elite has either changed allegiance, or become more critical of the government and its policies. At the same time, a new breed of pro-China power elite has been created as advocates and defenders of China's policy on Hong Kong, while serving as vehement critics of the colonial government. The days of quiet containment have long gone and the colonial government has suffered from continued erosion of political authority over both the influential elite class and the public at large. The legitimacy problem which was submerged in the 1950s through the 1970s re-emerged as a real and serious issue for the government. It is becoming more difficult for the government to convince the people of its legitimacy. It is therefore no exaggeration to say that the government has been facing a legitimacy crisis.[16]

The gap that existed between an advanced economy and a relatively backward polity has been an act of design by the British Government and the future sovereign, China. In the eyes of both governments, such arrangement can make Hong Kong more governable and thus serves the interests of the state better. This has firmly set the bounds within which political development as democratization as well as other autonomy development can be allowed.

---

[16] Ian Scott, *Political Change and the Crisis of Legitimacy in Hong Kong* (Hong Kong: Oxford University Press, 1989).

Political Development since 1984

Political reform was brought about basically by the 1997 issue. What was agreed by the Sino-British deal was to allow Hong Kong a kind of self-rule and maintain its capitalist system unchanged for fifty years. The development of representative government began after the Sino-British Agreement on the future of Hong Kong. In 1985, the Legislative Council was to have elected members from the electoral colleges of District Boards and nine functional constituencies. The subsequent attempt to a further introduction of direct elections of a small number of seats in the Legislative Council was abandoned due to China's opposition.[17] The year 1991 was a year where Hong Kong had its first directly elected legislature. The election was held in the aftermath of the June 4th Tiananmen incident. Pro-China candidates were all defeated, whilst the Democrats won a landslide victory.

Governor Christopher Patten, in an apparent bid to further democratization of Hong Kong, initiated a reform package which had the following elements: adoption of a single-seat single vote system; lowering the voting age to eighteen; abolishing the appointed membership in the municipal councils; creating nine new constituencies; individuals and not groups are eligible to vote in all the functional constituencies. As a result, the electoral base of the political system was significantly enlarged, allowing a wider political participation. China objected the reform package vehemently, fearing that such reform would upset the smooth transition.

On 29 June 1994, the reform bills were passed by a narrow margin. The 1995 election was undertaken under the reformed political system. Such an attempt angered China so much that it immediately set up a Preliminary Working Committee (PWC) to counter the Patten's reform, including planning for the replacement of the 1995-elected legislature by a provisional legislature in 1997. China had also made it clear that there would be no "through train" for the 1995-elected legislature through 1997. A series of proposals by the PWC, including the reinstitution of those laws which contravened the Bill of Rights, caused widespread condemnation and uproar in the community.

---

[17] It was later disclosed that the British and Chinese Governments had secretly agreed in 1987 to have a small number of directly elected seats in 1991.

Two parties, the Democratic Party (DP) and the Democratic Alliance for Betterment of Hong Kong (DAB), dominated the election.[18] The China factor in fact played an important part insofar as the election result was concerned. In terms of absolute numbers, this election had 1,338,205 voters casting their ballot, quite a significant increase of voters, though the turnout rate remained low. This means that more people have been drawn into the political process as a result of the widening access to political participation. As a result of the widening of access to the political process, the people have been politicized. The political implication of this increase of political participation should not be underestimated. Once the political aspirations of the people have been raised, it may not be so easily suppressed without causing social resentment, tensions and conflicts.

Constraints, Problems and Risks

Autonomy: Forms, Constraints and Risks

As autonomy is seen here as one salient feature of the civil society, it is important to probe further into this aspect of the civility of Hong Kong society. There are at least two aspects of autonomy that need to be discussed: the objective and subjective aspect of autonomy. The objective aspect of autonomy refers to the institutional aspect of autonomy, which includes the constitutional as well as the legal or organizational aspect of autonomy. It can also be referred to as the conditions of autonomy. The subjective aspect of autonomy referred to the subjects who initiate or undertake autonomous actions or activities. It includes the awareness, desires, felt needs, expectations, and commitments in connection with the pursuit of autonomy by the subjects of autonomous action, whether they are individual, groups or peoples. In this section, I discuss the conditions of autonomy and the problems and risks involved.

In both the Joint Declaration (Section 3 (1) and Section I of Annex I) and the Basic Law (Article 12), Hong Kong as a SAR of the People's Republic of China has been promised "a high degree of autonomy." There is no doubt that the Joint Declaration and the Basic Law define the limits of autonomy that Hong Kong can enjoy. Within the Basic Law, autonomy

---

[18] In the 1995 election, the DP won a total of 17 seats from 24 candidates it fielded, where the DAB only got 5 of the 11 candidates they sent to run for office.

can be further defined and delimited by different provisions. It is obvious that the Basic Law sets the constitutional constraints for the autonomy of Hong Kong. But autonomy referred to here can mean several things, with the exception of independence from China. Indeed, autonomy takes several forms: non-sovereign autonomy, legal autonomy, political autonomy, among others, which are discussed as follows.

Non-Sovereign Autonomy

Hong Kong as a British colony has been enjoying a form of non-sovereign autonomy granted by the British Government. It was allowed to exercise a limited autonomy at various historical stages. After the change of the sovereignty, this pattern of development is expected to continue as prescribed by the Basic Law.

According to Kuan,[19] the delegation of authority to Hong Kong to manage its economic affairs set the stage for a long process of limited autonomy. After that, the autonomy gained in the financial sector was extended to foreign economic relations. This allowed Hong Kong to negotiate and do business directly with its global trade partners on its own. Hong Kong's subsequent acceptance as member in other international organizations, including being a member of GATT, was a clear display of its status of non-sovereign autonomous entity. Foreign states, like Canada and the United States do have legislation to recognize such a status of Hong Kong.[20] The Basic Law pays due recognition of this form of autonomy in its provisions:

> The Hong Kong Special Administrative Region may on its own, ... , maintain and develop relations and conclude and implement agreements with foreign states and regions and relevant international organizations in the appropriate fields, including the economic, trade, financial and monetary, shipping, communications, tourism, cultural and sports fields. (Article 151)

---

[19] H. C. Kuan, "Escape from Politics: Hong Kong's Predicament of Political Development" (paper presented at the International Conference on Political Development in Taiwan and Hong Kong, co-sponsored by the Centre of Asian Studies, The University of Hong Kong and Institute for National Policy Research, Taipei, Taiwan, 8–9 February 1996), pp. 6–8.

[20] Canada's revised Foreign Missions and International Organizations Act in 1991 and the United States' Hong Kong Policy Act in 1992 both recognized Hong Kong's non-sovereign status. See *ibid.*, p. 7.

Apart from the non-sovereign autonomy that Hong Kong has so far enjoyed, it is also important to see what other forms of autonomy would be allowed in the future SAR.

Legal Autonomy

Although Hong Kong has been promised a high degree of autonomy, there are provisions in the Basic Law which make people worry about how genuine the promise is. It has been widely noted that Article 17 and Article 160 open the gate for China's intervention into the legal autonomy of the future SAR. Article 17 states that the Standing Committee of China's National People's Congress (NPC) has the power to invalidate Hong Kong's legislation. Article 160 gives the Standing Committee a similar power to veto existing legislation in Hong Kong. Other provisions in the Basic Law also raise concern about China's ease of intervention into the internal affairs of Hong Kong. For example, Article 18 states that the Standing Committee has the power to apply China's national laws in "turmoil" situation. But the meaning of the word "turmoil" is so loose and easy to be manipulated. Article 19 stipulates that matters related to "acts of state" should remain a matter for the central government to decide and these are outside the jurisdiction of Hong Kong courts. There is no clear definition of the "acts of state" in the provision. If the "acts of state" do not confine only to defence and foreign affairs, but include other activities of the government, this means that the activities of the central government, which may include those which interfere into the affairs of the SAR, are beyond the laws of the SAR. Therefore, it is clear that Article 19 and other provisions of the Basic Law could set the stage for China's intervention into Hong Kong affairs. Furthermore, what makes one worry is that the power to interpret the Basic Law remains in the hands of the Standing Committee. Given these legal gaps and apparent deficiencies, the Basic Law poses a risk that Hong Kong's autonomy be compromised.[21]

---

[21] The Foreign Affairs Committee (FAC) of the House of Commons in a report published on 23 March 1994, stated that "Articles 18 and 158 of the Basic Law are grave potential threats to the autonomy of the Hong Kong SAR after 1997 and to the implementation of the Joint Declaration." See Christine Loh, "The Implementation of the Sino-British Joint Declaration," in *The Other Hong Kong Report 1994*, edited by D. H. McMillen and S. W. Man (Hong Kong: The Chinese University Press, 1994), p. 68.

Political Autonomy

The kind of political autonomy as democracy allowed by the future sovereign as defined by the Basic Law is quite limited. Under the Basic Law, of the 60 seats in the legislature, 30 will be elected through functional constituencies for all three terms through 2007, and 10 and 6 seats by a election committee for the first and second term respectively. In a nutshell, it will take a full decade for the legislature to be half directly and half indirectly elected. Such a blueprint for political development is indeed very restricted and conservative. But it is in line with China's wish to contain and suppress the democratic development of Hong Kong. To amend this restricted political design in the Basic Law requires the approval of two-thirds of the future legislature, the chief executive and the Standing Committee of the NPC of China. Apart from restricting the number of the directly elected members to remain permanently as a minority, Annex II of the Basic Law is also designed to restrict the influence of the legislature. It requires for motions proposed by individual members, a simple majority vote of each of the two groups of members returned by functional constituencies and members returned by geographical constituencies.

Legal Entitlements of Rights and Liberties of Citizens

Both the Joint Declaration and the Basic Law recognize the basic rights of Hong Kong citizens. In Part XIII of Annex I of the Joint Declaration, it stated clearly that "The provisions of the International Covenant of Civil and Political Rights and the International Covenant on Economic, Social and Cultural Rights as applied to Hong Kong shall remain in force." Chapter III of the Basic Law listed the provisions for the fundamental rights and obligations of residence of Hong Kong, which broadly conform with standard basic human rights provisions. From Article 25 through Article 41, the commonly accepted basic human rights are prescribed. Article 39 restated the two international covenants of human rights as recognized in the Joint Declaration.

However, despite these provisions, there is genuine worry about its enforcement. Without an effective enforcement, it is doubtful whether the human rights of the citizens of Hong Kong will be protected. The reason is obvious and simple. China is not a signatory of these two international covenants. It has therefore no obligation of accountability to the United

Nations Human Rights Committee (UNHRC).[22] Any human rights violations in the future SAR will be treated as a domestic matter by China.
Whether China will succumb to international pressure on the human rights
issue has been amply demonstrated by its past record. The facts show that
there is little effect on China insofar as the international condemnation of
human rights violation is concerned. Is there a chance that China will
become a signatory of the two covenants before the hand-over? It seems
less likely. As a result, what are stated as human rights protections in the
Joint Declaration and the Basic Law may turn out to be empty promises.
The protection of human rights as prescribed in the Joint Declaration and
the Basic Law is not enforceable.

In 1992, the Hong Kong Government passed the Bill of Rights into
law. It seems that the protection of basic rights and liberties has begun to
take root in Hong Kong.

However, there are doubts and worries about the effectiveness of this
legal protection of rights. Since the introduction of the Bill of Rights in
1992, the Chinese Government has made it very clear that it will be repealed after the hand-over, as the Bill of Rights was seen by the Chinese
Government as a unilateral decision without consulting the Chinese
Government. The fate of the Bill of Rights therefore was clouded with
uncertainty from the start. There is evidence to show that the Chinese
Government is serious in overturning the Bill after 1997. The proposal by
the PWC to reinstate seven legislation which were scrapped because they
were found to be contravening the Bill of Rights is a case in point.

The PWC legal sub-group recommended to the NPC's Standing Committee in mid-October 1995 that key provisions of the Bill of Rights in
relation to its overriding status over existing or new laws should be
scrapped after 1997 because they violated the Basic Law.[23] The PWC also
proposed that seven laws which were scrapped because they were found
contravening the Bill of Rights be reinstated.[24] The proposal was in effect

---

[22] Lu Ping, the Head of the Hong Kong and Macau Affairs Office, in a visit
to Hong Kong in May 1994, said that Beijing was not obliged to report to the
UNHRC after 1997. See *ibid.*, p. 73.

[23] *South China Morning Post*, 19 October 1995.

[24] The following Ordinances were proposed to be scrapped: Societies
Amendment Ordinance 1992, Television Amendment Ordinance 1993, Telecom-
munication Amendment Ordinance 1993, Broadcasting Authorities Amendment

tantamount to the reinstatement of the draconian colonial laws which were intended to restrict the rights of the people in Hong Kong.

It was widely known that without Articles 2(3), 3, and 4, which the PWC proposed to scrap, the Bill of Rights would become meaningless. The articles in effect say that no law enacted before or after the Bill of Rights can violate it. The proposal was also seen by legal experts as an attack on the Judiciary's authority to implement human rights protection.[25]

How did China react to this event? A senior mainland source was reported to say that China was doing nothing more than reinstating laws that the Hong Kong Government has been using until just a few years ago. Shen Guofang, the Chinese Foreign Ministry spokesman reiterated on 24 October that laws modified unilaterally by the Hong Kong Government would not be recognized. He said that the modification "seriously contravened the Sino-British Joint Declaration and the principles enshrined in the Basic Law that the existing laws in Hong Kong should basically remained unchanged."[26] Expectedly, as mentioned above, these proposals aroused an uproar. But China has taken a firm stand on this issue. The fate of the Bill of Rights has been put into great uncertainty.

Britain's House of Commons Foreign Affairs Select Committee recommended in April 1994 the setting up of a human rights commission in Hong Kong to safeguard the protection of human rights. China's NPC reacted strongly against the recommendation and saw it as an infringement of China's internal affairs. To avoid antagonizing China, the Executive Council rejected the recommendation but put aside HK$20 million over the years 1995 to 1997 for human rights development and set up a human rights sub-committee under the auspices of the Ombudsman. It will

---

Ordinance 1993, Public Order Amendment Ordinance 1995, Amendment to the Emergency Regulations in 1995, Legislative Council Commission Ordinance 1994, Amendment to the New Territories Land (Exemption) Ordinance 1994, and to be replaced by their old version.

[25] Professor Raymond Wacks of Hong Kong University Law Faculty was reported to have said that proposed change would lead to "constitutional terror" and the proposal would reduce the Bill of Rights to an "empty vassal" "if all amended laws are restored the previous decision of courts will be undermined." *South China Morning Post*, 19 October 1995.

[26] *South China Morning Post*, 25 October 1995.

have the powers to look into government violations of human rights of citizens.[27]

On 23 February 1997, the Standing Committee of the NPC of China passed a resolution that under Article 160 of the Basic Law, three sections of the Hong Kong Bill of Rights Ordinance (BORO) and major amendments to the Societies Ordinance (Cap. 151) and the Public Order Ordinance (Cap. 245) which were introduced in 1992 and 1995 respectively would be scrapped. The NPC resolved that the Hong Kong SAR should enact laws on its own to avoid any legal vacuum arising on 1 July 1997. To follow up the NPC's decision, the Office of the Chief Executive (CE) Designate proposed amendments to these two ordinances and issued a hastily prepared consultation document "Civil Liberty and Social Order" to the public in April 1997. The intent of the amendment is apparent in restricting the civil liberties of the Hong Kong people in forging ties with overseas groups or organizations and in their freedom of assembly.[28]

---

[27] John D. Ho, "The Legal System: Are the Changes Too Little, Too Late?" in *The Other Hong Kong Report 1994*, pp. 20–21.

[28] The 1992 amendments of the Societies Ordinance which were proposed to be amended are: (a) removal of the provision to refuse to register a society which is connected with any political group established outside Hong Kong; and (b) replacement of the registration system with a notification system. The proposed amendments to the Societies Ordinance were: "(a) to reintroduce registration of societies, but restricting the grounds for refusal of registration to those which are provided for in the ICCPR [International Covenant on Civil and Political Rights], namely, national security, public safety, public order, protection of public health or morals, and protection of the rights and freedoms of others; (b) to include a provision which prohibits societies from establishing ties with foreign political organizations or bodies.... Societies breaching the Ordinance are liable to refusal for or cancellation of registration." The proposed amendments to the Public Order Ordinance were: "(a) in normal circumstances, the Commissioner of Police must be notified of a public procession at least seven days before the procession. The Commission of Police must reply, stating clearly whether he has any objection to, and whether he will impose conditions on, the procession; (b) in exceptional circumstances, the Commissioner of Police may accept shorter notices which, however, must not be less than 48 hours prior to the procession." See *Civil Liberty and Social Order: Consultation Document* (Hong Kong: Chief Executive's Office, Hong Kong Special Administrative Region, The People's Republic of China, April 1997), pp. 13 and 16.

The proposed amendments immediately created widespread uproar and criticisms that the future SAR government wanted to restrict the civil liberties of the people of Hong Kong. The Hong Kong Government, in an unusual manner, also distributed a *Commentary* criticizing the proposed amendments.

In response to the serious criticisms and popular protests against the amendments, the CE Office scaled down the amendments on 15 May. Yet it failed to allay fears that civil liberties in the future of Hong Kong may be under constant threat. Indeed, this incident deepened people's ongoing concern over the erosion of their civil liberties in the future.

Conclusion

In his classic study of class, Marx makes the celebrated distinction between *class in itself* and *class for itself*. To paraphrase Marx, I see civil society can be likewise be categorized: *civil society in itself* and *civil society for itself*. By civil society in itself, I mean the institutional aspect of civil society, including the constitution and other institutional aspects of civil society. On the other hand, civil society for itself refers to the social consciousness aspect of it. It means in civil society the conscious and voluntary pursuit of rights and liberties and other public causes by its citizens with respect to its goals and ideals. Civil society can only be fully realized by converging both the full realization of its institutional and consciousness aspects of civil society. In such a full realization, civil society will be *in and for itself*.

What is the state of civil society in Hong Kong? From the above discussion, it seems that the civil society in Hong Kong is pretty much a civil society in itself, with all its problems and risks. Is civil society in Hong Kong a civil society for itself? Though we have not discussed this part of the issue, we can make a general observation on this aspect. To deny Hong Kong civil society has its growing self-awareness seems not fair, but to say that it has full awareness as a society is also an overstatement. It seems civil society in Hong Kong has just crossed the threshold to self awareness and has been more and more conscious of itself from the mid-1980s onward. Though it still has a long way to go in fully conscious of itself as a society, the process of self-awareness has been going on for over a decade and will continue to grow in future. Even though the civil society in Hong Kong is still far from the stage of converging institutions and consciousness, yet the path towards this stage has been set and the journey has started.

The Joint Declaration and the Basic Law has set for Hong Kong civil society the constraints for its future development. As indicated above, there are gaps and deficiencies in both the Joint Declaration and the Basic Law in safeguarding both the autonomy and the rights of citizens. The constitutional loopholes and gaps as indicated in effect open up the possible floodgate for interference from the central government. The civil society in Hong Kong has come a long way. But its future is full of risks and uncertainty. Will the civil society be suppressed? restrained? or crushed?[29]

Since the introduction of direct election in the legislature, the Pandora's box of democratization has been opened. For better or worse, Hong Kong has been politicized. The people have been enfranchised. Political parties are maturing and socially accepted. Public space becomes more entrenched and pronounced. Hong Kong civil society seems set for

---

[29] Professor S. K. Kuan, in a recent discussion of the political development of Hong Kong, argues that a political society has been borned and developed in Hong Kong. According to Kuan, "a political society is an independent arena mediating between the society at large and the polity. No political society could develop as the colonial government was effectively secluded from the society and when all social-economic elites could be successfully co-opted into the government's machinery of consultation." See H. C. Kuan, "Escape from Politics," p. 20.

He poses a similar question about the future of the political society and concludes that (pp. 23–24): "[the political society] can at best be tamed. The most important factor lies in the fact that the polity can no longer be secluded from the society. The people of Hong Kong have been psychologically inducted into the political process. Unlike their forefathers, they no longer rely solely on individual and familial self-help for a living, but entertain increasing expectation from the government and are ready to join collective actions to press demands on the government. The government has also changed in their attitudes and policies toward interest group activities from suspicion and distrust to accommodation and cooperation. Besides, the Hong Kong government in general and the top leadership in particular has become increasingly localized, with its members coming from the general society, bringing with them the latter's ethos and aspirations. This will provide a positive backdrop for participation by elements of the political society in the formation of public agenda and the general will."

However, the development of political society would also depend on certain antecedent conditions, including development of free and fair elections, political parties and public space, and a free press, among others. The political society was

further development. Of course, there are risks and uncertainties. However, given the existence of the factors and circumstances as canvassed, the civil society will not be easily suppressed or crushed without causing social turmoil and conflicts. The road for civil society will be bumpy. But the people of Hong Kong seem determined to push it forward. It seems that Hong Kong civil society will at best be tamed, but not be crushed.[30]

Bibliography

The Basic Law of the Hong Kong Special Administrative Region of the People's Republic of China. Hong Kong: The Consultative Committee for the Basic Law of the Hong Kong Special Administrative Region of the People's Republic of China, 1990.

Chamberlain, H. B. "On the Search for Civil Society in China." *Modern China* Vol. 19, No. 4 (1993), pp. 199–215.

Chan, W. K. *The Making of Hong Kong Society: Three Studies of Class Formation in Early Hong Kong.* Oxford: Clarendon Press, 1991.

Chandhoke, Meera. *State and Civil Society: Explorations in Political Theory.* New Delhi: Sage, 1995.

Cheek-Milby, Kathleen, and Miron Mushkat. *Hong Kong: The Challenge of Transformation.* Hong Kong: Centre of Asian Studies, The University of Hong Kong, 1989.

Cheng, Joseph Y. S., and Sonny S. H. Lo. *From Colony to SAR: Hong Kong's Challenges Ahead.* Hong Kong: The Chinese University Press, 1995.

---

still small, fragmented and weak on the eve of the Sino-British negotiations over the future of Hong Kong. It has grown substantially ever since.

Though political society as envisaged by Kuan is not the same as civil society as proposed here, there is some overlapping of features that should not be overlooked. It seems that political society represents some political portions of civil society which has a high level of autonomy and voluntary elements in them. If that is the case, what can be said of the political society can well be said of that portion of civil society. To go back to the three major features that characterize civil society: autonomy, legal entitlements of rights and liberties and social pluralism, it is obvious that each has close relationships with those factors, including free elections, public space, political parties, free press, which enhance the development of political society.

[30] This chapter has benefited from two recent discussions on this subject by Ian Scott, 1996 and H. C. Kuan, 1996. I would also like to thank the two anonymous reviewers for their helpful comments.

Cheung, Stephen Y. L., and Stephen M. H. Sze. *The Other Hong Kong Report 1995*. Hong Kong: The Chinese University Press, 1995.

Civil Liberty and Social Order: Consultation Document. Hong Kong: Chief Executive's Office, Hong Kong Special Administrative Region, The People's Republic of China, April 1997.

Habermas, J. *The Structural Transformation of the Public Sphere — An Enquiry into a Category of Bourgeois Society*. Translated by Thomas Burger with the assistance of Frederick Lawrence. Cambridge, MA: MIT Press, 1989.

Hall, John A. *Civil Society: Theory, History, Comparison*. Cambridge: Polity Press, 1995.

Ho, John D. "The Legal System: Are the Changes Too Little, Too Late?" In *The Other Hong Kong Report 1994*, edited by Donald H. McMillen and S. W. Man, pp. 9–22. Hong Kong: The Chinese University Press, 1994.

Hook, Brian. "Political Change in Hong Kong." *The China Quarterly*, Vol. 136 (1993), pp. 840–63.

Huntington, Samuel P. *Political Order in Changing Societies*. New Haven: Yale University Press, 1968.

Ip Po-keung. "Civil Society — The Liberal Conception." In *Human Rights and the Development of Civil Society*, edited by S. W. Man and C. F. Cheung, pp. 73–82. Hong Kong: Hong Kong Humanity Press, 1996. (in Chinese)

Keane, John. *Democracy and Civil Society*. London and New York: Verso, 1988.

Kuan Hsin-chi. "Escape from Politics: Hong Kong's Predicament of Political Development." Paper presented at the International Conference on Political Development in Taiwan and Hong Kong, co-sponsored by the Centre of Asian Studies, The University of Hong Kong and Institute for National Policy Research, Taipei, Taiwan, 8–9 February 1996.

———. "Power Dependence and Democratic Transition: The Case of Hong Kong." *The China Quarterly* Vol. 128 (1991), pp. 774–93.

Kwok, Rowena, Joan Leung, and Ian Scott. *Votes without Power, The Hong Kong Legislative Council Elections 1991*. Hong Kong: Hong Kong University Press, 1992.

Lau Siu-kai. "Decline of Governmental Authority, Political Cynicism and Political Inefficacy in Hong Kong." *Journal of Northeast Asian Studies*, Vol. 11, No. 2 (1992), pp. 3–20.

——— and Kuan Hsin-chi. *The Ethos of the Hong Kong Chinese*. Hong Kong: The Chinese University Press, 1988.

——— and Louie Kin-sheun. *Hong Kong Tried Democracy: The 1991 Elections in Hong Kong*. Hong Kong: Hong Kong Institute of Asia-Pacific Studies, The Chinese University of Hong Kong, 1993.

Lethbridge, Henry. *Hong Kong: Stability and Change*. Hong Kong: Oxford University Press, 1978.

Leung, Benjamin K. P., and Teresa Y. C. Wong. *25 Years of Social and Economic Development in Hong Kong*. Hong Kong: Centre of Asian Studies, 1994.

Loh, Christine. "The Implementation of the Sino-British Joint Declaration." In *The Other Hong Kong Report 1994*, edited by Donald H. McMillen and S. W. Man, pp. 61–74. Hong Kong: The Chinese University Press, 1994.

McMillen, Donald H., and S. W. Man. *The Other Hong Kong Report 1994*. Hong Kong: The Chinese University Press, 1994.

McMillen, Donald H., and Michael DeGolyer. *One Culture, Many Systems: Politics in the Reunification of China*. Hong Kong: The Chinese University Press, 1993.

Miners, N. *The Government and Politics of Hong Kong*. Hong Kong: Oxford University Press, 1986.

————. *Hong Kong under Imperial Rule: 1912–1941*. Hong Kong: Oxford University Press, 1987.

Mouzelis, Nicos. "Modernity, Late Development and Civil Society." In *Civil Society: Theory, History, Comparison*, edited by John A. Hall, pp. 224–49. Cambridge: Polity Press, 1995.

Rankin, Mary Backus. "The Origins of a Chinese Public Sphere: Local Elites and Community Affairs in the Late Imperial Period." *Etudes Chinoises*, Vol. 9, No. 2 (1990), pp. 13–60.

Rowe, W. T. "The Public Sphere in Modern China." *Modern China*, Vol. 16, No. 3 (1990), pp. 309–29.

————. "The Problem of 'Civil Society' in Late Imperial China." *Modern China*, Vol. 19, No. 2 (1993), pp. 139–57.

Scott, Ian. *Political Change and the Crisis of Legitimacy in Hong Kong*. Hong Kong: Oxford University Press, 1989.

————. "The State and Civil Society in Hong Kong." Paper presented at the International Conference on Political Development in Taiwan and Hong Kong, co-sponsored by the Centre of Asian Studies, The University of Hong Kong and Institute for National Policy Research, Taipei, 8–9 February 1996.

Seligman, A. *The Idea of Civil Society*. New York: The Free Press, 1992.

Sinn, Elizabeth Y. K. *Power and Charity: The Early History of the Tung Wah Hospital. Hong Kong*. Hong Kong: Oxford University Press, 1992.

The Sino-British Joint Declaration on the Future of Hong Kong. Hong Kong: Government Printer, 1984.

Stillman, P. "Hegel's Civil Society: A Locus of Freedom." *Polity*, Vol. 12 (1980), pp. 622–46.

Tang, James T. H. "Hong Kong's International Status." *The Pacific Review*, Vol. 6, No. 3 (1993), pp. 205–15.

Tsang, Steve Y. S. *Democracy Shelved: Great Britain, China and Attempts at Constitutional Reform in Hong Kong, 1945–1952*. Hong Kong: Oxford University Press, 1988.

Weigle, Maria A., and Jim Butterfly. "Civil Society in Reforming Communist Regimes: The Logic of Emergence." *Comparative Politics*, Vol. 23, No. 4 (1992), pp. 1–23.

8

The Hong Kong Fiscal Policy: Continuity or Redirection?

Tang Shu-hung

Introduction

The Sino-British Joint Declaration (1984) resolved that China will reassume its sovereignty over Hong Kong on 1 July 1997. The Basic Law (1990) of the Hong Kong Special Administrative Region (HKSAR) stipulates the political framework and budgetary policy. However, political and financial transition is both difficult and delicate. On the financial aspect, the Hong Kong government and the Chinese authority have to cooperate to draft the 1997–1998 Budget since the period of this financial year falls within the two sovereignties. The financial relationship between the present Hong Kong Government and the future HKSAR Government goes back as early as setting up the Land Fund in 1985 for the future HKSAR Government, according to Annex III of the Joint Declaration. The Memorandum of Understanding (MOU) on constructing the new airport in Hong Kong and other related matters signed in September 1991 also specified the financial obligations of the Hong Kong Government. In addition to these formal financial relationships and obligations, the Chinese authority has been regularly criticizing that the spending and revenue proposals of the Hong Kong Government's financial budgets since 1991–1992 have undermined the financial stability of, and imposed heavy financial burden on, the future HKSAR Government.[1] In particular, it was pointed out that

---

[1] Q. S. Yuen, "Betraying Conventional Budgetary Principles, Laying Hidden Disaster on the Future SAR," *Bauhinia Monthly*, Vol. 67 (1996), pp. 24–26. (in Chinese)

these budgetary measures did not conform to the principle of "keeping expenditure within the limits of revenues" as stipulated in Article 107 of the Basic Law.

Repeatedly, the Hong Kong Government has maintained that its financial budgets since 1990–1991 are consistent with the budgetary principles of the Basic Law.[2] The general public is very confused by these divergent interpretations, especially when these controversies are loaded with political connotation. At this crucial stage of sovereignty transfer, the general public is anxious to know how these controversies would affect Hong Kong's fiscal policy. This chapter tries to address this issue. Section II describes the fiscal philosophy and budgetary guidelines of the Hong Kong Government. Section III describes the formal financial relationship between the Hong Kong Government and the future HKSAR Government. Section IV presents an assessment of the fiscal performance of the Hong Kong Government according to the prevailing fiscal philosophy. Section V discusses the new development of the Hong Kong fiscal policy. The last Section discusses how these performance and development affect the fiscal policy in the transition period and beyond.

Fiscal Philosophy and Budgetary Guidelines

Colonial Regulations

In early years after the Hong Kong Government was set up in 1843, the philosophy and management of the Hong Kong fiscal system was governed by the Financial Procedures stipulated in the Colonial Regulations. The ultimate fiscal principle was self-support and balanced budget such that there was no need for the Exchequer of the United Kingdom to subsidize the colony. These financial procedures controlled the scope and scale of public expenditure and the financial reporting system of the colony. In 1855, the Hong Kong Government had reached the goal of financial self-support. However, the Hong Kong Government still adhered to these stringent financial procedures. In 1870, the Hong Kong Government was

---

[2] Sir Hamish emphasized in the 1995–1996 Budget that the prevailing fiscal policy and budgetary measures are consistent with the budgetary principles of the Basic Law (See Paragraph 7, 1995–1996 Budget). But he did not provide any explanation for such conclusion.

released from Treasury control of the United Kingdom and was given a greater degree of autonomy over its own finances. Treasury control was reintroduced in 1946 after Britain regained the control of Hong Kong from the Japanese occupation, and it was again relinquished in 1948 when the Hong Kong Government realized a budget surplus in 1947–1948. It was ten years later that the Hong Kong Government was granted quasi-full financial autonomy in view of its prudential financial management. The remaining control reserved by the Secretary of State of the United Kingdom was that prior approval should be obtained for raising loans by the Hong Kong Government when a guarantee by the United Kingdom may be required.[3] This was quite reasonable because it could serve as an indirect measure to control the unwarranted use of the deficit financing method. In fact, even this remaining control did not effectively diminish the degree of financial autonomy of the Hong Kong Government because it had already accumulated huge fiscal reserves which enabled it to obtain loans without collateral or guarantee from the United Kingdom.

Increasing financial autonomy does not mean relaxing prudential financial management procedures. Contrarily, even heavier pressure was exerted implicitly on the Hong Kong Government to obtain even better financial position than before the 1958 period. The Hong Kong Government adhered to the principles of financial management stipulated in the Colonial Regulations consistently throughout the post-World War II period, even after obtaining financial autonomy status in 1958. This implies that the Hong Kong fiscal system should generate budget surplus as much as possible in order to achieve financial stability. This is very different from the Keynesian theory which argues for using deficit budget to increase the level of aggregate demand such that the economy could be fine-tuned to reduce its cyclical fluctuation.[4] In other words, the objective of achieving financial stability is more important in Hong Kong than achieving economic stability as pursued in many Western industrialized countries.

---

3 A. Rabushka, *Value for Money: The Hong Kong Budgetary Process* (Stanford, CA: Hoover Institution Press, 1976), pp. 33–34.

[4] This explains why the most important objective of the Hong Kong tax system is to generate sufficient recurrent tax revenue to finance a major proportion of total expenditure and to maintain fiscal reserves at a satisfactory level.

Budgetary Guidelines since the 1970s

Budgetary Guidelines of the 1970s

To ensure the principle of "living within our means" be adhered to, the tax system must generate sufficient recurrent revenues and maintain fiscal reserves at a satisfactory level. At the operational level, successive financial secretaries had developed and refined budgetary guidelines to define the level of "sufficiency" and being "satisfactory." Sir Philips Haddon-Cave, the then financial secretary of the 1970s, systematically revised and extended these budgetary guidelines.[5] These guidelines are summarized as follows (Paragraphs 91–107, 1977–1978 Budget):

1. Recurrent expenditure should absorb no more than 80% of recurrent revenue and at least 60% of capital expenditure should be financed by the surplus on recurrent account. Recurrent expenditure should not be more than 70% of total expenditure.

2. The residual deficit on capital account should at least be financed half by capital revenue and no more than half with debt.

3. Annual debt service charges should not, at any time, exceed income earned on our fiscal reserves.

4. Recurrent revenues should at least be 88% of total expenditure.

5. The balance of the fiscal system is defined by the following two ratios: the ratio of direct to indirect taxation be targeted at 55:45; and the ratio of direct and indirect taxation taken together to all other recurrent revenue be targeted at 70:30.

6. The rate at which total expenditure by the public sector can grow annually in real terms, based on historical experience in the 1970s, can be taken to be about 10%.

7. The free fiscal reserves at the beginning of the financial year should at least be 15% of estimated expenditure.

In addition to these guideline ratios, Sir Philips also developed the

---

[5] Budgetary guidelines had been used before the 1970s to assist budgetary planning. In the 1970s, Sir Philips Haddon-Cave reviewed and refined these budgetary guidelines systematically and further developed them as an important fiscal discipline of the prudential budgetary management philosophy in Hong Kong. The development of the Hong Kong fiscal system is to a large extent directed by these budgetary guidelines which have been subject to periodic review.

following six requirements of the tax system (Paragraph 160, 1978–1979 Budget):

1. The tax system should help generate sufficient recurrent revenue to finance a major proportion of a given level of total expenditure and to maintain fiscal reserves at a satisfactory level.
2. The tax system is as neutral as possible as regards the internal cost/price structure, the supply of human effort and private investment decisions.
3. The laws governing the tax system are adopted from time to time to make them compatible with changing commercial practices.
4. Each and every levy is simple and easy (and therefore inexpensive) to administer for both the government and the taxpayer, and does not encourage evasion.
5. The tax system is equitable as between different classes of taxpayers or potential taxpayers and between different income groups.
6. Exceptionally, the tax system is capable of being used to achieve non-fiscal objectives when necessary.

The objective of these budgetary guidelines and requirements of the tax system is intended to impose a degree of fiscal discipline so as to achieve budget surplus and to follow the principle of "living within our means." Table 1 summarizes some important guideline ratios.

These budgetary guidelines are grounded in historical experience. Sir Philips emphasized that "none of them is absolute and they are no substitute for common sense, acceptance of economic reality, recognition of social needs, imaginative decision-making and a continuing emphasis on cost-effectiveness and cost-efficiency."

Budgetary Guidelines of the 1980s and 1990s

Under pressure of events, these budgetary guidelines have frequently been breached and are therefore subsequently be revised to better reflect the recent economic and financial reality. These budgetary guidelines were revised in 1982–1983 when Sir John Bremridge presented his maiden Budget Speech. This revision is summarized in Table 1 on budgetary guideline ratios, and in Table 4 on growth of public expenditure. The purpose of this revision was to reduce expenditure growth and to relax the constraint on the deficit level.

Table 1: Budgetary Guideline Ratios of Hong Kong

Guideline ratios		Before 1975–76	1975–76 to 1981–82	1982–83 to 1985–86	1986–87 to 1994–95
1. *Recurrent Revenues* Total Expenditure	At least	—	88%	77%	—
2. *Recurrent Expenditure* Recurrent Revenues	Not more than	70%	80%	85%	—
3. *Surplus in Recurrent* *Account* Non-recurrent Expenditure	At least	75%	60%	33%	50%
4. *Recurrent Expenditure* Total Expenditure	Not more than	—	70%	65%	—
5. *Non-recurrent* *Revenues* Non-recurrent Expenditure	At least	25%	20%	20%	—

Sources: S. H. Tang, *Issues of Public Finance in Hong Kong* (in Chinese) (Hong Kong: Wide Angle Press, 1988), p. 6. and *Budget*, Hong Kong Government, various issues.

In 1986–1987, the Medium Range Forecast (MRF) was introduced. The MRF is a medium term budgetary strategy comprising general economic assumptions and a wide range of detailed assumptions relating to developing expenditure and revenue patterns over the forecast period, and budgetary criteria (Appendix A, 1986–1987 Budget). The following are the more important budgetary criteria:

1. *Total cash flow surplus/deficit*
   The government aims to maintain adequate reserves in the long term.

2. *Operating surplus*
   A substantial element of capital expenditure must be financed from a surplus on operating account (recurrent revenue in relation to recurrent expenditure). A broad target of at least a 50% funding of capital expenditure from the operating surplus is adopted.

3. *Total expenditure growth*
   It is intended that, over time, expenditure growth should not exceed the assumption as to the trend growth in GDP.

4. *Capital expenditure growth*

By its nature some fluctuations in the level of capital expenditure are to be expected. However, over a period the aim is to contain capital expenditure growth within overall expenditure guidelines, i.e. within the assumption as to the trend GDP growth but allowance is made for unavoidable expenditure on exceptional projects. Allowance is also made for a number of major projects due to start in the forecast period. In planning the size of the capital programme regard has to be paid to the recurrent consequences of capital works (staffing, maintenance, etc.).

5. *Revenue policy*

The projections reflect the revenue measures introduced in this year's budget. Account is taken of the need to maintain the real yield from fees and charges, fixed duties etc., and to review periodically the various tax thresholds in the light of inflation.

The first two budgetary criteria deserve more discussion. Table 2 gives the budgetary guideline on total cash flow surplus/deficit. Since the public sector employs cash-based accounting system, total cash flow surplus/deficit thus in fact denotes budget surplus/deficit. The budgetary guideline on total cash flow surplus/deficit was first proposed in 1986–1987, though the principle of "living within our means" had been used long before. Table 2 shows the evolution of this new guideline. It is interesting to note that the budgetary guideline ratio given in Table 1 does not rule out the possibility of having a deficit budget. But the budgetary guideline on total cash flow surplus/deficit first emphasized obtaining annual cash flow surplus (from 1986–1987 to 1992–1993) in order to maintain the real value of the total balance of the General Revenue Account and the Funds Account (i.e. fiscal reserves). In 1993–1994, the focus of this guideline shifted from short-term emphasis to long-term consideration. It states that the Hong Kong Government aims to maintain adequate reserves in the long term. The effect of the 1993–1994 version of the budgetary guideline on total cash flow surplus/deficit is to give the financial secretary more flexibility in formulating budgetary policy, as long as it satisfies the guideline on fiscal reserves. However, the degree of "adequacy" of fiscal reserves is undefined and the short-term policy prescription is unspecified.

Table 3 shows the evolution of the guideline on the "satisfactory" level of fiscal reserves. It was first tied to budget revenues, then to recurrent expenditure, and then switched to tie to total expenditure since 1988–1989.

Table 2: Budgetary Guideline on Total Cash Flow Surplus/Deficit: 1986–87 to 1993–94

Period	Guideline on total cash flow surplus/deficit
1986–87 to 1987–88	As a general aim, a cash flow balance is sought, although erring on the side of surplus, to ensure that total balances in General Revenue Account and in the Funds gradually increase to maintain their real value.
1988–89	As a general aim, a cash flow surplus is sought each year to ensure that total reserves in General Revenue Account and in the Funds maintain their value in real terms. On the basis of the current level of reserves an annual surplus of $2.0 billion is necessary to achieve this objective.
1989–90	As a general aim, a cash flow surplus is sought each year to ensure that total reserves in General Revenue Account and in the Funds maintain their value in real terms. On the basis of the current level of reserves annual surplus of around $3.0 billion is necessary to achieve this objective.
1990–91 to 1992–93	As a general aim, a cash flow surplus is sought so that in the long term adequate reserves are maintained.
1993–94 to Present	The government aims to maintain adequate reserves in the long term.

Sources: *Budget*, Hong Kong Government, various issues.

Table 3: Guideline on Fiscal Reserves of Hong Kong

Period	Guideline
1947–48 to 1961–62	At the beginning of the financial year, the fiscal reserve should not be less than the revenue estimate of that financial budget.
1962–63 to 1976–77	At the beginning of the financial year, the fiscal reserve should not be less than 50% of the recurrent expenditure of that financial budget.
1977–78 to 1987–88	At the beginning of the financial year, the free fiscal reserve should not be less than 15% of the total expenditure of that financial budget.
1988–89 to Present	At the beginning of the financial year, the reserve balance should not be less than 50% of total public expenditure of that financial budget. (Informal Guideline)

Sources: S. H. Tang, *Hong Kong Public Finance in the Transitional Period* (in Chinese) (Hong Kong: Joint Publishing, 1992), p. 179 and *Budget*, Hong Kong Government, various issues.

The purpose of this guideline ratio is to set the minimum level of fiscal reserves. One of the functions of fiscal reserves is to finance deficits. Tying the minimum level of fiscal reserves to a specific level of total public expenditure would impose an additional internal constraint on the growth of total public expenditure. When Sir John adopted a new set of budgetary guideline ratios in 1986–1987, the guideline ratio on fiscal reserves was not mentioned explicitly. It was argued that there had no absolute rule as to the correct level of fiscal reserves (Paragraph 68, 1987–1988 Budget). The present Financial Secretary, Mr. Donald Tsang refused to give a formula on determining the minimum level of fiscal reserves, regardless of repeated request from the legislative councillors, general public, political parties and the business sector. In the 1996–1997 Budget, Mr. Tsang reiterated that "the appropriate level of reserves over the long run can be a matter for debate. But let me state unequivocally. This is not the time, with all its inherent uncertainties, to reduce the cushion of healthy reserves that Hong Kong at present enjoys. Our reserves underpin the soundness of our financial system and must be maintained." (Paragraph 51, 1996–1997 Budget).

Notwithstanding these repeated statements of giving no official guideline on the minimum level of fiscal reserves, there were some hints given in the MRF discussions of the 1988–1989 and subsequent budgets on this issue. My research suggests that the new guideline could be as follows: "At the beginning of the financial year, the reserve balance should not be less than 50% of total public expenditure." This is only my interpretation. I therefore call it an "informal guideline." Detailed calculation shows that the required minimum level of fiscal reserves derived from this informal guideline is very similar to those obtained under the 1977–1978 to 1985–1986 guideline.[6]

Linking the objective of the guideline on total cash flow surplus/deficit to maintaining adequate reserves reflects the conservative approach of budgetary management in Hong Kong. The guideline on expenditure growth also follows the same philosophy. Table 4 shows the evolution of the budgetary guideline on total expenditure growth since the 1970s.

---

[6] S. H. Tang, *Guideline on Fiscal Reserves in Hong Kong and Its Implication on Funding the New Airport Project* (BRC Working Paper ES 91017, School of Business, Hong Kong Baptist University, 1991); S. H. Tang, *Hong Kong Public Finance in the Transitional Period* (in Chinese) (Hong Kong: Joint Publishing, 1992), pp. 164–80.

Table 4: Budgetary Guideline on Expenditure Growth of Hong Kong

Period	Guideline ratio
1972–73 to 1982–83	The real growth rate of total expenditure is 10%. (Haddon-Cave Guideline)
1983–84 to 1985–86	The nominal growth rate of total expenditure is 10%. (Bremridge Guideline)
1986–87	Total expenditure growth in real terms should not exceed the growth in GDP. (Bremridge Guideline)
1987–88 to Present	It is intended that, over time, expenditure growth should not exceed the assumption as to the trend growth in GDP. (Jacobs Guideline)

Sources: S. H. Tang, *Issues of Public Finance in Hong Kong*, and *Budget*, Hong Kong Government, various issues.

The 1987–1988 guideline on expenditure growth is still in force. The trend real growth rate refers to the average real GDP growth rate of each financial budget's MRF five-year period. For planning purpose, the trend expenditure growth is held to be slightly below GDP growth to provide room for manoeuvre in the face of unforeseen circumstances (Appendix C, 1987–1988 Budget). However, the interpretation and assessment of this guideline has always been problematic. First, the guideline does not clarify whether it refers to "public expenditure" or "government expenditure." Government expenditure is the sum of expenditure charged to General Revenue Account in accordance with the Appropriation Bill, excluding transfers to funds and expenditure charged to statutory funds. Public expenditure comprises government expenditure and other public bodies expenditure.[7] From the nature of the Jacobs expenditure guideline and the

---

[7] Defining "expenditure" has always been problematic since there is no unique definition adopted internationally. In Hong Kong, expenditure by those organizations including statutory organizations, in which the government has only an equity position, such as Mass Transit Railway Corporation and the Kowloon–Canton Railway, is not included. There were heated debates between the legislative councillors and Sir John in the mid-1980s on this official definition. The councillor Ms. Lydia Dunn suggested that it should be included. This controversy remains unresolved. Similarly, equity injection by the Hong Kong Government to these statutory organizations also subject to the same definitional debate. Previously they

data and diagrams given in the financial budget, it is the common under-standing of the general public that the guideline qualifies public expendi-ture growth, not government expenditure growth. Since the real growth of public expenditure is in general higher than government expenditure and GDP, especially for the two deficits budgets in 1993–1994 and 1995–1996, Sir Hamish Macleod, the former Financial Secretary was criticized for violating the guideline on expenditure growth. Sir Hamish did respond to these criticisms but did not clarify the true interpretation of the guideline. In the 1995–1996 Budget, Sir Hamish argued that the budget deficit did not arise from higher expenditure growth than what the guideline permitted. He clarified that the guideline referred to government expenditure because it has under the control of the government and subject to the scrutiny of the legislature, and not to public expenditure because some public bodies were self-financing. He also argued that the test for compliance with this guideline could not be concluded by simply looking at two years' figures because the concepts of "trend" and "over time" extending to at least five years. Sir Hamish's clarification was viewed as relaxing some-what the guideline on expenditure growth (Paragraphs 8–15, Financial Secretary's concluding remarks on the 1996–1997 Budget Debate).

With increasing electoral representation in the Legislative Council, the government is more specific in describing its policy stance. In the 1995–1996 Budget, Sir Hamish identified the following seven fundamentals of the prevailing fiscal and budgetary policies in Hong Kong, and labelled it the Hong Kong approach "Consensus Capitalism" (Paragraph 5, 1995–1996 Budget):

1. I have held fast to the living-within-our-means rule of public expenditure. This most vital of all our principles ensures that over time government spending grows no faster than the economy as a whole. It is a delightfully simple concept which has proved to be remarkably effective in avoiding a bloated bureaucracy.

---

were treated as non-recurrent expenditure which was a component of government expenditure. But starting from 1991–1992, the Capital Investment Fund was set up to finance equity injection into these statutory organizations. Since then, ad-vances and equity investments from the Capital Investment Fund are excluded from government expenditure, but they are included in the calculation of the consolidated cash flow surplus/deficit.

2. I have planned for the long term whilst dealing prudently and realistically with the actual circumstances that face us.
3. I have kept in mind the simple principle that, to quote last year's Budget Speech, the government should leave money where it can do most good, in the pockets of the taxpayers.
4. I have held firm to my belief in private enterprise and small government. Because, again to quote myself, only in this way can we ensure that business will have the freedom and the opportunity to generate the wealth Hong Kong needs.
5. But I also accept that we cannot leave everything to the private sector. The government has a plain duty to provide the social, physical and regulatory infrastructure which supports the private sector.
6. I share the community's belief that the government has special social responsibilities, in particular towards the disadvantaged, the disabled and the vulnerable. This priority is demonstrated by the fact that no less than 45% of our recurrent expenditure is devoted to health, social welfare and education. And this is in addition to our massive housing programme.
7. I also believe that fair and orderly markets are essential to our economic success. And, of course, the linked exchange rate is a vital ingredient in ensuring the stability which investors need.

What makes these seven fundamentals important is its emphasis on the government's responsibility in providing the social, physical and regulatory infrastructure, and the spending priority in social services. This is the first time Sir Hamish mentioning the spending priority issue, an issue which has not been dealt with by the previous expenditure guidelines. It thus provides a basis for further discussion on spending priority, especially on funding the social and economic development of the next decade.

Revenue policy is one of the MRF's budgetary guidelines. But it only focuses on maintaining the real yield of tax revenues and revenues from fees and charges. It is therefore far from being a comprehensive tax policy with multiple objectives. The controversies on the appropriate levels of personal allowances, the direct tax rates, the fiscal reserves, and the contribution from each financial resource, etc. remain unsettled mainly because of the lack of a comprehensive official tax and revenue policy and the accompanying support from the general public. In the 1996–1997 Budget, Mr. Donald Tsang stated the following seven principles, also labelled as the "seven heavenly virtues," of the tax and revenue policy in Hong Kong (Paragraph 47, 1996–1997 Budget):

1. retain a low, simple and predictable tax regime;
2. raise sufficient revenue to meet known spending commitments;
3. maintain a rigorous "user-pays" system for setting fees and charges so as to keep tax rates low;
4. keep adequate fiscal reserves to provide a cushion against future uncertainties;
5. combat tax avoidance and evasion;
6. provide concessions where most needed; and, finally,
7. minimize the inflationary impact.

The nature and function of these seven heavenly virtues are very similar to Sir Philips' six requirements of the Hong Kong tax system, except that the seven heavenly virtues mention nothing about tax equity, but emphasize the relationship between user-pays principle on government services and low tax rate policy. The emphasis on user-pays principle and full cost pricing reflects the government's intention to shift the burden more to indirect taxation. Moreover, the shifting emphasis from "sufficient recurrent revenue" to "sufficient revenue" is also a major policy change.

Formal Financial Relationship between the Hong Kong Government and the Future HKSAR Government

Before assessing the performance of the Hong Kong fiscal system against these budgetary guidelines and policies, we have to describe and discuss the financial relationship between the present Hong Kong Government and the future HKSAR Government.

The Land Fund of the HKSAR Government

According to paragraph 6 of the Annex III of the Sino-British Joint Declaration on Hong Kong's future, from the entry into force of the Joint Declaration until 30 June 1997, premium income from land transactions of the Hong Kong Government, after deducting the land development cost, are shared equally between the Hong Kong Government and the future HKSAR Government. The future HKSAR Government's share is credited to the Land Fund, which is administered by the Chinese side. Since premium income allotted to the future HKSAR Government could not be treated as non-recurrent revenues of the current financial budget of the Hong Kong Government, it thus introduces a new element of conservatism into the already over-prudential philosophy of budgetary management in Hong Kong.[8]

Building the New Airport: Memorandum of Understanding (MOU) and Financial Arrangement

The Hong Kong Government decided in October 1989 to build a new airport at Chek Lap Kok. Since this is a long-term and massive investment infrastructure project, it will extend beyond the sovereignty transfer in 1997. The endorsement and blessing from the Chinese Government is essential for securing long-term contractual and funding (borrowing) arrangements for the new airport project. The Chinese negotiation team came to Hong Kong in October 1990 to discuss the technical issues and economic viability of the new airport, and the financial obligations of the Hong Kong Government. After intensive negotiations and secret diplomatic talks, the "Memorandum of Understanding Concerning the Construction of the New Airport in Hong Kong and Related Questions" (MOU) (1991) was signed on 3 September 1991 in Beijing. The following two understandings specify the financial relationship between the Hong Kong Government and the future HKSAR Government:

1. The Chinese Government will adopt a positive attitude to necessary and reasonable borrowing by the Hong Kong Government to be repaid after 30 June 1997. If the total amount of debt to be repaid after 30 June 1997 will not exceed HK Dollars 5 billion, the Hong Kong Government will be free to borrow as necessary while informing the Chinese Government. If the total amount of such debt will exceed HK Dollars 5 billion such borrowing will only proceed if a common view has been reached concerning the proposal.

2. On the basis of the above understanding the Hong Kong Government will plan its finances with the firm objective that the fiscal

---

[8] S. H. Tang, "A Critical Review of the 1995–96 Budget," in *The Other Hong Kong Report 1995*, edited by Stephen Y. L. Cheung and Stephen M. H. Sze (Hong Kong: The Chinese University Press, 1995).

reserves on 30 June 1997 to be left for the use of the Hong Kong Special Administrative Region Government will not be less than HK Dollars 25 billion.

The effect of these two understandings is to give $20 billion net to the future HKSAR Government, in addition to completing the ten new airport projects as much as possible before 30 June 1997. The MOU gives only the broad provisions of the financial relationship between the two governments, while the actual financial arrangement for the new airport and airport railway has to be resolved by the Airport Committee of the Sino-British Joint Liaison Group. The following Financial Arrangement, signed on 4 November 1994, specified the amount of equity injection and debt ceiling:

> *Arrangements for Equity and Debt*: The Hong Kong Government will make arrangements to inject equity of not less than $60.3 billion into the new airport at Chek Lap Kok (first runway and associated facilities) and the airport railway. The total borrowings in respect of the two projects outstanding at the time the projects shall have been completed will be not more than $23 billion. Such borrowings will not need to be guaranteed or repaid by the Government, and the statutory body currently known as the Provisional Airport Authority and the Mass Transit Railway Corporation will be liable for the repayment of such debts in full.

The MOU and Financial Arrangement set limits on fiscal reserves, equity injection and debt ceiling. All these have important fiscal implications on the financial budgets of the 1990s.

Assessment of Fiscal Performance

Budget and Actual Surplus/Deficit

There are many criteria in assessing whether the budgetary performance achieves the objective of financial stability. The most important one is the actual surplus/deficit of the financial budgets. Table 5 compares the budget and actual surplus/deficit of the financial budgets since 1946–1947. Since the very objective of financial management of the Colonial Regulations is to avoid deficit, Table 5 shows the relationship between total expenditure and GDP. Among the 51 financial budgets since 1946–1947, there were 23 deficit budgets, i.e. 45%, and only 7 realized actual deficits. The realized deficits in these seven years were due mainly to economic recessions, rather than to adopting expansionary fiscal policy to stimulate the

Table 5: Comparison of Budget and Actual Surplus/Deficit of
Hong Kong (in HK$ million)

Financial year	Budget surplus (+) or deficit (−)	Budget deficit as a % of budget total expenditure	Budget deficit as a % of forecast GDP by the budget	Actual surplus (+) or deficit (−)	Actual deficit as a % of actual total expenditure	Actual deficit as a % of final GDP estimates
1946–47	−116.5	69.4%		−3.5	4.0%	
1947–48	0.0			+36.6		
1948–49	+1.1			+35.0		
1949–50	+0.2			+82.1		
1950–51	+3.3			+40.0		
1951–52	+13.1			+32.7		
1952–53	+2.1			+72.8		
1953–54	+20.5			+41.5		
1954–55	+1.2			+61.1		
1955–56	−35.4	7.9%		+52.3		
1956–57	−43.3	8.8%		+40.1		
1957–58	−53.7	8.6%		+51.1		
1958–59	−94.1	14.5%		+39.4		
1959–60	−92.4	13.3%		−45.3	6.4%	
1960–61	−226.1	24.1%		+13.9		
1961–62	−160.9	15.0%		+77.2		
1962–63	−163.9	13.4%		+139.8		
1963–64	−163.0	12.0%	12.0%	+98.5		
1964–65	−114.3	7.6%	7.6%	+77.8		
1965–66	−60.0	3.5%		−137.4	7.8%	1.0%
1966–67	−94.1	5.0%		+11.7		
1967–68	−37.0	1.9%		+133.5		
1968–69	−13.0	0.7%		+208.1		
1969–70	+53.4			+448.5		
1970–71	+191.1			+618.7		
1971–72	+256.0			+640.0		
1972–73	+47.0			+636.0		
1973–74	+200.0			+71.6		
1974–75	+12.0			−378.0	5.6%	0.8%
1975–76	−431.0	6.5%	1.3%	+232.0		
1976–77	−355.0	4.9%	0.9%	+917.0		
1977–78	+30.0		0.03%	+1225.0		
1978–79	−20.0	0.2%		+1488.0		
1979–80	+2318.0			+2975.0		
1980–81	+9323.0			+10512.0		

Table 5 (Cont'd)

Financial year	Budget surplus (+) or deficit (−)	Budget deficit as a % of budget total expenditure	Budget deficit as a % of forecast GDP by the budget	Actual surplus (+) or deficit (−)	Actual deficit as a % of actual total expenditure	Actual deficit as a % of final GDP estimates
1981–82	+7881.0			+6535.0		
1982–83	+2326.0			−3500.0	9.8%	1.8%
1983–84	−3167.0	7.5%	1.8%	−2993.0	7.8%	1.4%
1984–85	−2091.0	4.8%	0.9%	−559.0	1.4%	0.2%
1985–86	−1155.0	2.5%	0.4%	+1443.0		
1986–87	+348.0			+4920.0		
1987–88	+2400.0			+10590.0		
1988–89	+5500.0			+18862.0		
1989–90	+11470.0			+11064.0		
1990–91	+720.0			+3967.0		
1991–92	+1300.0			+22508.0		
1992–93	+7550.0			+21979.0		
1993–94	−3360.0	2.2%	0.4%	+19164.0		
1994–95	+7660.0			+10843.0		
1995–96	−2620.0	1.4%	0.2%	−2465.0*	1.3%	0.2%*
1996–97	+1600.0					

Notes: (1) Budgetary figures before 1989–1990 are from General Revenue Account, and from Consolidated Accounts since 1989–1990.

  (2) Total expenditure before 1986–1987 refers to total public expenditure, and to total government expenditure since 1986–1987.

  (3) "*" denotes revised estimate.

  (4) 1996–1997 is budget estimate.

Sources: Calculated from *Budget and Estimates of Gross Domestic Product*, Hong Kong Government, various issues.

economy. It has been emphasized repeatedly by successive financial secretaries that one of the objectives of the annual budget is to ensure that Hong Kong is not in danger of "living beyond our means." However, the philosophy of "living within our means" does not imply that there should not be any deficit budgets, but the way in which the deficit is financed in Hong Kong is very different from Western countries. In Western industrialized countries, budget deficits are either financed by bond issuing or money printing. But in Hong Kong, the government prefers to use fiscal reserves rather than issuing public bonds to finance budget deficits.[9] This is in line with the financial principle of the Colonial Regulations to avoid bond issuing as much as possible.

As evidenced from Table 5, the actual budget outcome is very different from the original budget estimate. Budget deficits usually turned out to be actual surpluses. The reasons for this sharp contrast had been identified as overestimating expenditure but underspending, and underestimating revenues in budgeting.[10] The underspending in some years had been as high as 10% of budget estimation and usually non-recurrent items absorbed much of the underspending. It thus reflected that the Hong Kong Government refrained from spending up to the approved amount in order to contain the deficit, or to turn the budget deficit into actual surplus so as to accumulate fiscal reserves. The Hong Kong Government has never used public expenditure as an instrument to stimulate the economy, in a strict Keynesian sense. The deficit budgets from 1955–1956 to 1968–1969 were derived mainly from increased public expenditure on social and economic services that were essential to Hong Kong's economic development. The proposed budget deficits could also be used as an excuse to raise tax rates or to levy new taxes. Since the Hong Kong Government refrained from spending up to the approved amount and the nature of the previous deficit budgets of the Hong Kong Government was very different from the Keynesian anti-cyclical expansion of aggregate demand, it could be argued

---

[9] In a widely quoted 1963–1964 Budget Speech, the financial secretary argued against using money-financed budget deficits. He said: "But I will not be proposing a course which has been under some public discussion recently — deficit financing. It is wholly inappropriate to our economic situation. In its least extreme form it is based on the theory that additional money generated by a government deficit (and given currency, as necessary, by use of the printing press) will stimulate consumption and thereby production, in time to match the excess money with goods before real inflationary harm is done. Unfortunately we don't, and can't, produce more than a small fraction of what we consume, and increased consumption would merely mean increased imports without matching exports; and a severe balance of payment crisis, which would destroy Hong Kong's credit and confidence in the Hong Kong dollar; and which we could not cure without coming close to ruining ourselves. Keynes was not writing with our situation in mind. In this hard world we have to earn before we spend." Quoted from *Hong Kong Hansard*, 1962–63, p. 50.

[10] A. Rabushka, *Value for Money*, p. 4.

that deficit budgets over the past five decades in Hong Kong did not violate the principle of "living within our means." Table 6 shows the extent of overestimating expenditure (i.e. underspending) and underestimating revenues in the financial years with deficit budgets. At the beginning of the 1996–1997 Budget, the fiscal reserves amount to $150 billion, which

Table 6: Budget and Actual Surplus/Deficit of Hong Kong
(in HK $million)

Financial year	Budget surplus (+)/ deficit (−)	Actual surplus (+)/ deficit (−)	Expenditure overestimation (Budget exp. − actual exp.)	Revenue underestimation (Actual revenue − budget revenue)
1946–47	−116.5	−3.5	+82.2	+30.8
1955–56	−35.4	+52.3	+46.5	+41.0
1956–57	−43.3	+40.1	+23.8	+69.8
1957–58	−53.7	+51.5	+28.5	+76.7
1958–59	−94.1	+39.4	+58.1	+75.2
1959–60	−92.4	−45.3	−17.0	+64.0
1960–61	−226.1	+13.9	+93.0	+147.0
1961–62	−160.9	+77.2	+121.4	+116.7
1962–63	−163.9	+139.8	+113.1	+190.6
1963–64	−163.0	+98.5	+64.6	+196.8
1964–65	−114.3	+77.8	+35.5	+136.6
1965–66	−60.0	−137.4	−57.7	−19.7
1966–67	−94.1	+11.7	+72.3	+33.5
1967–68	−37.0	+133.5	+156.6	+13.9
1968–69	−13.0	+208.1	+92.4	+128.8
1974–75	+12.0	−378.0	−7.0	−383.0
1975–76	−431.0	+232.0	+592.0	+49.0
1976–77	−355.0	+917.0	+635.0	+637.0
1978–79	−20.0	+1486.0	−690.0	+2196.0
1982–83	+2326.0	−3500.0	+902.0	−6728.0
1983–84	−3167.0	−2993.0	+2044.0	−1870.0
1984–85	−2091.0	−559.0	+383.0	+1149.0
1985–86	−1155.0	+1443.0	−1490.0	+4088.0
1993–94	−3360.0	+19614.0	+5952.0	+16572.0
1995–96	−2620.0	−2465.0*	+8369.0	−8214.0

* Revised estimate

Sources: *Budget*, Hong Kong Government, various issues and *Annual Report of the Director of Accounting Services and the Accounts of Hong Kong*, Hong Kong Government, various issues.

is equivalent to 81.7% of the estimated total government expenditure, more than satisfying the guideline on fiscal reserves.

Real Growth of Total Expenditure and the Size of the Public Sector

The guideline requires that, over time, total expenditure growth should not exceed the assumption as to the trend growth in GDP. Sir Hamish has clarified that total expenditure refers to total "government expenditure." Table 7 shows the real expenditure growth since 1986–1987, the first year adopting the MRF budgetary guideline. It is not easy to assess whether the expenditure growth conforms to the guideline because of the difficulty in obtaining the data on expenditure growth; and the ambiguity in interpreting the guideline. First, the financial budget does not give the growth rate, nominal or real, on either the estimated or actual government expenditure. The financial budget gives only the nominal estimate of the government expenditure for the same financial year. Having no information on the revised estimate of the government expenditure of the last financial year, and knowing nothing about the implicit price indexes for different categories of government expenditure, it would be impossible to construct the accurate time series of the real growth rate of government expenditure. On the other hand, the annual financial budget gives both the nominal and real growth rates of the public expenditure, although it is not referred by the budgetary guideline. The data on real growth rate of actual government expenditure in Table 7 was in fact given by the Secretary for the Treasury, Mr. K. C. Kwong in his reply to the Honourable Dr. Huang Chen-ya's written enquiry on the time series of government expenditure. Since this is not part of the time series data given regularly in the appendix of the Budget Speech, there is no guarantee that it will be available in the future and to the public. Second, the concepts of "trend" and "over time" may subject to different interpretations. Since one financial year involves in six MRFs which could extend its relationship to eight other financial years, the guideline does not specify clearly how this trend is defined and measured.

Without a clear definition and published data, there are bound to be many criticisms levelling against the government for violating the expenditure guideline. After avoiding to address to these criticisms for many years, Sir Hamish Macleod, in the concluding remarks on the debate of his last budget, i.e. the 1995–1996 Budget, did clarify two ambiguities: (1) the guideline applies to government expenditure only, and (2) the concepts of

Table 7: Real Expenditure Growth of Hong Kong, 1987–88 to 1996–97

Financial year	Total public expenditure		Recurrent government expenditure	Total government expenditure	Real gross domestic product (GDP)			Size of the public sector	
	Budget estimate %	Actual %	Budget estimate %	Actual %	MRF trend growth rate %	Budget estimate %	Actual %	Budget estimate %	Actual %
1987–88	4.9	3.5	—	2.5	5.5	6.3	13.0	16.6	13.9
1988–89	7.0	8.0	—	5.8	5.5	5.0	8.0	15.6	14.2
1989–90	9.0	10.7	—	11.8	6.0	6.0	2.6	16.4	15.6
1990–91	9.4	2.3	—	2.5	5.5	3.0	3.4	18.8	16.3
1991–92	8.2	2.9	—	3.1	5.5	3.5	5.1	19.3	16.2
1992–93	7.7	3.2	—	4.9	5.0	5.0	6.3	18.8	15.8
1993–94	12.5	15.5	5.2	17.3	5.0	5.5	6.1	18.5	17.3
1994–95	1.2	−2.2	5.0	−2.2	5.0	5.5	5.4	18.1	16.3
1995–96	9.3	8.3	5.9	5.0	5.0	5.5	4.6	17.6	17.6*
1996–97	7.6		5.6	5.7	5.0	5.0		18.0	

Notes: (1) "*" denotes revised estimate.

(2) The size of the Public Sector is measured by the proportion of total public expenditure to Gross Domestic Product in nominal terms. Since expenditures incurred by statutory organizations such as Kowloon–Canton Railway (KCR) and Mass Transit Railway (MTR) are not included in calculating total public expenditure, the actual size of public sector in Hong Kong is thus underestimated by about 2% on average.

(3) Starting from the 1993–1994 Budget, real growth rate of recurrent government expenditure is given in the MRF. But real growth rate of total government expenditure is still not announced yet.

Sources: (1) Budget, Hong Kong Government, various issues.

(2) Annual Report of the Director of Accounting Services and the Accounts of Hong Kong, Hong Kong Government, various issues.

(3) The data on real total government expenditure growth was given by the Secretary for the Treasury in his reply on 27 March 1996 to the Honourable Dr. Huang Chen-ya's enquiry.

"trend" and "over time" extend to at least five years. Sir Hamish gave the following summary statistics to substantiate his conclusion that the expenditure guideline is being firmly adhered to (Paragraph 15, Financial Secretary's Concluding Remarks on the Debate on the 1995 Appropriation Bill):

1. Since the introduction of the MRF in 1986–1987, total government expenditure has increased in real terms by 68% compared to cumulative GDP real growth over the same period of 69%.
2. Over the three years to 1995–1996 (in other words using 1992–1993 as the base year) recurrent government expenditure will have grown by 16% compared to the real growth in GDP of 17%. Over the same period, government spending on capital works (at 1994–1995 prices) will be $83.2 billion against a permitted expenditure ceiling of $93 billion.
3. Public expenditure in 1995–1996 will be only 17.6% of GDP and is forecast to remain below 18% for the remainder of the forecast period to 1998–1999.

Sir Hamish was referring to the ten years period starting from 1986–1987, the year when MRF was first introduced, to 1995–1996. One could argue that this ten-year period could be divided into two five-year MRF periods, i.e. from 1986–1987 to 1990–1991, and from 1991–1992 to 1995–1996. Calculating the accumulated growth rates of these two five-year periods shows that both MRFs satisfy the expenditure guideline. Since Sir Hamish uses the actual value in assessing the conformity to expenditure guideline, it does cast doubt to the relevance of the annual budget debate which discusses mainly the estimated real expenditure growth of a financial budget.

Table 7 also shows the size of the public sector since 1987–1988. Small government is one of the objectives of the Hong Kong fiscal system. The size of the public sector has never exceeded 20%. In 1986–1987 when the MRF was first launched, the size of the public sector was 16.7% in the budget estimate and 15.3% in the final value. Since the accumulated real growth rate of government expenditure from 1986–1987 to 1995–1996 is smaller than the corresponding GDP real growth rate, it follows roughly that the size of the public sector in 1995–1996 should not deviate much from the 1986–1987 actual value. But in 1995–1996, the size of the public sector rose to 17.6%, which is 2.3% higher than the 1986–1987 figure. There are two reasons explaining for this increase. First, there has been substantial increase in non-public bodies (i.e. statutory organizations) expenditure since the early 1990s, especially after several government departments establishing their respective Trading Funds. Consequently the growth of public expenditure is greater than that of government expenditure. Second, the implicit price deflator for government expenditure is in general greater than that for GDP. Thus, satisfying the guideline on government expenditure growth does not prohibit the size of the public sector from rising. Nevertheless, the size of the public sector in 1996–1997 is estimated at 18.0%, which is still within the 20% ceiling, even after massive spending on the new airport project.

Spending Priority

One of the seven fundamentals in budgetary planning, as described in the 1995–1996 Budget, is the government's special social responsibilities, especially towards the disadvantaged, the disabled and the vulnerable. It states that "[T]his priority is demonstrated by the fact that no less than 45% of our recurrent expenditure is devoted to health, social welfare and education." This policy sets the minimum percentage of recurrent public expenditure on three important social services. Table 8 gives the time series of these percentages. Data on recurrent public expenditure by policy area groups was first given in the 1993–1994 Budget, and traced back to 1988–

Table 8: Recurrent Public Expenditure by Policy Area Groups as a % of Total Recurrent Public Expenditure

	Social Welfare (SW)	Health (H)	Education (E)	Total of SW, H and E
1988–89	7.8	10.6	21.4	39.8
1989–90	7.9	10.9	20.4	39.2
1990–91	7.2	11.3	21.7	40.2
1991–92	7.8	11.8	20.8	40.4
1992–93	7.7	13.5	21.3	42.5
1993–94	8.4	13.8	21.4	43.6
1994–95	8.7	14.2	21.9	44.8
1995–96*	9.4	14.1	21.5	45.0
1996–97**	10.1	13.8	21.0	44.9

 * Revised estimates
** Budget estimates
Sources: *Budget*, Hong Kong Government, various issues.

1989. It is interesting to note that from 1994–1995 to 1996–1997, the percentage is around 45% which is the minimum level stated in the 1995–1996 Budget. Two observations could be raised from Table 8. First, there has been continuously shifting of spending priority among the three social services since 1988–1989. Spending percentage on social welfare has been increasing from 7.8% in 1988–1989 to 10.1% in 1996–1997. It is predicted that the trend in social welfare spending will be continuously increasing due to the ageing population and worsening unemployment and underemployment situation. Spending percentage on health also experiences similar rate of increase but starting from 1995–1996, the upward trend since 1988–1989 is reversed. It is unclear whether this represents a major policy shift. On the other hand, spending percentage on education maintains a rather stable 21% throughout the period, despite the pledge from the government to increase education spending. Second, there is no discussion on the underlying rationale for the 45% criterion. Apparently, it is based on the estimates of the 1995–1996 Budget, reflecting more on historical development than on any consensus or justifiable reasons on the development of these three social service areas.

Adding Land Fund: The True Financial Position

Based on the above assessment, it is evident that the conservative fiscal discipline has been firmly adhered to since 1946–1947. All budgetary guidelines have been followed. Both the size of the public sector and the tax rates of direct taxation are less than 20%.[11] The amount of fiscal reserves is more than adequate. However, it was argued that the fiscal and budgetary policy since the mid-1980s became more conservative because the Land Fund institutionalized a conservative element into the already over prudential fiscal system in Hong Kong. Table 9 presents the true financial position of the Hong Kong Government after including the annual income of Land Fund into the consolidated account. The last column of Table 9 shows that if the annual incomes of the Land Fund were added on, the government would have achieved huge surplus budgets for the past ten

---

[11] It was proposed in the 1960s that the ceiling for the size of the public sector and the direct tax rate in Hong Kong should not be more than 20%. For detailed discussion and reference, see S. H. Tang, *Issues of Public Finance in Hong Kong*, pp. 119–45.

Table 9: The Financial Position of the Land Fund, 1985–86 to 1996–97 (in HK $million)

Financial year	Budget estimate of land premium income alloted to Land Fund	Actual amount of land premium income alloted to Land Fund	Actual interest income of Land Fund	Actual land premium income and interest income of Land Fund	Budget surplus/ deficit (before adjustment)	Budget surplus/ deficit (after adjustment)	Actual surplus/ deficit (before adjustment)	Actual surplus/ deficit (after adjustment)
1985–86		423.0	2.0	425.0	–1155.0	–1155.0	1443.0	1868.0
1986–87	1404.0	1871.0	87.0	1958.0	348.0	1752.0	4920.0	6878.0
1987–88	1698.0	2940.0	309.0	3249.0	2400.0	4098.0	10590.0	13839.0
1988–89	3530.0	5710.0	435.0	6145.0	5500.0	9030.0	18862.0	25007.0
1989–90	6320.0	6447.0	1992.0	8439.0	11470.0	17790.0	11064.0	18703.0
1990–91	4150.0	2950.0	2006.0	4956.0	720.0	4870.0	3967.0	8923.0
1991–92	5300.0	7475.0	1873.0	9348.0	1300.0	6600.0	22508.0	31856.0
1992–93	7960.0	7592.0	3005.0	10597.0	7550.0	15510.0	21979.0	32576.0
1993–94	11360.0	16893.0	4315.0	21208.0	–3360.0	8000.0	19164.0	40372.0
1994–95	20261.0	16354.0	3064.0	19418.0	7660.0	27921.0	3791.0	23189.0
1995–96	19538.0	17032.0**			–2620.0	16918.0	–2465.0**	14567.0**
1996–97	23438.0				1600.0	25038.0		

* Budget estimates

** Revised budget estimates

Sources: Calculated from various issues of *Budget*, Hong Kong Government, and *Hong Kong Special Administrative Region Government Land Fund Annual Report*, Hong Kong, various issues.

years. Prudential budgetary management should take into account of all sources of revenues and should present the true financial position in the financial budgets. This is not the case in Hong Kong. Since premium income allotted to the future HKSAR Government could not be treated as non-recurrent revenues of the current financial budget of the Hong Kong Government, thus the budget surplus/deficit from 1985–1986 to 1996–1997 distorted the true budgetary position and underestimated the financial strength of the Hong Kong Government. With a smaller revenue base, successive financial secretaries still strove to present surplus budgets. The small deficit budgets in 1993–1994 and 1995–1996 were criticized by the Chinese authority as violating the principle of "living within our means." This exerts tremendous pressure on Sir Hamish to control expenditure growth and achieve actual surpluses. Many new programmes on social and economic development were either delayed or cancelled so as to follow strictly the expenditure guideline. Since 1985–1986, the Hong Kong Government has already accumulated $115.8 billion fiscal reserves, about 77% of the current $150 billion total fiscal reserves. This remarkable achievement in building up the financial wealth of the government reflects the fiscal conservatism of the government.

Sovereignty transfer would not change this conservative stance. The 1996–1997 MRF projection of the next three financial budgets substantiates this argument. It is projected that all are having over $20 billion budget surpluses for the next three financial years.

Table 10 presents the calculation of the consolidated cash flow surplus/deficit for the remaining three financial years of the 1996–1997 MRF. Previously this was an important component of Section II of the MRF in the Appendix A of the financial budget. Starting from 1994–1995, a new presentation format was adopted. Details of the consolidated cash flow surplus/deficit for the last three MRF financial years are no longer given compactly and explicitly in Section II, though data are scattered in different tables and in footnotes. Several observations could be noted from Table 10. First, there will be substantial budget surpluses for the next three financial years. This is mainly because all premium income of land transaction will be credited to the Capital Works Reserve Fund (CWRF) and the interest income generated from the previous Land Fund will now be credited to the General Revenue Account (GRA) after transferring Land Fund to the Fiscal Reserves on 1 July 1997 immediately following the sovereignty transfer. Second, according to Annex III of the Joint Declaration, "from the entry into force of the Joint Declaration until 30 June 1997,

Table 10: Projection of the 1996–1997 MRF Budgetary Position
(in HK$ million)

	1996–97	1997–98	1998–99	1999–2000
Revenue				
General Revenue Account	163,695	187,680	216,460	243,290
Capital Works Reserve Fund	27,595	45,680	40,630	48,430
Capital Investment Fund	2,820	3,860	4,070	5,010
Civil Service Pension Reserve Fund	500	540	570	610
Loan Fund	2,185	6,320	4,890	4,910
	196,795	244,080	266,620	302,250
Expenditure				
General Revenue Account	142,125	162,920	186,120	213,400
Capital Works Reserve Fund	35,910	45,770	53,450	61,490
(Works Account & Reserve Account)				
Loan Fund	5,705	3,320	2,260	3,410
	183,740	212,010	241,830	278,300
Cash surplus/(deficit) before budget revenue measures	13,055	32,070	24,790	23,950
Less: Effect of budget revenue measures	(1,095)	(—)	(—)	(—)
Cash surplus/(deficit) after budget revenue measures	11,960			
Less: Advances and equity investments from the Capital Investment Fund	(10,340)	(2,200)	(2,300)	(2,410)
Less: Injection into Mandatory Provident Fund Authority		(5,000)		
Consolidated Cash Surplus/(Deficit)	1,620	24,870	22,490	21,540

Note: Effect of budget revenue measures will be announced when the actual budget speech is delivered.
Source: Calculated from *The 1996–97 Budget.*

new leases of land may be granted by the British Hong Kong Government for terms expiring not later than 30 June 2047. Such leases shall be granted at a premium and nominal rental until 30 June 1997, after which date they shall not require payment of an additional premium but an annual rent equivalent to 3 percent of the rateable value of the property at that date, adjusted in step with changes in the rateable value thereafter, shall be charged." It is estimated that income from this source in 1997–1998 will be around $3,600 million. Third, nominal growth of government expenditure follows roughly the guideline. Fourth, as the effect of budget revenue measures on budget surplus or deficit is given only in the financial budget, so it is not included in Table 10. Given the windfall gain in government revenues, it is foreseeable that more tax concessions will be given. Fifth, there has been over $10–$20 billion annual equity investments and advances for funding the new airport from the Capital Investment Fund (CIF) since 1991–1992. As the new airport project is entering into the final stage, there will be no need to inject huge money into either the Airport Authority or the Mass Transit Railway Corporation. Thus the advances and equity investments from the CIF will be reduced substantially to around $2,200 million for the remaining MRF years. But this figure does not include the CIF's investment in the North-West Railroad to proceed to the construction stage either in 1997 or in 1998. Taking into account of the last two factors, the consolidated annual cash surplus in the forecast period will be reduced to around $10 billion.

After adding the Land Fund account, revenue from land transaction accounts for about 15% to 20% of total government revenues, and the proportion would go up to 35% if revenues from Profits Tax paid by realty and property development companies are included. Because of the excessive dependence on land-based revenues, it is argued that the government's revenue base becomes very unstable and is vulnerable to economic recession. Thus, a conservative stance in controlling spending growth and in maintaining huge fiscal reserves is absolutely necessary and prudent, regardless of the existing huge level of fiscal reserves. The business community is very much subscribed to this viewpoint. The following arguments however present an alternative stance on this controversial issue. First, the duration of business cycle in Hong Kong is in general very short. Second, the government has been very effective in controlling spending growth and in minimizing budget deficits during the recession years. Third, housing property becomes an important instrument to hedge against inflation which could not be effectively constrained under the prevailing linked Exchange Rate regime. With rising population and scarce land supply, the land transaction generates stable annual revenue for the government, even at recessionary years. Fourth, the huge fiscal reserves can cushion temporary budget deficits. These counter-arguments suggest that excessive land-based revenues should not be a reason for maintaining an over-conservative budgetary policy.

While high land-based revenue contributes to building up fiscal reserves, it also makes the low-tax rate policy possible in Hong Kong, a virtue which Mr. Donald Tsang professed and valued very much in the

1996–1997 Budget. However, it is not without costs. First, a high land-based revenue needs a high land price policy to support, which inevitably fuels inflation. Second, a high land-based revenue reduces the role of taxation in the fiscal system in achieving stabilization and equity objectives. When the goal of financial stability has long been achieving, the government should conduct a comprehensive review of the existing fiscal system and policy, so as to make it more accommodative to funding social and economic development in Hong Kong. Unfortunately, the government did not take this approach and still maintains financial stability as the most important objective of the Hong Kong fiscal system. The following section describes some recent developments of the fiscal policy to strengthen the government's financial stability.

New Developments of the Hong Kong Fiscal Policy

After suffering from unexpected heavy deficits in 1982–1983 due to world economic recession, the Hong Kong Government started considering ways of reforming the fiscal system so as to achieve a more stable revenue base. One proposal was to introduce a comprehensive sales tax, either at the retail or wholesale level. This could increase the importance of indirect taxation in the overall tax system since indirect taxes are less elastic (i.e. more stable). Because sales tax is regressive and inflationary, and the government refused to conduct a comprehensive review of the tax system, the proposal to introduce the sales tax could not obtain the necessary support from the Legislative Council. Sir John Bremridge reiterated that policy formulation was the sole responsibility of the government and he did not like the idea of having to set up an independent tax review commission. It is because of this rigid stance on policy formulation and review that the sales tax proposal was shelved. It is ironic that an executive-led colonial government does not have the political clout and determination to reform its fiscal system. In fact, the Hong Kong tax system has not changed much since the inception of the Inland Revenue Ordinance in 1947.

The objective to make the fiscal system more stable has very much remained unchanged. In the 1990s, the government tries to increase revenues from fees and charges, i.e. non-tax revenues; to shift public sector's responsibilities to the market; and to reform funding policies for subvented organizations. These new developments are discussed in the following subsections.

Establishing Trading Funds

Various government departments supply more than 4,000 items of services on fees and charges basis. Some government services are mainly provided to the business community and are therefore suitable to be operated on a commercial basis. This would lead to more efficient use of resources and improve efficiency in the public sector. The Trading Fund Ordinance was passed in 1994, and starting from 1994–1995, several Trading Funds are being set up. There are several budgetary implications. First, a Trading Fund has independent finance. There is no need to go through the Appropriation Bill for spending approval, and revenues do not need to be credited to the General Revenue Account. As such, spending of the Trading Fund is no longer grouped under the "government expenditure" category but becomes a component of "public expenditure." In other words, spending of the Trading Fund is no longer regulated by the budgetary guideline. There has been an upward trend of the percentage of Trading Fund spendings to total public expenditure since 1994–1995. For example, the percentages are 0.86%, 1.2% and 2.95% from 1994–1995 to 1996–1997 respectively. With a smaller spending base, the interpretation and assessment of the expenditure guideline should be carefully handled. Second, being self-financing, Trading Fund revenue is no longer part of recurrent revenues of the General Revenue Account. In general, departments setting up Trading Funds are those experiencing departmental budget surpluses. Moving these contributing departments to self-financing may adversely affect the financial position of the traditional annual budget. Third, according to the Ordinance, each Trading Fund has a target rate of return. It means that fees and charges have to be increased substantially in order to achieve the target rate of return. This becomes very controversial since there is no clear relationship between the General Revenue Account and the Trading Fund. In particular, the general public does not comprehend the objective of self-financing of the Trading Fund when the government has already accumulated huge fiscal reserves.

The Sewage Trading Fund is a good case in point. The Fund was set up with an objective of launching a massive sewage treatment programme as a vital environmental protection and cleaning of the Victoria Harbour. Since the Fund is to be self-financing, the large-scale investment has to be financed through raising fees and charges substantially and continuously on water and sewage treatment. The general public is angered at such fees and charges policy, especially at the need to pay for the target rate of return.

The Ordinance Amendment to raise the fees and charges was defeated at the Legislative Council in June 1996. The government was asked to inject money into the Fund and to reconsider the financial implications of the Trading Fund. But the government refused the request of injecting money to the Fund, arguing that it would violate the very objective of self-financing and full-cost recovery. The government even threatened that in view of the upcoming deficit of the Fund, it is impossible to improve the quality of services and only emergency maintenance and repair work is to be provided. The coexistence of huge fiscal reserves of the Consolidated Account and deficit of this Trading Fund seems somewhat unreasonable. It nevertheless tells the simple fact that the government wants to escape from its funding responsibility and to benefit financially from the approved target rate of return.

The User-Pays Principle and Full-Cost Recovery of Government Utilities and Services

Fees and charges on utilities and services provided by government departments are important sources of recurrent revenue in Hong Kong. They accounted for 13% to 16%, and 11% to 14% of recurrent revenues in the 1980s and the 1990s respectively. Fees and charges are the price paid for government utilities and services. The general principle is for the users to pay for the full cost of providing these services, except for some services which are of merit goods nature justifying government subsidies. Starting from the early 1990s, the government initiated the public sector reform to increase departmental efficiency and value for money. Recovering full cost from fees and charges is one of the main objectives of such reform.

In October 1994, the government published the Report on "Review on Government Utilities" (1994). It was argued that a target rate of return was necessary to reflect the cost of capital employed in providing utility services. The Report suggested a series of target rates of return for five government utilities. A general comment from the business sector and the legislative councillors was that the target rate of return of above 10% was too high. It should be equivalent to the long-term bond rate. Some even argued that the government should not apply the private sector's target rate of return to government utilities.[12] In 1994–1995, two government utilities

---

[12] *Hong Kong Economic Times*, 10 November 1994.

achieved rates higher than their respective target rates of return, while two had lower rates. Only the Post Office experienced –0.1% rates of return, and in August 1995, a Trading Fund was established for the Post Office to enable it to operate on a commercial basis.

The most controversial issue is on the fees and charges policy on government services. There are about 3,400 items of government services on fees and charges at the end of 1995. At present, the actual fees and charges for government services in general are less than full-cost recovery because of underdeveloped accounting system, inefficient financial management and delayed revision. Starting from 1992–1993, the government has been adopting a more proactive policy of raising fees and charges. Mr. Donald Tsang justified this policy in the 1996–1997 Budget. He said that (Paragraph 50, 1996–1997 Budget):

> I mentioned earlier the need to maintain a rigorous user-pays principle for setting government fees and charges. Our policy on this issue is simple, practical and, I believe, fair. Where there are overwhelming social considerations, we subsidise heavily, providing services free or at a tiny fraction of their cost. This is the basis on which we provide hospital services, education and public housing. But for other services which the Government provides, where there is no overriding social need, we must maintain the principle of user pays and full cost recovery. Those who use these services, often for commercial purposes, should pay the full cost. I can see no case for taxpayers subsidising such services. The user-pays principle is an integral part of our system of public finances. It is part of the balance we have to strike if we are to go on providing heavily-subsidised services while, at the same time, keeping taxes low. Short-term gestures made at the taxpayers' expense would only jeopardise the fundamentals of our public finances.

The general public does not concur with this policy because it fuels inflation and operating cost. A ramification of this policy is the potential threat of reducing the rate of subsidy given to many social services such as education, health and housing. The legislative councillors refused to pass many amendments to raise many fees and charges of government services in late 1995 and early 1996. The Hong Kong General Chamber of Commerce (the Chamber) supports the user-pays principle in paying for the supply of government services to the public, but argues that "full cost recovery" should be on a transactional basis, i.e. the cost of actually completing or processing the transaction. Thus, general overhead costs should not be included in "full cost recovery," and should be paid out of general revenue. Moreover, the Chamber argues that "if the Government is intent on full cost recovery on everything it does, there should be less need to pay profits and salaries taxes."

The Chamber's viewpoints on fees and charges principle are both practical and stimulative. Regrettably, Mr. Donald Tsang avoids deliberately addressing to these fundamental issues. It seems that the government's objective to increase revenue from fees and charges remains unchanged. The ratio of revenues from fees and charges to total recurrent revenues amounts to 5.0%, 7.9% and 6.7% on average for the 1970s, 1980s, and 1990s (1990–1991 to 1996–97) respectively. These ratios are higher than many developed and developing economies. The future role of fees and charges hinges on the interpretation of the following issues: (1) How would strict adherence to user-pays principle affect revenues from fees and charges and inflation rate? (2) What is the proper role of fees and charges in the overall financial position of the government?[13]

Review of the Funding Policy of the NGOs: Social Welfare and Education Subvention Systems

Social welfare spending as a percentage of either total government expenditure or total public expenditure has been increasing substantially over the last three years, partly due to an ageing population's increasing demand for social security support, and partly due to improving quality of social welfare services. These social welfare services are mainly provided by nongovernmental organizations (NGOs) under a subvention funding system through the Social Welfare Department (SWD). Under the current system, the amount of funds paid by SWD to NGOs is worked out by looking at the actual costs they incur (over 85% of their total costs is on personal emoluments). This gives rise to levels of subvention which vary considerably between similar service units. To ensure value for money from these NGOs, a consultancy firm was commissioned by the government in 1995 to review the SWD's subvention system.

The first part of the Consultancy Report,[14] published in February 1996, focused on value for money and accountability of these NGOs. The Report proposed that "all departmental and subvented services will be asked to

---

[13] S. H. Tang, *The 1996–97 Budget: Some Observations on Revenue Issues* (BRC Working Paper No. 96018, School of Business, Hong Kong Baptist University, 1996).

[14] Coopers & Lybrand, *Review of the Social Welfare Subvention System — Changing the Way NGOs Are Funded* (Hong Kong: Coopers & Lybrand, 1996).

give definitions of the purposes and objectives of a service unit; to manage its resources effectively and to improve the quality of services. Service units should identify and respond to specific client needs and respect clients' rights. Each service unit will have to conduct an annual self-assessment and a departmental assessment will be done every three years. Service units which fail to comply with the standards will be asked to prepare an action plan setting out steps and a deadline for improvement." Assistant Director of Social Welfare Mr. Paul Wong warned that "subsidy may be cut and we may not allow such agencies to run new service units if they still fail to meet the targets."[15]

The second part of the Consultancy Report was published in April 1996. It proposed to change the current funding system for NGOs. The Report suggested that service units should be provided with a single grant to cover all of their needs. This is called the Unit Grant approach. There are three advantages of this approach: (1) it would make subvention system simpler; (2) it would give NGOs the flexibility to make the best use of the funding; and (3) it would give greater prominence to the quality and quantity of the service actually being delivered.

The Report proposed a three-stage and six-year process of implementing this new Unit Grant approach. Setting a cost neutral benchmark is the most important element of this approach. By cost neutrality, it means that the total cost of social welfare subvention under the Unit Grant system must be no more or no less than it is under the current system. According to the implementation scheme, "the Unit Grant will be calculated at the end of Year 3. To ensure cost neutrality, the total amount of subvention paid to the sector in Year 3 will form the basis of comparison. This overall level of funding will be adjusted for inflation, incremental creep and claw-back of surplus to produce a benchmark level of funding for Year 4. This is the level of total funding which is available for distribution to service units as Unit Grants. Whilst there are different ways in which this distribution can take place, the overall amount of funding will remain unaltered in order to preserve cost neutrality."

The Unit Grant approach encounters great resistance from social workers because one of the objectives of this approach is to delink salaries

---

[15] Jessica Tang, "Costly Standards for Welfare," *Hong Kong Standard*, 9 February 1996.

scales between subvention employees and civil servants. Only existing staff can follow, as they are now, the Civil Service-related salary scales. Existing staff are the staff of a NGO who, without a break, have been employed: (1) in subvented posts; (2) by the same organization; and (3) in the same rank, before the first day of the implementation process. In other words, staff on promotion would not qualify for existing staff status. NGOs will be free to set their own salary levels for newly promoted or appointed staff. It means that NGOs will be free to continue to follow Civil Service salary scales, but they are no longer required to do so. Moreover, for new staff, NGOs will be responsible for meeting their financial requirements out of the subvention paid to them on Unit Grant basis. There will be no access to additional financial support. The Hong Kong Council of Social Service argues that additional resources should be provided, if it is proven necessary to improve the quality of services. The Council does not agree to the proposal that "the overall cost of subvention neither increases nor decreases as a result of changing the way in which it is paid." On the other hand, the social workers profession strongly protests that their benefits and livelihood will be gravely affected by the new approach.[16]

The new Unit Grant approach was under public consultation for three months. Assistant Director of Social Welfare Mr. Paul Wong said that if there was too much resistance from the social welfare organizations and social workers profession, the SWD may consider to abolish the proposal.[17] It seems that the government is determined to reform the funding policy for the NGOs so as to improve value for money and to contain expenditure growth. The government may amend some recommendations but would not shelve the proposal.

Similar drastic reform proposal is being contemplated in education spending, the largest single item of government expenditure. The Task Group on School Quality and School Funding of the Education Commission has published a report in June 1996 on "Quality School Education. Ways to Improve Performance." The general public is invited to submit comments before 31 July 1996 to the Task Group.[18] The present funding

---

[16] Hong Kong Council of Social Service, *Welfare Digest*, 26 June 1996.

[17] *Ta Kung Pao*, 23 June 1996.

[18] The Task Group on School Quality and School Funding is one of the task groups of the Education Commission. The Task Group will consider all views expressed and make recommendations to the Education Commission, which will

arrangements do not relate the level of funding to school performance. About 90% of current school funding is used for the salaries of teachers and non-teaching staff. The number of teachers that a school can employ is largely determined by the number of classes, regardless of enrolment. The remaining 10% or so of funding is divided into tightly defined categories and, in general, resources cannot be transferred from one category to another.

The Task Group aims to build up a culture of quality school education through designing a new funding policy which relates to school performance. The Task Group is considering ways of providing incentives to enhance and award performance and to deal with underperforming schools. It is anticipated that the upcoming new funding policy will introduce drastic reform of the current teachers' salary system. The official and overt objective, of course, is to introduce greater flexibility and accountability into the funding and school management systems. While agreeing to relate funding to school performance, many educationists query whether this is to be achieved through reallocation of the fixed amount of resources but not with increasing provision from the government?[19] In view of the objective of the new funding policy proposal for social welfare NGOs, it would not be unfounded to speculate that the hidden agenda of "Quality School Education" is to control education spending growth.

A similar review has recently been underway on the health care system in Hong Kong. The review is being conducted by the Health and Welfare Branch of the government. There are many issues under review. It is expected that by the end of the second quarter of 1996, the review on public health care expenditure should have been completed. Specifically, it focuses on whether public health care expenditure should be pegged to GDP or to total public expenditure? Or should it be necessary to impose a

---

publish a consultation document on Education Commission Report No. 7 (ECR7) in late 1996. Since ECR7 will be the last report published by the Education Commission before the sovereignty transfer, it will have added significance and importance to link the new education policy on the social and economic strategy and development to lead Hong Kong entering into the next decade.

[19] B. S. Chik, "Could Cutting School Funding Improve Education Quality?" *Hong Kong Economic Times*, 28 June 1996 (in Chinese); Y. S. Tsang, "Is It Feasible to Allocate Resources to Schools According to Their Performance?" *Ming Pao*, 27 June 1996 (in Chinese).

global cap on public health care spending? By the end of 1997, the comprehensive review should have been completed, including issues on fee-charging structure and funding policy.[20]

This review focuses mainly on spending and funding issues. The forthcoming recommendations on the relationship between public health care expenditure, GDP and total public expenditure would be particularly crucial to the future public health care spending growth. This could be interpreted as an extension of the total expenditure budgetary guideline to specific programme area. A possible global cap on specific programme area spending, or pegging its growth to that of GDP, adds a new constraint on shifting spending priority due to changing social and economic conditions. But it will help restraining spending growth in specific areas.

Articles 107 and 108 of the Basic Law: Fiscal Constitution and the 1997–1998 Budget

The following two articles of the Basic Law specify the budgetary policy of the future HKSAR Government:

> *Article 107.* The Hong Kong Special Administrative Region shall follow the principle of keeping expenditure within the limits of revenues in drawing up its budget, and strive to achieve a fiscal balance, avoid deficits and keep the budget commensurate with the growth rate of its gross domestic product.

> *Article 108.* The Hong Kong Special Administrative Region shall practise an independent taxation system. The Hong Kong Special Administrative Region shall, taking the low tax policy previously pursued in Hong Kong as reference, enact laws on its own concerning types of taxes, tax rates, tax reductions, allowances and exemptions, and other matters of taxation.

Article 107 is the so-called balanced budget article and Article 108 is the so-called low tax policy article. There had been several stages of consultation and revision before the final versions of these two articles were adopted. It was argued that the wording and spirit of these two policy articles followed more or less the same fiscal philosophy of the Hong Kong Government. Theoretically speaking, it should not generate any significant disagreement to incorporating the prevailing fiscal discipline into the Basic Law. On the contrary, these two policy articles were among the most

---

[20] *Hong Kong Economic Journal*, 25 July 1996.

controversial and debatable ones during the drafting and consultation periods. Apart from the technical difficulties of interpreting and implementing the earlier versions of these two policy articles, the most debatable issue is their underlying philosophy. The wording of Articles 107 and 108 were proposed by the Hong Kong drafters of the Economy Special Issues Subgroup of the Drafting Committee of the Basic Law who were representing the interests of the business community. There are three implicit reasons for their proposal. First, a rapid democratization of the Hong Kong political system may develop after 1997 whereby over half of the legislative seats would be elected by universal suffrage. Second, the freely elected seats of the legislature would be dominated by democrats since they are more appealing to ordinary households. Third, the democrats would advocate for increasing spending on social welfare which is detrimental to the prudential management of public finances in Hong Kong. In other words, the hidden objective is to restrict the political influence of the democrats through constraining their ability to increase social welfare spending in the financial budgets.[21]

It is obvious that when issue of class interest is involved, the debate on the appropriateness of the objective and on the wording of these two policy articles becomes heavily value-laden. The democrats argued that giving the prevailing budgetary principles a constitutional status would unnecessarily impose a rigid constraint, affecting the capacity and flexibility of the future HKSAR Government in adjusting fiscal policy to accommodate for social and economic developments. The democrats also criticized that the built-in anti-social welfare stance in Article 107 would distort the spending priority of the future HKSAR Government which should be determined according to changing social and economic situations. The business community defended its proposal by citing Buchanan's constitutional economics philosophy.[22] Fiscal constitution is one of the main components of constitutional economics. The main thrust of fiscal constitution is to impose legally and morally binding constitutional rules so as to limit the government's fiscal capacity and its interference in the private sector. It is argued that Buchanan's recommendation has been

---

[21] S. H. Tang, "Fiscal Constitution, Income Distribution and the Basic Law of Hong Kong," *Economy and Society*, Vol. 20, No. 3 (August 1991), pp. 288–92.

[22] J. Buchanan and R. Wagner, *Democracy in Deficit: The Political Legacy of Lord Keynes* (New York: Academic Press, 1977).

gaining tremendous support in the United States as a last resort to solve its chronical deficit and public debt crisis. Hong Kong as the most competitive and freest economy of the world should get its constitution right by incorporating the balanced budget element of fiscal constitution in the Basic Law.

When interest conflict of different classes of the society was involved in the debate, it would be detrimental to social stability if an extreme position were taken in drafting these policy articles. This was also the position taken by the Basic Law Drafting Committee. The final versions of Articles 107 and 108 could be regarded as a compromise to the conflicting views on fiscal constitution. For example, Article 107 only states that the HKSAR shall "strive to achieve a fiscal balance," specifying neither the time frame nor the consequence of achieving/violating the principle of "living within our means." Article 108 only states that the HKSAR shall "taking the low tax policy previously pursued in Hong Kong as reference...." In other words, the vagueness of the wording may give the HKSAR Government more room to manoeuvre. Some officials of the Hong Kong Government tend to take this rather optimistic viewpoint. But it is also plausible that a more conservative stance be taken, either by the Standing Committee of the National People's Congress or by the HKSAR Government. This is to be reflected by and interpreted from the 1997–1998 and subsequent budgets.

The 1997–1998 Budget is a very special one because the sovereignty transfer on 1 July 1997 effectively divides the 1997–1998 Budget into two parts. It would be to the best interest of the economy and the society if the 1997–1998 Budget could be drafted, passed and implemented in the normal way without any unnecessary and undesirable interruption. A Budget Expert Group has been set up under the Sino-British Joint Liaison Group (JLG) to work on the 1997–1998 Budget. On 14 March 1996, the following consensus was reached at the Budget Expert Group meeting (Paragraph 20, Financial Secretary, Speech, 1996–1997 Budget Debate):

1. The detailed compilation of the 1997–1998 Budget will remain the responsibility of the relevant Hong Kong Government departments.

2. The prudent financial principles and the system of financial management which the Hong Kong Government has followed in the past have proved effective and are consistent with the spirit of Articles 107 and 108 of the Basic Law. They should continue to be the guiding principles for preparing the 1997–1998 Budget.

3. The two sides will strengthen cooperation in order to ensure that the preparation of the 1997–1998 Budget will proceed in an orderly manner. We view the two sides of the JLG expert group as equal partners in this joint endeavour.

4. So far as possible we will aim to keep to the budget timetable by reaching an early consensus on each major issue as it arises.

5. Given the tight time-frame, the expert group will meet frequently, normally once a month (but more than if necessary).

6. The JLG confidentiality rule will continue to apply strictly to protect the market-sensitive budget deliberation.

After the tenth round of meetings of the JLG expert group on the 1997–1998 transitional budget held on 10 July 1996, the Chinese team leader Mr. Chen Zuo'er said both sides had reached consensus on all items of discussion and were progressing step by step in the drafting of the budget.[23] Apparently, the Hong Kong officials have succeeded in convincing the Chinese experts that the prevailing fiscal discipline and budgetary guidelines are consistent with the spirit of Articles 107 and 108 of the Basic Law. This is a very significant breakthrough because the Chinese authority has been criticizing the financial budgets since 1991–1992 as violating the principle of "living within our means" of the Basic Law.

Concluding Remarks: Continuity or Redirection of Fiscal Policy?

Our analysis shows that the fiscal policy in the 1990s is even more conservative than in the previous decades. There is no doubt that the Hong Kong Government has firmly maintained continuity of its prudential management of public finances throughout the period since 1946–1947. Contrary to the common expectation or allegation that the Hong Kong Government will increase spending for gaining political support from the Hong Kong people, the fiscal policy in the transition period is even more conservative. The size of the public sector has been tightly controlled. Fiscal reserves have been accumulating to an unreasonable level. During the last stage of sovereignty transfer before 1997, government officials tend to take a more conservative stance in budgetary management than they

---

[23] *Hong Kong Standard*, 11 July 1996.

used to be, avoiding the danger of being criticized later by the HKSAR Government.

This conservative fiscal stance is in fact institutionalized by the Land Fund which was set up in 1985 exclusively for forced public saving in the transition period for the future HKSAR Government. This fiscal conservatism is reinforced by Articles 107 and 108 of the Basic Law. The general public does not comprehend or support this over-conservative budgetary policy. In fact, the budgetary guideline is so rigid that it becomes constraining rather than accommodating the efficient use of financial resources for social and economic developments in Hong Kong. For example, the expenditure guideline prohibits the government from spending more than what the GDP trend growth rate permits, regardless of the urgent need for such expansion in spending and availability of excessive financial resources. This is what happens in the drafting of the 1997–1998 Budget. The expenditure guideline is being used by Mr. Donald Tsang as a shield to guard off any demand for more rapid expansion of social services from the general public. These demands are being viewed by the government as motivated by political considerations.

As suggested by Sir Philips Haddon-Cave, there is nothing sacrosanct about these budgetary guidelines and they should be subject to critical and systematic review so as to better reflect the evolving role of public finances in Hong Kong. This is not the case in the 1990s. Expenditure guideline has been treated as a sacred cow for the executive-led colonial government. Mr. Donald Tsang refused to review and amend the budgetary guidelines which have been adopted since the 1986–1987 MRF. Mr. Chen Zuo'er, a senior Chinese representative to the JLG, emphasized that the 1997–1998 Budget should preserve the prevailing proven effective fiscal system and prudential budgetary guidelines.[24] In fact, the consensus reached by the Budget Expert Group of the JLG on 14 March 1996 has effectively treated the prevailing budgetary guidelines as an important interpretation of Articles 107 and 108 of the Basic Law, making it even more difficult to conduct periodic review of the budgetary guidelines. Moreover, the Chinese side may adopt an even narrower viewpoint on these guidelines. For example, Mr. Guo Shangquan, the Vice-Director of the Economic System Reform Committee of the People's Republic of China and the

---

[24] *Wen Wei Po*, 15 March 1996.

Chinese Convenor of the Economy Special Issues Subgroup of the Preparatory Committee of the future HKSAR Government, argued that excessive growth of social welfare spending of the 1996–1997 Budget violated the spirit of Article 107 because its real growth was far higher than that of the trend GDP. He suggested that it should be discussed in the JLG.[25] But Mr. Donald Tsang argued that the expenditure guideline applies only to total government expenditure, not to individual programme area. It is foreseeable that in the future HKSAR Government, Mr. Guo's interpretation of expenditure guideline would be gaining support from the legislature.

The 1997–1998 Budget would most probably be a caretaker budget. As the caretaker of the future HKSAR, the Chinese authority will avoid taking new and bold policy initiatives that have long-term financial and economic implications. As officials of the outgoing government that has only three-month jurisdiction, they are unwilling and do not have the mandate to launch any drastic reform of the prevailing fiscal system and policy in the 1997–1998 Budget. A caretaker budget cannot give adequate attention to the prevailing social and economic problems, e.g. worsening income disparity, higher unemployment and underemployment, declining growth potential of the economy, and the ageing population, etc. If not given immediate attention and action, these problems will be deteriorating and perpetuating.[26] At this crucial juncture, Hong Kong fiscal policy needs a comprehensive and systematic review and redirection. Regrettably, political considerations dominate policy formulation in the transition period and beyond. Demands for conducting a comprehensive review of the fiscal system and policy have repeatedly been rejected by the Hong Kong Government, simply because of the fear that these may destabilize the

---

[25] *Ming Pao*, 4 March 1996.

[26] S. K. Lau has monitored on a continuous basis the general public's attitude towards the economic functions of the Hong Kong Government. He finds that in 1994, more people support setting minimum wage, establishing unemployment benefit and taxing the rich more than in 1988. Lau argues that public pressure on the government will become even stronger in the years ahead, and there is increasing probability that it will and has to respond to such public demand. Lau warns that the fraying of the socioeconomic fabric of Hong Kong should not be taken lightly. See S. K. Lau, "The Fraying of the Socioeconomic Fabric of Hong Kong," mimeo. (Hong Kong: The Hong Kong Institute of Asia-Pacific Studies, The Chinese University of Hong Kong, 1996).

existing equilibrium of political power, profit, income and wealth distribution. Without a comprehensive review, many policy initiatives of the government during the transition period have been proven ill-designed, uncoordinated, and adversely affecting the livelihood of the ordinary households. Worse still, the Chinese authority is taking a "minimalist stance" on the role of the future HKSAR Government.[27] It is hoped that the new HKSAR Government will take initiatives to conduct a comprehensive study of the relationships between the budgetary guidelines, Articles 107 and 108, and the funding needs for social and economic developments in the territory for the next decade.

Bibliography

Agreed Minutes of the Airport Committee of the Sino-British Joint Liaison Group, 4 November 1994 and 30 May 1996, Hong Kong.

The Basic Law of the Hong Kong Special Administrative Region of the People's Republic of China, 4 April 1990, Beijing.

The Budget, Hong Kong Government, Hong Kong, various issues.

Buchanan, J., and R. Wagner. *Democracy in Deficit: The Political Legacy of Lord Keynes*. New York: Academic Press, 1977.

Chik, B. S. "Could Cutting School Funding Improve Education Quality?" *Hong Kong Economic Times* (in Chinese), 28 June 1996.

Coopers & Lybrand. *Review of the Social Welfare Subvention System — Changing the Way NGOs Are Funded*. Hong Kong: Coopers & Lybrand, 1996.

Hong Kong Council of Social Service. *Welfare Digest*, 26 June 1996, pp. 1–2.

Hong Kong Economic Journal (in Chinese), various issues.

Hong Kong Special Administrative Region Government Land Fund: Declaration of Trust, 13 August 1986, Hong Kong.

Hong Kong Standard, various issues.

Joint Declaration of the Government of the United Kingdom of Great Britain and Northern Ireland and the Government of the People's Republic of China on the Question of Hong Kong, 26 September 1984, Hong Kong.

Lau Siu-kai. "The Fraying of the Socioeconomic Fabric of Hong Kong," mimeo. Hong Kong: The Hong Kong Institute of Asia-Pacific Studies, The Chinese University of Hong Kong, 1996.

---

[27] S. K. Tsang, "The Economy," in *The Other Hong Kong Report 1994*, edited by Donald H. McMillen and S. W. Man (Hong Kong: The Chinese University Press, 1994), pp. 146–47.

Memorandum of Understanding Concerning the Construction of the New Airport in Hong Kong and Related Questions, 3 September 1991, Beijing.

Ming Pao (in Chinese), various issues.

Rabushka, A. *Value for Money: The Hong Kong Budgetary Process.* Stanford, CA: Hoover Institution Press, 1976.

Ta Kung Pao (in Chinese), various issues.

Tang, Jessica. "Costly Standards for Welfare." *Hong Kong Standard*, 9 February 1996.

Tang Shu-hung. *Issues of Public Finance in Hong Kong* (in Chinese). Hong Kong: Wide Angle Press, 1988.

———. *Guideline on Fiscal Reserves in Hong Kong and Its Implication on Funding the New Airport Project.* BRC Working Paper ES91017, School of Business, Hong Kong Baptist University, 1991.

———. "Fiscal Constitution, Income Distribution and the Basic Law of Hong Kong." *Economy and Society*, Vol. 20, No. 3 (August 1991), pp. 283–305.

———. *Hong Kong Public Finance in the Transitional Period* (in Chinese). Hong Kong: Joint Publishing, 1992.

———. "A Critical Review of the 1995–96 Budget." In *The Other Hong Kong Report 1995*, edited by Stephen Y. L. Cheung and Stephen M. H. Sze, pp. 157–82. Hong Kong: The Chinese University Press, 1995.

———. *The 1996–97 Budget: Some Observations on Revenue Issues.* BRC Working Paper No. 96018, School of Business, Hong Kong Baptist University, 1996.

Task Group on School Quality and School Funding. *Quality School Education — Ways to Improve Performance.* Hong Kong, 1996.

Tsang Shu-ki. "The Economy." In *The Other Hong Kong Report 1994*, edited by Donald H. McMillen and Man Si-wai, pp. 125–48. Hong Kong: The Chinese University Press, 1994.

Tsang Yiu-sang. "Is It Feasible to Allocate Resources to Schools According to Their Performances?" *Ming Pao* (in Chinese), 27 June 1996.

Wen Wei Po (in Chinese), various issues.

Yuen, Q. S. "Betraying Conventional Budgetary Principles, Laying Hidden Disaster on the Future SAR." *Bauhinia Monthly* (in Chinese), Vol. 67 (1996), pp. 24–26.

9

Evolution of the Contractual Nature of Land Use Control in Hong Kong[1]

Lai Wai-chung, Lawrence

This chapter depicts the contractual nature of the leasehold land system of Hong Kong as it evolves in terms of property rights. The matters discussed in this chapter are relevant in the light of the introduction of modern planning regulations and the proposals in the consultative document *Comprehensive Review of Town Planning Ordinance*[2] and the ensuing *Consultation Paper on Town Planning Bill*, which contains a draft *Town Planning Bill*.[3]

Contractual Planning

The land system in Hong Kong since 1842 has been leasehold with the government being the landlord or lessor of virtually all lands. Under this

---

[1] This chapter was first presented to the International Conference on Political Order and Power Transition in Hong Kong at Lingnan College, 18–19 September 1996. It was later incorporated in Chapter 3, "Evolution of the Contractual Nature of Land Use," in *Town Planning in Hong Kong: A Critical Review* (Hong Kong: City University of Hong Kong Press, 1997), written by the same author.

[2] Hong Kong Government Planning, Environment and Lands Branch, *Comprehensive Review of the Town Planning Ordinance — Consultative Document* (Hong Kong: Government Printer, July 1991).

[3] Hong Kong Government Planning, Environment and Lands Branch, *Consultation Paper on Town Planning Bill* (Hong Kong: Government Printer, July 1996).

system, land parcels are allocated from the government to individuals by competitive auction or tender or by private treaty grant. The property rights of the land owner (strictly speaking, the lessee) are defined explicitly by the conditions of sale and terms of the lease document and those understood in common law. The conditions of sale specify obligations the lessee must fulfil (say the carrying out of development for a specified use within a given period of time) before legal title is formally transferred from the government. The conditions of sale refer to the lease, the formal title document, to be issued afterwards.

The property rights over leasehold land refer generally to the exclusive right to use land for specific purposes (as defined by the "user" clause), the exclusive right to derive income from the use of land (such as rent) and the exclusive right to transfer the whole or part of the use or income rights to another individual (such as assignment or re-assignment) during the period of the lease. The oldest lease is the "999-year" unrestricted lease which is the near equivalent of a freehold for a human person. It is said to be unrestricted because it does not specify any user restriction other than restriction on offensive or obnoxious trades.[4] The exclusivity of the three types of right means, under the doctrine of privity of contract, that a third party has no right to interfere with such enjoyment of rights. To enjoy his rights as a lessee where building development is required, the proprietor needs to apply to the Building Authority for building permission through an Authorized Person (AP).

The development bulk of the land under the Buildings Ordinance since the 1962 has been governed by the plot ratio control stipulated in the Building Regulations. The plot ratio is the ratio between gross floor area (GFA) of a building and gross site area (GSA) of the building plot. The higher the ratio, the greater will be the value of the site.

The lease document is a civil contract between an individual and the

---

[4] For instance, in the Crown Lease for Inland Lot No. 243, the user clause states that the lessee and the successor "shall not nor will, during the continuance of this demise, use, exercise of follow, in or upon the said premises or any part thereof, the trade or business of a Brazier, Slaughterman, Soap-maker, Sugar-baker, Fellmonger, Melter of tallow, Oilman, Butcher, Distaller, Victualler, or Tavern-keeper, Blacksmith, Nightman, Scavenger, or any other noisy, noisome or offensive trade or business whatever, without the previous licence of His said Majesty, His Heirs, Successors."

government over a specific land parcel. The individual voluntarily enters in to this contract in full recognition of the consideration, benefits and obligations defined or agreed with the government under the prevailing development bulk or plot ratio control under the Building Regulations. Once the land parcel is assigned, the terms of this civil contract can be subsequently modified by mutual agreement between the lessee and the government. The lessee is required to pay the government a premium if the "after value" of the modification is greater than the "before value." Land sale proceeds and modification premium form a major source of government revenue.[5]

The land contract for private development is one allowing for maximum development. When land for private development is allocated by the government through competitive public auction or tender, the consideration paid by the successful bidder is at market price. The policy of charging modification premium by reference to the "after value" of redevelopment also reflects that land revenue is predicated on the maximum development potential. The right of development according to the "particulars and conditions of sale" or lease document is enforceable at common law, although it can be overridden by legislation such as the Town Planning Ordinance. It is an inherent right of a civil contract between the government and an individual, and the contractual nature of land development is a characteristic, not a mere "by-product of the leasehold system."[6]

The right to maximum development is implicit in the particulars and conditions of sale and lease terms. In fact, the government always imposes a contractual obligation on the purchaser of land lease to commence building development within a specified time period.[7] A complete waste of land

[5] See Anthony Walker, K. W. Chau, and Lawrence W. C. Lai, *Hong Kong in China: Real Estate and the Economy* (Hong Kong: Brooke Hillier Parker, 1994); see also Samuel. R. Staley, *Planning Rules and Urban Economic Performance — The Case of Hong Kong* (Hong Kong: The Chinese University Press, 1994), pp. 32–34.

[6] Samuel R. Staley, *Planning Rules and Urban Economic Performance*, p. 100.

[7] For instance, in the Particulars and Conditions of Sale by public auction held on 18 March 1996 for Tai Po Town Lot No. 141, the purchaser "shall develop the lot by the erection thereon of a building or buildings complying in all respects with these Conditions and all Ordinances, by-laws and regulations relating to building,

will attract re-entry by the government.[8] However, there is nothing at law to disallow development to a lower intensity. The property right to use resources includes the right to waste resources. The implication of any state compulsion of maximizing resources use efficiency for property rights will be akin to forced slavery for human rights. The freedom to maximize resource use and income is as important as the right of not doing so.

The government sometimes has good grounds to break the land contract by re-entering land before the lease expires for a "public purpose," which is intelligible in terms of the public goods concept in economics. The building of military camps, hospitals, reservoirs, highways and public open space are cases in point. When that happens, the affected proprietor is compensated the "market" value[9] of the existing building under the

---

sanitation and planning which are or may at any time be in force in Hong Kong, such building or buildings to be completed and made fit for occupation on or before 31st day of March, 1999." (Special Condition No. (2)) and failure or neglect by the purchaser to comply with this condition shall entitle the government to re-entry without refund according General Condition No. 21.

[8] In the Particulars and Conditions of Sale for Tai Po Town Lot No. 141, referred to in Note 7 above, General Condition No. 17(b) specifies that "In the event of demolition as aforesaid the Purchaser shall within one month of such demolition apply to the Director for consent to carry out building works for the redevelopment of the lot and upon receiving such consent shall within three months thereof commence the necessary works of redevelopment and shall complete the same to the satisfaction of and within such time limit as is laid down by the Director." Otherwise, the government shall be entitled to re-entry under General Condition No. 21.

[9] For the meaning of "open market value," the Lands Tribunal has accepted the definition of Swinfen Eady LJ in *IRC* v. *Clay*: "A value, ascertained by reference to the amount obtainable in an open market, shows an intention to include every possible purchaser. The market is to be the open market, as distinguished from an offer to a limited class only, such as the members of the family. The market is not necessarily an auction sale. The section means such amount as the land might be expected to realise if offered under conditions enabling every person desirous of purchasing to come in and make an offer, and if proper steps were taken to advertise the property and let all likely purchasers know that the land is in the market for sale." See *IRC* v. *Clay* [1914] 3 *King Bench* 466, 475. Such "market" value understood by surveyors is not the same as market value understood by economists.

Crown Lands Resumption Ordinance. The lost redevelopment value is ignored in the valuation. Such infringement of private property rights is avoided in the resumption of agricultural lease in the New Territories where a system of certificate of future entitlement to lost land area has been used instead of cash compensation.[10]

Rural land was acquired by the government by the "Letter A / Letter B" resumption through which the land owners surrender 5 units of rural land in exchange of a future claim of 2 units of urban land in the new town according to a pre-determined schedule of prices. A Letter A / B is a certificate issued by the government to the rural land owner for such exchange of rights. This system has been abandoned by the government and all residual claims had been settled by a buy-back before July 1997.[11]

As the original land parcels in urban leaseholds are invariably pre-specified by reference to a street block or subdivision plan based on government land surveys, the leasehold system described above can be regarded as a kind of planning by contract or consent. The elements of planning conducted by the government include laying out, setting out, levelling of land and stipulation of user restrictions and obligations by the government having regard to the general character of the street block or subdivision. The situation for rural land in the New Territories is different. Such land was by legal fiction converted in 1897 as Crown land and then "leased back" to indigenous proprietors. The lot boundaries of such agricultural lots, as recorded in the Demarcation District (DD) Plans and, in the case of New Kowloon, Survey District (SD) Plans. Such lots are highly irregular. The DD and SD Plans were produced after a survey of uses and lot boundaries by Indian surveyors before the turn of the century.[12] Owing

---

[10] R. D. Pope, "A History of Letter A / B Land Exchange Policy," *The Hong Kong Surveyor*, Vol. 1, No. 1 (May 1985), pp. 7–9; E. G. Pryor, "The Acquisition of Land for Urban Use by Exchange in Hong Kong and Taiwan," *New Zealand Town Planning Quarterly* (December 1975), pp. 27–29.

[11] New Territories Land Exchange Entitlements (Redemption) Bill.

[12] The Demarcation District (DD) Sheets were produced in 1898, initially at the scale of 16 inches to the mile (or 1/3960). However, it was soon realized that the scale was too small to show the fragmentary form of occupation in the New Territories and a larger scale, of 32 inches to the mile (or 1/1980), was adopted for the remaining sheets. See W. J. Newland, *A General Report on the Survey of the New Territories from November 1899 to April 1904* (Hong Kong, 11 May 1904).

to technological constraints at that time, the DD and SD Plans should at best be a topological representation[13] of land ownership pattern. The uses surveyed were recorded in the agricultural lease.

Modern planning arose mainly on the grounds that such contractual planning control could not effectively pre-empt externalities. Nor could it allow for the provision of public goods. It emerged more than a century after 1842 after the system of planning by contract described above had been in place. While the Town Planning Ordinance was passed in 1939, actual plan preparation within its ambit did not start until after the Second World War. In 1959 a new section 16(1)(d) was introduced to the Buildings (Administration) Ordinance which required the refusal of building consent when a proposed building development did not conform to the land use zoning of plans prepared under the Town Planning Ordinance.

The most significant economic impact of the inception of modern planning, where it is superimposed on pre-existing leaseholds, is that the private property rights of the lessees are often attenuated, i.e. subtracted, reduced, restricted or even nullified, by the government unilaterally. This general characterization of modern planning, however, covers a number of situations in which the exact relationship between land use control by lease and modern planning as well as its property rights implications vary from one to another. The variation depends not only on the types of town plans but also on the timing of the introduction of the town plans in question. Before the relationship between the lease and town plans and their impacts on property rights is examined, an outline reference to the types of town plans and their functions is made below.

The Plan Hierarchy

Town plans in Hong Kong are conceived of in a four-tier hierarchy (Figure 1) covering the territorial, regional, district and site levels in an ascending order of greater geographical and operational details. At the territorial or "strategic" level is the administrative Territorial Development Strategy (TDS) which defines broad areas of future urban and suburban growth,

---

[13] See S. C. Leung, "The ABC of Land Parcels," *Journal of the Hong Kong Institute of Land Surveyors* (1984), Section 12, p. 26.

Figure 1: Hierarchy of Town Plans

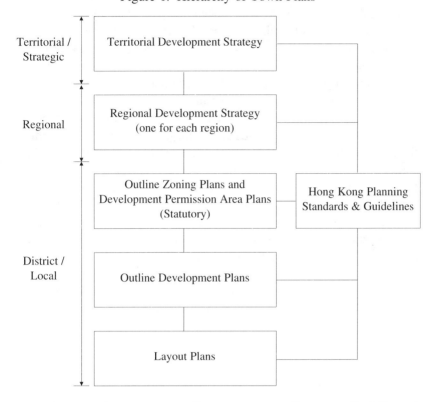

Source: Adapted from Hong Kong Government, *Town Planning in Hong Kong: A Quick Reference* (Planning Department, 1995), p. 7.

conservation areas as well as the spatial pattern of the desired infrastructural network.

Within the ambit of TDS and other major territorial development strategies are five administrative Regional Development Strategies (with those for the Metro Area — Metroplan, the South-western New Territories and the North-western New Territories having been completed). Each regional development strategy consists of a number of development statements for plan preparation and interpretation at the lower levels.

At the district level are the administrative Layout Plans (LPs) (1:500 to 1:2,000) and Outline Development Plans (ODPs) (1:2,000) and the statutory Outline Zoning Plans (OZPs) (1:7,500 to 1:20,000) (and Development

Permission Areas Plans (DPA plans) (1:5,000) for rural New Territories before OZPs are prepared). DPA plans evolved from the rudimentary Interim Development Permission Area (IDPA) plans. LPs are mainly used for engineering purposes such as the levels and scope of land formation (by reclamation or terracing), alignments of roads, sewers and drainage reserves and major delineation of major land parcels and their broad land use zoning. ODPs are drawn to a smaller scale than LPs showing more details of intended land uses for both private and public development.

The zoning in LPs and ODPs, like those in Regional Development Strategy (RDS), is said to be administrative because it binds the land authority in the drafting of lease documents for new land to be allocated. Besides, it could affect government decisions about and the appropriateness as well as the terms of lease modification for land already allocated. The administrative town plans are also the basis for public spending development programming and for land sale programming. They do not however alter legally any existing rights over land.[14]

OZPs and DPA plans are the only statutory, as compared to administrative, town plans in Hong Kong. Zoning in statutory town plans override the user of any pre-existing leases upon redevelopment, dictate the user

---

[14] However, the government may use the argument of "public purpose" to resume land for the implementation of a layout plan. A scandalous case is the resumption of land falling within the Chung Uk Tsuen Layout Plan. Such land was resumed under the Road (Works, Use and Compensation) Ordinance and the Crown Lands Resumption Ordinance. The land resumed was indeed more than sufficient to form a public road network. In fact, the ulterior objective was to implement the "Rural Development Area" zone which is for the development of "small houses" for "indigenous villages." The effect was the transfer of wealth from the non-indigenous villagers to indigenous villagers. As the land possessed by the non-indigenous villagers had been purchased from the latter, the resumption is extremely unethical. The official argument of improving the "village environment" is avoiding the basic issue of taking one party's property and transferring to another party instead of the public domain. See Lawrence Wai-chung Lai, *Doubts on Private Property Rights* (Hong Kong: Qin Jia Yuan Publishing Co., 1993), pp. 175–77; Dorothy Yeuk-yu Chow, "An Examination of the Property Rights Implication of Existing Planning and Compensation System" (unpublished B.Sc. (Surveying) dissertation, Department of Surveying, University of Hong Kong, April 1996), pp. 86–90.

for new leases or modified leases and prescribe the need for planning application or the otherwise for land covered.

As a matter of policy, a planning study will be carried out before a draft plan is actually prepared. The public have the first chance to look at the plan when it is gazetted and exhibited.[15] Any member of the public, whether or not he is the lessee, has a right to object to the zoning and provisions in a draft statutory town plan when it is gazetted. However, the government has no legal duty or policy of finding out or informing directly individual proprietors affected by the draft plan, which has immediate legal effect although there is no statutory time limit on hearing objection.

Planning as a Prelude to the Initial Allocation of Contractual Rights

The exact relationship between government leases and town plans can be conveniently discussed under two broad scenarios. The first scenario is that of a new development area, such as one obtained by reclamation or terracing the hillside owned by the government, without any pre-existing private land interests.

Private development in the past under this scenario was simply a matter of voluntary contract between the government and the lessee by reference to the lease document. The introduction of modern planning does not in practice alter this contractual nature of development as far as the initial allocation of land parcels is concerned. For a new development area, say a "package area" in new town, the statutory OZPs will not be necessary right at the beginning of the land conversion process. Instead, the government needs initially only a large-scale LP for engineering works of land formation, infrastructure construction and broad categorization of land for inclusion in the land sale programme and for general public uses. Then, an ODP with more details about land subdivision for more exact private and public uses is produced. The land authority will draft the conditions of sale, the lease document (for private land uses), and engineering conditions (for government uses) in accordance with the zoning of the ODP. The property rights of land allocated from the government for private development in this manner remain purely contractual. The lessees know in advance the

---

[15] *Comprehensive Review of the Town Planning Ordinance*, Section 5.

nature of the administrative zoning as reflected in the conditions of sale and the lease document. However, such rights will ultimately be affected by an OZP which is usually produced after actual building development is completed.

The small-scale OZP, within the context of the TDS and relevant RDS, will govern the prospect of the future change in use intended by the lessee. The property rights implications of the OZP are best discussed in the next scenario because the first OZP for a new development area will not normally create much disturbances to the rights predicated on the government lease, given the recent period of the actual development. In the first scenario, it is where the user becomes non-viable or obsolete due to economic changes and the statutory zoning remains the same as the user will problems arise for the lessee.

Subsequent Attenuation and Extinction of Pre-existing Private Property Rights

The second scenario is that of modern town plans being imposed on developed land parcels with pre-existing leases. Where they are administrative or non-statutory by nature, the zoning of the town plans (say RDS, ODP, LP) will not affect redevelopment rights unless the intended uses require lease modification or resumption for "public purpose."[16] These plans are not produced under the Town Planning Ordinance. When lease modification is sought, the land authority is administratively bound to follow the use zoned on the administrative town plan. In the past, the land authority tended to take a liberal view about non-statutory zoning and might in some circumstances proposed a change in the administrative zoning to meet the request for lease modification. As a consequence, the administrative town plan did not alter the contractual nature of private development. However, this flexible approach is no longer in practice for private development not only because, increasingly, administrative zoning is taken as given but also because very few places with administrative town plans have not yet been covered by statutory plans, i.e. OZPs or DPA plans.

Where a statutory town plan prepared under the Town Planning Ordinance is imposed on land with existing rights defined by the government

---

[16] See Note 14.

lease, a number of potential problem areas may be created for the proprietor. The first problem area is that any intended redevelopment or change in use would need to be checked against the statutory plan even where there is no need for lease modification. The statutory town plan in law consists of two parts: an annotated zoning map and an accompanying set of "Notes." The Notes, stated expressly as part of the plan, indicate (a) in the paragraphs of the covering pages uses (and, in the case of a DPA, also temporary uses) always permitted in all zones; (b) in Column 1, uses always permitted for each given zone; and (c) in Column 2, uses which may be permitted for each given zone (Table 1). Such Notes were introduced after the Singway Case which ruled that all statutory town plans were null and void for uncertainty.[17] The "Explanatory Statement," stapled together with the "Notes," do not form part of the plan and shall have no legal effect. It describes the physical and socio-economic background, zones and government programmes within the "planning area" of the OZPs or DPA plans. In DPA plans and rural OZPs which replace the former, the "planning intention" for individual zones is often specified. The Column 1 and Column 2 uses vary not only according to zone but also according to plan. The same zoning in different OZPs or DPA plans may have different uses under either column.

In case an intended use is a Column 2 use (or a temporary change in use or development in a DPA plan), then planning permission must be obtained from the Town Planning Board (TPB) before lease modification, if required, and building permission may be sought. Planning permission is in this situation necessary even if the use is permitted by the government lease. While it is the usual case that the applicant is in fact the proprietor, his agent or consultant, any member of the public is entitled to make an application.

When the TPB makes a decision, it has the benefit of having the recommendations of a Town Planning Board Paper prepared by the government's town planners in consultation with relevant government departments and public utilities. If the application of such permission under s.16 of the Town Planning Ordinance is rejected, the applicant is entitled by law to apply for a s.17(1) review by TPB and then finally a s.17B appeal to the Town Planning Appeal Board. If the s.16 application is

---

[17] *Singway Co. Ltd. v. A.G.* [1974] *Hong Kong Laws Report (HKLR)* 275.

Table 1: An Example of Column 1 and Column 2 Uses for a
Residential (Group B) Zone

Column 1 Uses always permitted	Column 2 Uses that may be permitted with or without conditions on application to Town Planning Board
Ancillary car park	Ambulance depot
Flat	Bank
Government staff quarters	Barber shop
House	Broadcasting, television and/or film studio
Police reporting centre	Clinic/polyclinic
Private swimming pool	Educational institution
Public library	Fast food shop
Residential institution	Government refuse collection point
Staff quarters	Government use (not elsewhere specified)
Utility installation for private project	Hawker centre
	Hospital
	Hotel
	Market
	Mass Transit vent shaft and other structure above ground level other than entrance
	Off-course betting centre
	Office
	Petrol filling station
	Photographic studio
	Place of public entertainment
	Place of recreation, sports or culture
	Post Office
	Private club
	Public car park
	Public convenience
	Public transport terminus or station
	Public utility installation
	Religious institution
	Restaurant
	Retail shop
	School
	Service apartment
	Service trades
	Showroom excluding motor vehicle showroom
	Social welfare facility

Source: Notes of the draft Sha Tin Outline Zoning Plan No. S/ST/5.

approved, the TPB may or may not impose planning conditions on the planning permission. The permission is valid normally for two years. It does not bind the applicant or any other person to develop. There is no statutory limit to the number of applications for a given site. There is also no statutory requirement that an applicant needs to instruct a professional town planner or any other kind of recognized professional registered by the government to lodge in an objection, an application, a review submission or an appeal.

Unlike the case of an objection to a draft plan where any person may have a right of hearing, only the applicant (even though he is not the proprietor), his representative and consultant are entitled to sit in a review or appeal session. There is no right for a third party to the application (who may in fact be the proprietor) to object to an application or attend a review, though the appeal session is open to the public.

In case an intended use is not found in Column 1 or 2, and is neither a use permitted in all zones nor, in a DPA plan, a temporary use which may be permitted and is so permitted, then that use cannot be developed even though the use is consistent with the government lease. The Building Authority will not give a permission to build if the requisite statutory use right or planning permission is not available.[18] The only way out for the proprietor is to wait or apply for rezoning in his favour. Where the zoning is for a public use (say open space), the proprietor usually would object in vain.

The institution of planning applications entails that private planning decisions are superseded by government planning decisions. This constitutes an attenuation of the rights of the proprietor to use land for the most profitable uses. Where the zoned use is for a "public purpose,"[19] such as the development of open space by the Urban Council or Regional Council, the government will as a matter of policy use the Crown Lands Resumption

---

[18] Section 16(1)(d), Buildings Ordinance, Chapter 123, Laws of Hong Kong.

[19] S.2(d) of the Crown Lands Resumption Ordinance reads "resumption for any purpose of whatsoever description whether ejusdem generis with any of the above purposes or not, which the Governor in Council may decide to be a public purpose." Its effect is that the Governor in Council has an unfettered discretion to declare any resumption to be for a public purpose (Gordon N. Cruden, *Land Compensation and Valuation Law in Hong Kong* (Singapore: Butterworths, 1986)), and this view was the *ratio decidendi* of *Chan Lau Fong and others v. The Attorney General* [1992] 2 *HKLR* 203.

Ordinance to take land at their existing value.[20] This means that the rights of the proprietor are extinguished unilaterally by the landlord (the government) before the lease expires naturally. The proprietor will as a result lose the difference between (1) the opportunity cost of land under the lease terms as controlled in development bulk by the prevailing Building Regulations and (2) the existing value. If a zoning proposal adversely affects the value of a land parcel, the proprietor(s) of that land parcel is not entitled to compensation. On the other hand, if a zoning proposal enhances the value of a land parcel, there is no betterment levy on the proprietor.

Notwithstanding their actual impacts on private property rights, OZPs are seldom announced as measures to extinguish existing rights. DPA plans for the rural New Territories, however, were produced expressly to extinguish the common law rights under agricultural leases, as affirmed in the Melhado Case,[21] to use land for open storage. The case ruled that the uses registered in the agricultural lease, as surveyed by the Indians, are matters of description and not restriction.

The second problem area is where the development intensity of the intended use, whether or not planning permission is required, is reduced or restricted in the relevant statutory zoning. The typical example is the stipulation in the statutory zone a plot ratio or building height lower than that permitted under the prevailing Building Regulations or lease document. The legal validity of plot ratio control as a "planning" matter was tested in the Crozet Case,[22] and affirmed in the CC Tse Case[23] and Auburntown Case.[24] This is another area attracting objections to zoning.

The best example is the downzoning of plot ratio from 15 to 9.5 in the industrial zones of Tsuen Wan New Town.[25] This means that any redevelopment of existing factory buildings could not exceed the now

---

[20] *Comprehensive Review of the Town Planning Ordinance*, Section 4(2).

[21] *A.G. v. Melhado Investment Ltd.* [1983] *HKLR* 327.

[22] *Crozet Ltd. v. A.G., High Court Miscellaneous Proceedings* (*HCMP*) 409/73.

[23] *CC Tse (Estate) Ltd. v. A.G., HCMP* 604/81.

[24] *Auburntown Ltd. v. T.P.B., HCMP* No. 222 of 1993.

[25] See Lawrence Wai-chung Lai, "Some Economic Consequences of Lowering Industrial Plot Ratios," *Hong Kong Economic Journal Monthly*, Vol. 166 (January 1991), pp. 98–99; Tsuen Wan Outline Zoning Plan No. S/TW/5, October 1990.

reduced plot ratio of 9.5, entailing a potential loss of 5.5. In value terms, there will be a 37% cut in the long-term stream of rental income. Plot ratio reduction can be regarded as taxation in kind, attenuating the rights of proprietors to derive the maximum amount of income from their property implied in the lease terms. Unlike real taxation, however, the income loss of the affected party does not go to the government as revenue but is lost. This implies economic waste is incurred by society.

The third problem area is where land under multiple ownership falls within a Comprehensive Development Area (CDA) designated in an OZP. Independent redevelopment of individual land parcels permitted by respective lease documents will no longer be realized by individual proprietors of the land parcels. Any redevelopment of the CDA must be comprehensive and unitary in accordance with a Master Layout Plan (MLP) submitted to and approved by the TPB under the planning application procedure. As multiple ownership effectively incurs prohibitively high transaction costs of arriving at mutual agreement to joint redevelopment according to a MLP, the government assigns the right to resort to resumption to public agencies for urban renewal. The agencies are the Land Development Corporation (LDC) and the Housing Society. This is another major area of objections to zoning.

CDA designation for land under multiple ownership in effect makes the freedom to use a proprietor's land contingent on the consent of another. It extinguishes the rights of proprietors to freely subdivide or combine property for the most profitable use. The CDA zoning creates difficulty for individual land owners because their investment horizons and expected returns may not necessarily be the same for all parts of their land or as those of other owners. The stipulation of negative prohibition against subdivision, as in the conditions of most modern leases, is less restrictive than positive requirements for joint development (as in the CDA concept) because in the second situation the land owner suddenly loses his autonomy in deciding the fate of *any* part of his land. As Cheung says in *The New Palgrave*, "private property rights offer the unique advantage of allowing individual property owners to option of NOT JOINING an organization."[26] The CDA concept compromises such an option in land because the owner

---

[26] Steven N. S. Cheung, "Transaction Costs and Economic Organization," in *The New Palgrave* (London: Macmillan, 1987), p. 57.

would have no option not to join with others if he wants to develop land in an organization involving third parties.

The success of CDA under single ownership in various cases of re-zoning of public utility property (originally used as dockyards or power houses) and the failure of the Tsim Sha Tsui CDA scheme under multiple ownership lend support to this theory. In the Tsim Sha Tsui scheme, a number of developed leasehold lots in the old commercial hub of Tsim Sha Tsui were grouped into a "Comprehensive Redevelopment Area" (later renamed CDA) in order to render development possible only if the lots were jointly redeveloped according to an approved MLP. The transaction costs involved in reaching a land assembly agreement in Hong Kong where land titles are stratified are phenomenal. This could easily frustrate the planners' intent for orderly comprehensive redevelopment: there could simply be no private redevelopment at all. Realizing such difficulties, the Hong Kong Government instigates the LDC which has the statutory power under the Crown Lands Resumption Ordinance to resume land for its CDA schemes which are approved by the TPB. Such schemes are to be imple-mented by LDC in joint venture with private developers.[27]

Where resumption under the Crown Lands Resumption Ordinance occurs for the purpose of urban renewal by government agencies, the property rights of proprietors are extinguished unilaterally by the landlord before the natural expiry of the lease. As far as the land owners are concerned, they are compensated according to the Pointe Gourde Rule,[28] constructing the object of profit-making redevelopment schemes as if it is for "public purpose." This common law rule pegs the value of compensa-tion at the existing level of the existing use but not the full potential value of land. The proprietor will lose the difference between the opportunity cost of land under the prevailing plot ratio control and the existing value of the property.

The fourth problem area is land subject to enforcement with in DPA plans. As mentioned previously, DPA plans are produced intentionally to

---

[27] In the Privy Council case *Silver Mountain Investment Limited and Another v. Attorney General and Another* [1994] 1 *HKLR* 137, it was ruled that LDC has no duty to consider participation of redevelopment by affected proprietors.

[28] See P. G. Willoughby, "Let The Land-Owner Beware," *Hong Kong Law Lectures* (1978), pp. 145–230; Albert H. Y. Chen, "The Basic Law and the Protec-tion of Property Rights," *Hong Kong Law Journal*, Vol. 23, No. 1 (1993), p. 42.

extinguish existing rights to open storage. The common law rights based on the agricultural lease to put land for open storage, excavation of earth and filling purposes now requires prior planning permission unless they are "existing uses." Non-compliance with this statutory requirement is an offence which attracts heavy fines. Although the Town Planning Ordinance provides for the exemption or defence of "existing use," the meaning of existing use is highly uncertain. This problem area is made more complicated by the fact that modern statutory zone boundaries often ignore the underlying irregular customary land ownership pattern. The artificial imposition of zone boundaries may produce zone identification problems for land literally covered by the zoning lines.

As a result of the superimposition of modern planning on existing leasehold land, the contractual nature of private development has been significantly altered. Private property rights freedom is increasingly subject to bureaucratic interference. Unlike a land sale or lease modification, neither a hearing of objection, planning application, review, or appeal nor a petition for rezoning is conducted between the government and the individual on an equal contractual footing. The TPB or the Town Planning Appeal Board (TPAB) is not allowed to negotiate with the applicant about the nature and content of a planning objection or application. Although the TPB (or TPAB) has a statutory duty to process objections, applications and reviews (or appeals) within legal time limits, the TPB is not obliged to approve an objection, an application for planning permission or even consider a petition for rezoning.

While bureaucratic interference of private decisions and activities may be a fact of modern living, it should be noted that those associated with zoning designation and planning permission are largely a matter of the exercise of discretionary power. Where the reasons for decisions thus made are unintelligible or are difficult to follow, and the institution of private property rights is weakened, the result will be the creation of great uncertainty in the land market, rent dissipation, opportunities for rent-seeking activities and an increase of the transaction costs of changes in land use and redevelopment. The development market in response will alter its mode of allocation from one based largely on price competition to one based also on non-price competition. Such non-price competition is often not to improve the quality of the output but to get through or bypass government procedures. This does not only undermine the institution of private property rights, affect the efficiency of the development market in responding to changing demand but could also frustrate the professed object of planning for a better sustainable living environment. At the extreme case of taking for purposes which are doubtfully "public," the whole root of the institution of private property rights is eroded. The economic concepts of rent dissipation and rent-seeking are explained below.

Rent Dissipation and Rent-seeking Activities Involved in Land Use Planning

Given the human propensity for competition, society in order to survive must have rules constraining competition. Property rights are a specific set of rules constraining the costs of competition. Private property rights as a specific form of property rights constitute the foundation for market transaction based on free contract. A contractual society is the ideological ideal of great political and economic thinkers like John Locke,[29] Adam Smith,[30] J. S. Mill,[31] Frederich von Hayek,[32] and Robert Nozick.[33] Where private property rights are attenuated by government regulation, rent dissipation will occur. Rent dissipation refers to the depreciation in the value of a resource by the costs of competition.[34] In the extreme case, where property rights are "common" in the sense that there are no agreed rules, rent dissipation is complete. This is best characterized by the Hobbesian "state of nature."

Where voluntary transaction based on predetermined rules is artificially restricted by subsequent regulation, rent dissipation is bound to

---

[29] John Locke, *Two Treaties of Government*, edited by P. Laslett (Cambridge: Cambridge University Press, 1964).

[30] Adam Smith, *An Inquiry into the Nature and Cause of the Wealth of Nations*, reprinted ed. (Oxford: Oxford University Press, 1976).

[31] J. S. Mill, *Principles of Political Economy* (New York: Appleton-Century-Crofts, 1897).

[32] F. A. Hayek, *The Constitution of Liberty* (London: Routledge & Kegan Paul, 1960); *The Road to Serfdom* (London: Routledge & Kegan Paul, 1976); and *The Fatal Conceit — the Errors of Socialism* (Chicago: Chicago University Press, 1988).

[33] Robert Nozick, *Anarchy, State, and Utopia* (Oxford: Basil Blackwell, 1974).

[34] Steven N. S. Cheung, "Common Property Rights," in *The New Palgrave*, pp. 504–5.1

occur due to attempts of parties affected to get through or bypass the regulations. Non-price competition is typical of situations where rent dissipation arises under regulation. Attributes other than price, such as status, personal influence, quality of public relations, and even corruption[35] will be used by competitors to gain advantages in bureaucratic processes. In the development market, zoning and development control are major causes of dissipation. The lost income stream as a result of regulation is "non-exclusive." It does not go to the government as tax revenue or to any pre-specified third party. Affected proprietors will not irrationally do nothing. They will try to object to or get through regulations imposed on their property in order to recapture their lost rights. Such attempts of the proprietors incur both costs of time (interest) and costs of professionals working on their behalf. In the field of planning application, review, appeal and rezoning, lawyers, consultant planners, transport engineers and environmental experts are typical characters whom the proprietors need to retain for performing the requisite professional work.

Rent-seeking refers to resource-consuming attempts by interest groups to define or redefine property rights (i.e. the prevailing rules of competition) in order to transfer other people's income or "rent" to themselves. Rent-seekers often seek to create non-price competition situations from which they have a comparative advantage to maximize their own income. Rent-seeking is intimately related to rent dissipation as the existence of "non-exclusive" income provides good opportunities for a scramble of resources. In land use planning, rent-seeking may be *ex ante*, through which politicians and professionals (notably the planners) invest real resources in an attempt to secure rent by regulation. It may be *ex post*, through which developers invest real resources to capture or recapture a larger share of the rent for themselves.[36]

The more complicated and *discretionary* is the planning process, the greater is the extent of rent dissipation or the scope of rent-seeking. In the

---

[35] In an opinion survey conducted by a student of the planning graduate school of the University of Hong Kong, *Urban Planning and Anti-Corruption Efforts in Hong Kong*, 25% of the respondents thought that "the extent of discretionary power found in the planning field in Hong Kong" is the most important factor that may lead to planning-related corruption in Hong Kong.

[36] Adam Gifford, Jr., "Rent Seeking and Non-price Competition," *Quarterly Review of Economics and Business*, Vol. 27, No. 2 (1987), pp. 63–70.

extreme situation, the gain by the applicant may be completely dissipated by the costs absorbed in the process, notably time costs and professional fees. Then, the only social group which reaps net benefits could well be the planning consultants.[37] Anticipating this consequence, proprietors may simply abandon any idea of maximizing the value idea of his resources, entailing loss of wealth to society as a whole. This scenario is one which is descriptive of the United Kingdom's "non" zoning planning regime.[38]

The British planning system apparently has no zoning in the sense that all development (except a few exempted "classes" of uses) within the Council district, other than some special areas, must go through the planning application procedure. In this procedure, the planner or indeed the District Council, filled by politicians, has great discretionary power. The use of this power is only constrained by the procedural law of natural justice. The planner may refuse or approve the application with or without planning conditions or obligations. The criteria of success in planning application are left almost entirely to the planner. While rent-seeking is not unlimited as a third party cannot participate in the planning application procedure and appeal is possible to the Secretary of State for the Environment, the situation creates a great scope of rent-seeking due to uncertainty about the rules of this non-price competition. Mills describes a rent-seeking development control system as one which "involves case-by-case deliberation in the merits of land owners proposals."[39] This kind of "zoning lotteries" is exactly the British "non-zoning" mechanism. The Conservative Government since the 1970s may be interpreted as making attempts to constrain rent-seeking in the process. They include:

1. presumption in favour of development;
2. establishment of "enterprise zones";
3. introduction of the Use Classes Orders; and
4. using the appeal process to support Central Government's liberalization policy.

---

[37] G. Tullock, "Rent Seeking and Zoning" (unpublished research paper, 1994).

[38] See Simon Ball and Stuart Bell, *Environmental Law* (London: Blackstone, 1991), Chapter 9.

[39] David E. Mills, "Is Zoning a Negative-Sum Game?" *Land Economics*, Vol. 65, No. 1 (1989), pp. 1–12.

It is ironical that the interventionist practices discarded by the British government has been dumped into the policy development agenda of Hong Kong's planner, as contained in the *Comprehensive Review of the Town Planning Ordinance* (Hong Kong Government, 1991) and the ensuing *Consultation Paper on Town Planning Bill* (July 1996). This latter document contains a draft *Town Planning Bill*, which is a White Bill.

Property Rights Implications of the Proposals in the Consultative Documents: *Comprehensive Review of the Town Planning Ordinance* and the Draft *Town Planning Bill*

The traditional conflictual model of a regulatory body regulating the applicant by granting or refusing permission is currently breaking down. Modern town planning may be seen as a negotiative process in which consultation between the prospective developer and the local planning authority in advance of the application is the norm, and in which proposals are both made and considered in the light of local and national policies. The local planning authority and the developer often have a community of interest in carrying out a particular development; the developer gets its proposal granted and the local authority obtains the revitalisation of the economy of an area, or the creation of jobs, or some other economic benefit.... In addition, agreements between developers and local authorities in which "planning gain" is bargained for are increasingly used to supplement the regulatory controls.[40]

The above negotiative or contractual approach now emerging in the United Kingdom is definitely not congruent with that adopted in the proposed planning reforms for Hong Kong. The consultative document *Comprehensive Review of the Town Planning Ordinance* recommends three proposals, adopted in the White Bill, with serious implications: (1) the universal requirement for a planning certificate for all uses (including Column (1) uses) before actual building development can be carried out;[41]

---

[40] Simon Ball and Stuart Bell, *Environmental Law*, p. 161.

[41] See *Comprehensive Review of the Town Planning Ordinance* (July 1991), paragraphs 5.24–5.27, pp. 57–59. The issue of planning certificates in respect of objection sites would be withheld, and similarly, consideration of planning applications in respect of these sites further deferred, until decisions had been made by the Governor in Council on the related objections. (*ibid.*, paragraph 3.25); see also *Consultation Paper on Town Planning Bill*, paragraphs 34–37. The legislative proposals are found in Part V of the draft *Town Planning Bill*.

(2) the statutory requirement for an exhibition and right of public hearing of the planning study;[42] and (3) the right for third party objection to planning applications.[43]

Under the existing planning regime, rent-seeking activities are restricted to statutory objection to zoning proposal; s.16 application and subsequent review and appeal procedures; and rezoning proposals. The above recommendations of the Comprehensive Review would expand vastly the scope of rent-seeking activities. The requirement for a planning certificate, in particular, renders the land use rights of lessees completely uncertain. It is akin to the "non-zoning" regime of the United Kingdom planning system mentioned above, the damage of which the Conservative Government has been trying hard to reduce by various measures of liberalization. The right to hearing of a planning study incurs extra costs of delays and the right of third party objection to planning application (made by the proprietor himself) violates private property rights by subjecting private's decision about the use of one's resources not just to the bureaucrat but also the rest of the world. This means the socialization of land use decision for property obtained at full market price.

Postscript

The collective prosperity and freedom of Hong Kong society are based on a market economy. Such an economy is in turn predicated on voluntary contract and the rule of law. Huge government welfare spending on housing, education and unemployment relief has been financed by an enviable low income tax regime, which is viable only because of the availability of handsome land revenues. The Hong Kong Government has been reaping such revenues, except during the period of Japanese occupation, since the earliest days of colonization. Land revenues in turns reflect the vitality of

---

[42] See *Comprehensive Review of the Town Planning Ordinance*, paragraph 3.22, p. 24; see also *Consultation Paper on Town Planning Bill*, paragraphs 18–22. The legislative proposals are found in sections 11–14, Part III of the draft *Town Planning Bill*.

[43] See *Comprehensive Review of the Town Planning Ordinance*, paragraph 4.11, p. 38; see also *Consultation Paper on Town Planning Bill*, paragraphs 31–32. The legislative proposals are found in sections 36–38, Part IV of the draft *Town Planning Bill*.

the land market, which depends on a contractual relationship between the government and individuals. Government planning can indeed establish, clarify and protect private property rights at the same time public interests are safeguarded.[44] However, an evaluation of the impact of planning in Hong Kong cannot ignore the contractual nature of the land market. Many proponents of modern planning legislation tend to not only undermine this contractual foundation of the market, but also ignore the fact that the leasehold land system is also a government planning system. The key feature of planning in the leasehold system is that of contractual agreement between the state and individuals. It is hoped that this chapter would stimulate thinking about the role of the leasehold system as a planning mechanism. Such thinking, or rethinking, is timely in the light of major planning legislation and housing policy proposals within the context of constitutional and political transition.

---

[44] Lawrence W. C. Lai, *Zoning and Property Rights: A Hong Kong Case Study* (Hong Kong: Hong Kong University Press, 1997) and "The Property Rights Justifications for Planning and a Theory of Zoning," *Progress in Planning*, Vol. 48, No. 3 (1997), pp. 161–246.